PRAISE FOR
VENGEANCE WALKING

"This secret campaign speaks volumes of the author's bravery and dedication to comrades and country by sharing his unimaginable story on history's forgotten truth. A powerful account of the human experience caught up in history's forgotten struggles."

— Douglas Carr, Civil Servant

"Excellent read that makes you feel like you're in the shoes of a Green Beret with the vivid portrayal of action during the chaos of armed conflicts."

— Sean Branson

VENGEANCE WALKING

THE LAKE OF TEN THOUSAND SOULS

DANNY BRYANT

Vengeance Walking:
The Lake of Ten Thousand Souls

First Edition

The views expressed in this work are solely those of the author and do not necessarily reflect the views of the publisher, and the publisher hereby disclaims any responsibility for them.

Published by Tactical 16, LLC
Monument, CO

ISBN: 978-1-943226-59-7 (paperback)

CONTENTS

ACKNOWLEDGMENTS

I would like to thank, with all of my heart, Reverend William Fowler for giving me the courage to write this book. I would never have been able to acknowledge, let alone face, the emotional and psychological damage that this mission unknowingly caused to me without Reverend Fowler's support. Even while writing it, I felt that I was reliving every moment to include the pain, anxiety, smells, and sounds that I had secluded in my mind, hoping to never experience again. It turned out to be one of the most therapeutic tools that I have experienced to date. I thank you with all my heart for allowing me to start the healing process and to show my family the father and husband that they all deserve.

To my brothers, David Badgley and Mike Shenk: for their unending and unjudged mental support. Without them I am sure I would have given up on life. The endless calls throughout every hour of the day, giving me optimism that everything would work out in the long run and that even though the fight was far from over, they were and would be there for me through all of it. Mike's numerous late hour fishing trips definitely helped clear out the cob-webs and bring me back to a calm reality.

I have to give a shout out to my brother Keith List, whose endless hours of patience have brought me into a new life with my new brothers. He helped me reach a huge and difficult goal I was worried I would never reach in this lifetime. Thank you for always being there and understanding, my brother.

I would like to send love and heartfelt prayers to my brother Kris, who we lost far too early and way before his time. He taught me a lot about life and what was really important. He also taught me how to cry like I have never done in my life. I learned the true meaning of "Awe" from this man and he put me in it so many times. I also learned that anyone can do anything, if they put their mind to it, regardless of the barriers. I thank you Kristopher and may God cradle your precious soul. Please come visit us as much as you can.

I wanted to give a shout out to the guys of the 160th Night Stalkers, brothers from another mother. Especially I Santiago, thanks for your support and brotherhood.

I would like to also extend my sincerest appreciation to Chris Schafer and the team at Tactical 16. Without their support and assistance in the editing and publication process, this story would have remained amongst a small group of family and friends. I am so blessed by all of those who have inspired and helped me to get this story out there for others to read and understand.

Lastly, but actually first. I would like to express the most humble and gratifying thanks to my family. To my wife, for forcing me to understand that I truly needed to die inside before I could get any better. She is my best friend and partner. Through years of unending injuries from military service, she has stuck by my side and been my hands when I couldn't use mine and my legs when I couldn't walk. Thank you, my love, for your unending service to me and your country. My twin boys, crazy and crazier, for giving me countless hours of free comedy. But most especially and specifically, to my daughter: she saved my life over and over again throughout the years, giving me the drive when I couldn't find any. She always wears a smile, even when I was grumpy for whatever reason, and truly filled my heart with unspeakable love and made me glow every day and minute I was with or around her. She has brought back a glow in my heart when all I had was gloom and anger. I thank you with every molecule of my soul and can never say I love you enough. Thank you and I love you. Always and Forever, Daddy.

In memory of Sergeant Todd F.
A great soldier, a great friend,
and a great Dad.
You are always missed.
May God rest your soul.

WRITER'S INTRODUCTION

My intention in writing this book was to tell the story of what my brothers and I endured in trying to ratify a very difficult situation. The other was to psychologically put down on paper what has for years been reoccurring in my mind and soul. Not only do I want to put my experience in the past, but I also want to educate the world on something so profound that the human race deserves to know and learn from the atrocities that have occurred. In concept, much like the Holocaust. Not in numbers, but in concept. The mass execution of people, their children, and the destruction of entire cultures needs to be examined so it ceases to happen in today's world and never happens again. Warning signs need to be recognized and acknowledged before any future lunatics are given the chance to advance in their unacceptable and disillusioned ideals.

This is a story of the horrors and the terrible things that human beings can do to one another and the motivation behind it. What lies in these pages might be somewhat incomprehensible to the average civilian, but this is my story and it needs to be finally told.

May God help the dead and their families find tranquility. May they rest in their eternal peace and may He help bring closure to the horrors that so many have had to endure without resolution and closure. May both sides finally find peace.

DISCLAIMER

I would like to add this disclaimer to make sure that everyone is on the same page. This book does not represent by any means, the United States Army, Navy, Marines, Department of Defense (DOD), any US National interests, or any US National occupation, United States or any branch or relation to any US Armed Service. It has no affiliation with the Central Intelligence Agency (CIA), the National Security Agency (NSA), or any agencies affiliated with the United States. This is just a book, people.

BRIEF HISTORY

Roughly, and somewhat officially, in the year 1979, the twelve-year-war in El Salvador began. The Farabundo Marti National Liberation Front (FMLN) was a combination of 5 guerilla factions that cumulatively came together under the pretense of the mutual interest of controlling the country and its rich coffee exports and labor.

The CIA started the United States involvement shortly after the unification of the FMLN by sending in its own operatives and hitting up Uncle Sam and Special Operations Command to use Special Forces Soldiers designated to that Area of Operations (AO), which was covered by 7th Special Forces Group (SFG.) Congress, in addition to the DOD, set limitations on the Green Berets requiring they were there for observation and intelligence purposes only and were not to engage with any hostiles under any circumstances and/or provide any aid or assistance to the host nation. Or at least, that's what they said and wanted you to believe on paper.

They were originally not to exceed 55 operatives or liaisons. The number 55 was set by US Congressional and DOD regulations. Shortly after getting advisors on the ground in El Salvador, the US realized the magnitude of what was happening and added units, expanding the forces to include but not limited to; training assistance in small unit tactics, internal command structure, squad level up to command and control centers, jungle and guerilla warfare tactics, training in counterintelligence, medical (in field) and advanced trauma, artillery, armor, and a huge number of pilots and aviation support.

After fighting started throughout the country, various corporations started to pay and hire private mercenaries and death squads to protect their corporate interests, to include the CIA.

Unknown to US intelligence at the time, many of the guerilla factions were heavily and intensely trained in Cuba. So as death tolls started to rise, the Pentagon, the US Embassy in San Salvador, the State Department, the Whitehouse staff and the Presidency masked, lied and misdirected the US involvement in El Salvador. Special Forces Commandos were then directed to a special training base in El Salvador called Atlacatl Battalion, a counter insurgency battalion. Here they were to bump up training in immediate reaction forces, counter insurgency, aggressive patrolling, ambushes, counter terrorism, hostage rescue, Very Important Person (VIP) protection, and reconnaissance.

At this point in the confrontation, it was very easy to find yourself on the receiving end of a grenade, bomb, or bullet. So, reports released by the US, were carefully written or disappeared into that great void of Washington D.C., where it was all covered up.

In 1980, Archbishop Oscar Romero was brutally shot and killed. In addition, four nuns were repeatedly raped, mutilated, and murdered.

In 1984, US Marines were executed at La Zona Rosa. The statement later released said that all of the Americans were "combatants," even though every Marine killed was unarmed. This is where I personally believe that the taste for vengeance and pay back entered into the mindset of American forces.

October 10, 1985, approximately 15 US advisors were killed in the guerilla attack at La Union.

In 1989, six Jesuit priests were horrifically and violently murdered.

El Salvador is bordered by Honduras, Guatemala, and the Pacific Ocean. The uprisings were said to have started because of tragic overpopulation and class struggles that had been growing for a said 100 years. Military nationals started forming death squads because of peasants and the indigenous people not making enough money. Coffee was 95% of the country's income and of that, only 2% of all incomes were being distributed throughout the population. Thus, guerilla safe houses were popping up in Honduras, as well as Guatemala, to fight the military onslaught.

The mass killing was later called La Matanza (the massacre). The victims were unionists, clergy, independent farmers, and university officials. 1000 people were murdered in the small village of El Mozote alone.

Some of the most atrocious acts caused by the El Salvadorian militants occurred when over 800 children disappeared in Tequcigalpa. The militants took them for their own or to sell them in illegal trafficking. They were also being sold to illegal adoption networks.

Can you justify our intervention? Maybe, maybe not? But years later is when my involvement began because of these acts.

Anything, Anytime, Anyplace.

VENGEANCE WALKING

1

BEFORE THE MAN

I THINK THAT ONE OF THE WORST PARTS ABOUT KNOWING YOU HAVE TO GET somewhere in a short amount of time is having to fly on a cheap ass civilian airline stuck sitting in coach. To top it off, we wouldn't get any alcohol on this flight, and we were flying all the way to Colorado Springs, Colorado, and there wasn't a good-looking girl in sight.

It was late December at about 0400 hours in 1994. The team had been called and deployed within six hours. Either this was something really important, or this was another fucked up training mission into the middle of Arizona or something. Upon arrival into the airport in Colorado, we were met by a little Air Force female and some class six Command Sergeant Major. We were in civvies and too tired to play any games with these two. We just wanted a bed and maybe a beer or two. Randie, our detachment Commander, was a first lieutenant closing in on captain. He had never served alone with us as our Commander before, and we weren't tagging along with a warrant officer, so we figured it was going to be some kiss ass exercise to help Randie get his second bar. I remember walking through the airport and there were motorcycles on display all over the place. They looked like Harleys, but they were of a different make... I can't remember.

After we got all of our luggage and A-Bags, we filed out to the front where we were greeted with four beautiful Air Force vans. The "A-Bag" (assault bag) is packed anticipating a minimum of a 24 to 48-hour operation. The bag should contain important essential items such as: tactical-vest (tac-vest), extra ammo, Kevlar helmet, extra batteries, communication gear, emergency shelter, poncho liner, ripcord, tools, cordage, extra water, e-tool, weapon cleaning kit with lube or break free, calorie dense food, and a first aid kit. Specifically, for me, I also carried advanced first aid and trauma kits. The rest of the items, including extra clothing, most importantly socks, toilet paper, hygiene requirements like toothbrush, razor etc., had to be packed carefully so that it can be thrown, take a round, have you jump on it, land on it, and throw it wherever when need be, and grabbed quickly in dire times. It also must have D rings placed along the outside so you can add things such as a Camelbak and other essential gear. We also carried Assault and Alice packs. The Assault pack is a very essential part of equipment for a Special Forces Soldier. The Alice pack is a very large pack that is for load bearing and a full-size pack with a capacity of around 45 or more liters and is for long range operations. The assault pack actually clips right on the back of the Alice pack.

Seeing the Air Force vans in front of us had me thinking that maybe this wasn't going to be that bad after all, because everyone knows that when the Air Force is footing the bill, we are going to have it in style. The air outside was pleasant, crisp, and truly refreshing compared to the plane and the stagnant air in the terminal. I got in the van with the lieutenant and asked what was going on and he said, "These desk jockeys don't have a clue. They're just here to give us a ride." I sat back and wondered, but really didn't care. I just wanted to get this thing over with so we could get back in time for the Super Bowl. The van ride was fairly short, thank God, but the smell of this Air Force female was driving me crazy. All I could think about the entire ride was trying to get a nut with her.

We stopped at this little rinky dink Comfort Inn out in the middle of nowhere. But tonight, we were sleeping in style. As we were unpacking the vans, the Lieutenant yelled that we were going to meet at the vans at 1800 (6pm for you non-military folks) hours and to be sober. I shared a room with Trout, which was great, but if I was not going to get in trouble in the next ten or so hours, I had better just go to bed. Trout and I had a long history together, and one thing that we were really good at besides combat was getting in trouble, so I jumped in the shower and hit the hay.

We met at the vans at about 1745, piled in, and drove out to the Air Force Academy. I'll tell ya, those fly boys don't have it that bad at all. One thing for sure was that you could definitely feel the air thinning as we were going higher in elevation. Upon arriving at the front gates, the lieutenant got out and met with a full bird colonel, talked for a couple of minutes, and sent us up to the northwestern corner of the base to a small, but very desolate, building. The air was cold enough that you could see your breath and there wasn't a single person in sight anywhere. It was as if the base and immediate area were deserted. I got an eerie feeling as we walked up to this unmarked brick three-story building. I couldn't help but look out into the night sky and the surrounding fence line. I did hear an elk with its loud squealing bellow, a sound that you could hear as it built in their lungs very distinctly before it pushed it out into the night air. This was definitely a very proper building to have a briefing. We went up the fire escape on the south side up to the second floor. As the lieutenant opened the fire door, there were about ten Air Force sky cops (the Air Force version of Military Police or MPs) standing there, armed to the hilt. This was business and you could read it on every one of their faces.

"What the hell is going on here?" I asked the lieutenant. "Don't worry about it, sergeant, and get out your DD Form 2," (which was our military identification (ID) cards).

The sky cops checked our IDs against what they called an Entry Authority List, which I hadn't seen since we did exercises at Kirtland Air Force Base on their nuclear facilities. After we had been cleared, we proceeded down the hall to a flight of stairs, went down, went down another hallway, went up and seemed to go in circles up and down, down hallways with no doors, until we finally went down this hallway that had one door on the left into what appeared to be like a huge classroom or hotel conference room. But in this conference room, there were no windows. There were several rows of chairs that had a wood top attached on the side that could be flipped up to use as a desk. They were all facing the front of the room where several long conference tables were lined up end-to-end which stood in front of a huge blackboard. Standing behind the tables was a two-star US Army general, a four-star Air Force general, the full bird we met earlier, an officer that looked to have on a South American Battle Dress Uniform (BDU) with badges and rank of the same, and two men in black civilian suits. This thing just got stepped up from being a stupid exercise to some serious shit. The Army and Air Force generals were standing talking as we entered, and the rest of the men were sitting down behind the table with their heads in a pile of papers, with the exception of the two men in civvies. They were just staring forward, leaning back in their chairs, with their arms crossed against their chest.

The colonel looked up and said, "Gentlemen, have a seat, we'll begin in a few minutes." I, as well as a few others, grabbed a pinch of chew and took out my empty water bottle that I had saved from the plane ride. As I put in the chew, I thought, "Awe heavenly," as I often do. Nothing like a quick pinch of nicotine before we get this thing started. All of us sat there in silence for about ten to fifteen minutes when the room was called to attention. In came a lieutenant colonel dressed in full Class As, with quite an impressive rack of ribbons to boot. I had seen this man somewhere before. Trout leaned over at about the same time I was thinking this and said, "That's General Stiner's right-hand man." I knew it! I had seen this guy at the Pentagon, at Fort Bragg, at Fort Benning, and even at Indian Springs Auxiliary Airfield. I hadn't ever really talked with him, but being that he was Stiner's right-hand man, this may be fun after all.

The lieutenant colonel bluntly said, "Please, take a seat." Everyone, to include the generals at the front of the room, then sat down.

"Sergeant, has everyone been cleared and have the premises been secured?"

We all turned towards the back of the room to where he was addressing the question. Two MPs, that I had not seen, stood at the hallway door and one replied, "Yes, sir, they have!"

The MPs then left the room and secured the door. I couldn't help but think, "man, this guy is serious;" I had been in a controlled, as well as secured, briefing, but this was the closest to Fort Knox that I had ever seen.

The lieutenant colonel then looked out amongst us and said, "Gentlemen, for those of you that do not know me, I am an aide to General Stiner and the Joint Chiefs of Staff. Colonel: Sir, if you would please hand out the briefing books."

The colonel stood with a large pile of papers and walked around to the front of the table and started to hand us a briefing packet consisting of several maps, intelligence reports, and an extensive amount of other information. The one thing that came to mind is that none of these guys had their nameplates on. Yeah, the ribbons and badges looked great, but who in the hell were these people and who were the Bobbsey twins at the end of the table?

"I understand that you are staying at the Comfort Inn. Enjoy your time there without having too much fun and I'll see you in about a week." The lieutenant colonel then walked out. I had seen some weird shit before, but I think that this had to take the cake.

The Army general then stood and said, "You will be confined to your quarters until told otherwise. We have a situation that we are dealing with and may, I repeat, may need to use you boys to help resolve it. It does have a certain amount of urgency and will be so treated. I would like now to get all of us introduced as we will be working together, probably for the next few months. As I call out your names, could you please rise for the rest of us?"

Picking up his clipboard, he called out, "Lieutenant Randie, who will be working as the Detachment Commander heading this A-Team."

Randie, a Green Beret, as were all of us, went straight to business, stood by the side of his desk, which was positioned at the front of the classroom to the far left, all nice and proper, snapped to attention and sat down. He had a medium size frame, with very black hair with a touch of salt. He had a tremendous amount of experience and was highly respected in the Special Forces. I will say that he had just as much of a confused look on his face as did the rest of us.

"Master Sergeant Koz, acting Operations Sergeant." Koz was a hardened veteran, a highly decorated three-term Vietnam veteran, and a guy that was as serious as death every minute of every day. He was a man of routine; he had been there, done that, and got the t-shirt. If you were going into the shit, he was definitely the man you wanted by your side.

"Sergeant First Class Tom, acting Operations and Intelligence Non-Commissioned Officer (NCO)."

Now, Tom was a big boy, but not in a bad way. You could have some great fun with him, but you had to know the boundaries. He never drank, never smoked, and knew his job and regulations better than anyone in the field. One of the many languages he spoke was Spanish and he knew it better than any of us. He was hardened and extremely strong, working construction on houses as a side job when he had the time. But Tom very rarely talked.

"Sergeant First Class Danny, acting Weapons NCO."

Danny was a breed all of his own. He could make anyone laugh and could crack a joke regardless of any situation. He was, and remains to this day, a great soldier and a very proud one. He was always, and still is, one goofy son of a bitch, but I would fight by his side anywhere, any time. If you had to look to anyone instantly for weapons information, identifying and the usage of foreign high-density light and heavy weapons or regulations of almost any kind, who definitely knew his shit, he was the one.

"Staff Sergeant Scout, acting Assistant Weapons NCO."

Scout was one of the best shots in the Army and everyone knew it, including himself. He was prior Marine Reconnaissance and had been to more sniper schools than almost anyone ever to serve in Special Forces. He was a gas, and I mean that in the humorous way, as well as the fact he could expel gas out of his ass that could easily clear a room the size of a coliseum. But he was one of those guys that if he believed something to be true no matter what the context, he was always up for an argument. He will always live the Marine motto, "*Semper Fi.*"

As Scout was sitting down, the colonel went back around the table and sat down, staring at us like he was about to rip into us like there was no tomorrow.

The general then called out, "Sergeant First Class Petie, acting Engineer NCO."

Petie was in charge of demolitions and construction projects. He was definitely a jolly old soul. Nothing ever bothered him; he was always cool, collected, and usually funny as shit. You would think that someone in his profession would be a little jumpier or on edge, but not Petie. You could just about strap a claymore to his ass and it wouldn't faze him a bit. He was one of only two of us who were married. And she was definitely the catch of the millennium. But that's a story for another time. The only thing about Petie was he could run and run. I mean better and farther than "Forest fucking Gump." It seemed like he could run forever.

"Staff Sergeant Trout, acting Assistant Engineer NCO."

Trout was the Italian Stallion. He was well-built, broad shouldered, and stronger than an ox. He had these 'Popeye' forearms that buckled out to his sides and a dark, thick, little moustache. He also had a lazy left eye, so every time he would make a strange or weird face his eye would start bouncing all over the place, making you just about heave from laughing so hard. He was a guy who could be one of the goofiest bastards you had ever met to being as serious as a blackened sky in a matter of a split second. He knew his job, he knew this business, and was by far one of the best out there.

"Sergeant First Class Dave, acting Medical NCO."

I stood up, snapped to attention at the left side of my desk, and sat down. It's weird to talk about yourself, but other than having the qualifications of a doctor or surgeon attending the 18 Delta Course, and attending four years of advanced medical training prior to that, I had pretty much been there and done that.

"Staff Sergeant Todd, acting Assistant Medical NCO."

Todd was kind of like a wound-up toy being held in your hand only an inch from the floor. He was always eager to help and ready from the word go. The one thing about Todd was, considering we were in medical, he was as ready to fire it up as anyone. His only vice was the booze. When he would drink, *he would drink,* and the worst thing was that after a good night of drinking, he would reek of it two or three days later, even if he didn't drink after that night.

"Sergeant First Class Rodge, acting Communications NCO."

Rodge was a great guy. He was misjudged or misinterpreted by a lot of people. Some were just too quick to judge, and after that first impression, they didn't allow for another. He was the type of guy that you needed to get to know. He was a hardened soldier with a very strong will but protected his heart and his true self from people who didn't take the time to get to know him or allow him to get to know them first. He had some amazing brains. I can't say that I know how or knew how it worked, but all I can say is that it definitely worked. He knew electronics, radio waves, radio signals, and basically all things communications. He was like "MacGyver" because it seemed like he could make a radio out of a Styrofoam cooler and talk to Tokyo. The one thing that Rodge and I had in common, that no one else had, was that we had both studied at the Kennedy Special Warfare Center at Fort Bragg and at the 7th Psychological Group at the Presidio in San Francisco, California. We also both went through special training in psychological warfare at Fort Campbell, Kentucky, with the 160th Special Operations Aviation Regiment. The course was originally designed to be a civil affairs course to form a unit that would restore order to villages and small towns after war.

"Staff Sergeant Ron, acting Assistant Communications NCO."

Ron: God, I don't know where to start. He grew up with a father who was a master electrician. He watched and learned through the years to almost becoming a master himself. He had round, thin wire glasses, fire red hair and, of course, the stereotypical freckles and fair skin. With him and Rodge, I swear they could do anything. It was truly amazing; between the two of them, I think that they actually could pull a rabbit out of their ass. He was the little red-headed step-child that everyone loved. He had the best sense of humor, unfortunately, leaving him to be the recipient of a majority of practical jokes. I would say between Trout and I, we did and played enough jokes on Ron to last he and his family for many generations to come. The best thing was that one of the things he wanted to do the most was grow his hair out and smoke a huge Cheech and Chong doobie if he ever got out.

"And last, but not least, Lieutenant Jesus (pronounced "hey-suse"), who you will meet in country. He will be acting Executive Officer, slash observer, slash mediator, slash partial interpreter. I'll brief Randie on the definition of that, and, I guess, slash guide. That will wrap up the team."

I liked how the general tipped his head back and forth a few times reading all the presumed jobs of this Jesus guy. It was somewhere between a slap in the face and a soft kick to the balls. We all sat up in our seats looking at each other like what in the fuck is going on here. All eyes eventually went to Lieutenant Randie. He sat and looked straight ahead and every one of us knew what that meant. It meant that we were professional soldiers, this is our job, and I am your CO (Commanding Officer), and that is what you have been dealt, so deal with it.

The first thing that came to my mind, and I'm sure everyone else's, was that we were going to have to have to lug around some "Candy Ass" Third Country National (TCN) that we were going to have to train as we went. To me, and to everyone else, that meant "baggage," and "baggage" meant slowing us down and making mistakes. And in this line of duty, and with the impressive board we have before us, this meant the difference between success and casualties. All we had ever been used to, and expected of us, was success. This was definitely not in the protocol. I hope these desk jockeys knew what they're doing, because none of us were going down for any "Candy Ass."

"We are going to conclude right here tonight and let Lieutenant Randie fill in the blanks tomorrow at o-dark thirty."

The room was then called to attention and the general said, "Dismissed. See you tomorrow."

None of the people at the front of the room moved. They didn't shift in their seats or anything. They just looked at us with blank stares, sizing up our every move. We then followed the lieutenant (LT) in single file out of the room as the MPs opened the door.

"I love the security around here," I said, considering the MPs had just a little too perfect timing in opening the door.

The MP stopped the LT and said, "All material stays in this controlled area."

The LT looked at the general for confirmation. He nodded and apologized for forgetting. I swear this thing just kept getting stranger by the minute. How in the hell was the LT supposed to brief us if he had nothing to brief us with? We walked down the hallway and back through the maze to the fire escape door; actually, I think that the fire escape door was the only way into the building let alone the conference room we were just in. And there wasn't a chance in Sam Hill I could have ever found my way through that maze again. Weird, but who knew, this was an Air Force Base. We met all the sky cops again, signed out, and then were released. When the door opened, the cold Colorado air came down the hallway. It smelled so fresh, so clean and crisp; you woke up, so to speak, and took in a deep breath. We were reminded that we were at a higher elevation; the air was slightly thin, but awesome, nonetheless. We piled back into the vans and were ready for a couple of cold ones.

As we arrived back at the hotel, it was about 2300 hours and the LT called out for us to meet in Tom's room. We dumped our stuff in our rooms, got changed, and walked down the hall to Tom's room. Everyone was in there already when we got there. Surprise, surprise. I swear whenever I'm with Trout, no matter what, we are always a day late or a dollar short. He started out by saying that the Air Force was going to give us one of their vans.

I laughed, "So much for being confined to quarters!"

The LT asked, "So, who's go'n to get the beer?" Todd looked at me and I nodded no. Not that I didn't trust him, I just wanted some to be left for the rest of us when he got back. Petie said that he was going to go get it, because he saw a stop and rob (convenient store) on the way in and he somehow knew that they sell beer until 0300 hrs.

The LT then said, "We're supposed to be talking about what is going on, but I'm not sure if they know what's going on. The information we were given in the conference room was about guerilla hostiles and something to do with a radar site. The topos (Topographical Maps) looked to be in a mountainous region. There wasn't any marking on the topos, which leaves me to suspect that they don't want us to know where we are going."

On military maps, there were numerous markings we used in reading them, including Sheet Name, Sheet Number, Scale, Edition Number, Index to Boundaries, Elevation Guide, Declination Diagram, Bar Scales and Contour Interval Note, to name a few. What we were given had nothing, so we just sat with some small talk and started a few games of "Spades."

When Petie got back, he had about six cases of Coors.

He said, "Since we're in the Rockies, we have to drink the beer of choice."

What he meant was the only place where they brew Coors is in Golden, Colorado. So that is why he chose it. God, I hate Coors. When I was in ninth grade, my friend's parents were out of town, and we drank all of his dad's Coors until we were all passed out in a puddle of our own puke. Ever since then, I will puke at even the smell of Coors.

I yelled out, "See you guys in the morning. I'm going to turn in."

The LT told me that we were to meet at the vans at 0830 hours. My first thought, and I'm sure everyone else's, was "Cool, we get to sleep in." I went to the room and turned in.

While I was lying in bed, I thought about a lot of different things. I thought about past missions and how great they went, as well as how some of them had some bad moments. I also thought about my home where I grew up. I thought about the pastures, my family, and a couple of girls I used to go out with.

I grew up in Southern Wisconsin, in the city of Madison. It had about a quarter million in population and was growing by the hour. My mother and father were originally from Chicago. They grew up during the Great Depression, so they were tight with food, money, and anything having to do with it. They had a very poor and difficult upbringing. And because of this, I was forced to start working as a porter at the ripe age of fourteen. We were three children, me being the oldest. I went to tough schools that had the problems of Chicago because of all the people coming up from there to take advantage of the welfare system Wisconsin had. The gangs and crime were getting to the point where Madison started making special task forces to deal with these growing problems. This, at that time, was really unheard of, especially in that area. I had to learn how to fight and how to survive young because of these difficult surroundings.

My father had a tendency to hit the bottle pretty hard and that meant he had to choose an outlet for all of his problems. That outlet was me. If he started in on my brother or sister, I would step in and take the blunt of it and get them away. There would be times that he would come into my room in the middle of the night and either beat the shit out of me or would take me by the hair, reminding me that he had told me to mow the grass. So, of course, I would be out there mowing the grass at three o'clock in the morning in my underwear. Because of my relationship with my father, I lived as an individual always trying to protect myself from him, or really, from everyone. I never felt that I was a real member of our family; I was there basically because I had to be by law, and we just went through the daily motions, and God forbid, we could not let the rest of our family find out how dysfunctional we were. We lived outside of reality, never able to admit the wrongs and/or face our real problems. We were never able to see eye-to-eye or able to really talk to one another. My parents didn't allow it. We had to keep all of our feelings inside because, according to my parents, our family didn't have any problems, only I did. It was all about an individual, not a unit. Because of my upbringing, I never thought I was a member of anything. I was always looking for something to belong to.

My father was a very popular and well-known realtor and property owner in the area. He seemed to be friends with just about everyone in the city, especially the wealthier and more predominant citizens. I spent my summers working a different job every year for one of my father's friends. One summer, it would be construction; the next would be plumbing, and so on. My father always said that I would never amount to anything, and I needed to learn a trade, because he sure as shit wasn't going to support me for the rest of his life. So, I got very well-rounded in doing different jobs of all kinds. I guess I do owe him that. But regardless of the job or who I was working for, I always exceeded expectations in my job performance for two reasons. One was that if I screwed up and it got back to my father, he was going to beat my ass; the other was because I always felt the need to compete with everyone, so I fought to win.

Because of this relationship I had with my father, I learned to hate. I hated the sheer thought of life. I played as many sports as I could when I was in school to stay away from the house. Mostly, I played football and swam mornings in the summer. I hated to go home. I knew that when I went home, my father was going to tear into me for one reason or the other. But I had football and I loved it. I would take all of the hate I had for my father and this life and literally go out and beat the shit out of people. I even made special steel sheaths in shop class for my lineman gloves that were definitely going to cause stitches. I fought in school almost every day. I built up a reputation for myself as being sort of a bad ass. This was good, because it helped in defending my brother and sister, but also sucked because everyone wanted a shot at "The Title" because I had never lost a fight. I can say that it was very rare that I would ever actually pick a fight. But they found me, that is for sure. Honestly, I was always quiet and more to myself.

When I was growing up, the only exposure to weapons I had was going out with my father's drinking buddies, and their sons, pheasant hunting and occasionally, squirrel hunting with my friends in Iowa. I had a Remington 12-gauge my father got for me. I was scared as hell sometimes to go squirrel hunting with my friends, because we would drink a few beers, and when things got boring for my friend, Loren, he would start shooting at us. There were many nights when we would sit in his father's living room picking the bird shot out of our backs and legs. It was truly a miracle that we never killed ourselves out there. Was it fun, you may ask? Yeah, I guess so, but now looking back, it was dumb as hell.

When I was seventeen, I signed up for the Army. I was at the Medical Evaluation Pre-evaluation (MEP) Station in Milwaukee for my evaluation when I saw a Green Beret for the first time. Whenever I thought about Green Berets, I always thought about "Rambo" or John Wayne, who never served in the military, by the way. But this guy was a true badass and that was what I wanted, no matter what. When I got my Armed Services Vocational Aptitude Battery (ASVAB) scores back, I was relieved that they were high enough for me to eventually work towards my final goal. I attended basic training at Fort Leonard Wood, also known as good ole "Fort Lost in the Woods," and then went through infantry training, completing both in a total of fourteen weeks.

After that, I went to Airborne school at Fort Benning, Georgia, for three weeks. We had ground week, tower week, and jump week. This is where we earned our "Silver Wings." We had a lot of washouts and we were told that our class had more than usual. I didn't know why, because not only was the training impressive, but it was fun as hell. I was lucky enough to go into Special Operations Preparation Course (SOPC) at Fort Bragg, North Carolina. Here we experienced intense physical training, a lot of land navigation, and some other prep work for the Special Forces Assessment & Selection (SFAS). I know that I am skimming through this rather fast, but if I go into a deeper description of these things, I feel I will be getting a call from "Big Brother," and I will also get into all sorts of stories, good and bad, making this chapter go on forever.

Following those training courses and assessments, I continued with Individual Skills, Military Occupational Specialty (MOS) Qualification (to include additional language training), Special Forces (SF) common tasks, Advanced Special Operations Techniques (ASOT), Interagency Operations, advanced language training in your specified language, and combative training. After Collective Training, we went into the Survival, Escape, Resistance, and Evasion (SERE) Course. This is the course that everyone loves to talk about. And yes, this was my favorite. We constantly, day in and day out, learned combat survival tactics. It was high-speed, violent, and honestly was the thing that started to "wind me up." This was a term we used when training that was making us itch almost out of our skins for combat or to fight. And last, but definitely not least, before we were assigned to our Active Duty SFG, we went to Live Environmental Training (LET). At LET, we would receive all the training we would use or need in interacting with another culture. We would learn to be totally fluent in that country's language, traditions, customs, and be able to mesh into that culture as a citizen or national of that specific area. This would help us use the natives for information, provide assistance in a foreign fighting force, and earn enough trust for the United States to utilize the region for future use politically, or just geographically. At the graduation dinner, on my plate was my Green Beret and on it, the blood red flash of 7th Group. Not only did I make it and was in, but I was now in the renowned Devil's Brigade 7th SFG. I was to be headquartered at Fort Bragg. 7th SFG was primarily responsible for Central and South America and parts of the Middle East and the Persian Gulf region. To say that my blood was pumping would have been an understatement. I made it!

It was 0530 hours the next day and Lieutenant Randie was pounding on our room door. First thing I did was roll over to see if Trout even made it back last night. He did and he looked like he was paying for it even more so. I went and answered the door; the LT stood there and said, "It's about fuckin' time! Tell Trout he can hit the rack for a couple more hours, our meeting this morning has been cancelled. The general's aide called about 45 minutes ago." This was either good or bad, there never was an in-between.

I jumped in the shower to come out to no towels. I yelled, "Trout, you fuck, where are the towels?" I stepped out of the bathroom and, of course, Trout was gone. I went around the corner outside our room to ask Rodge for a towel, and yes, the damn door closed. Here I was, standing in the middle of the hall, butt naked, knocking on Rodge's door.

He yelled, "We are doing the dishes," in a high-pitched, female-like voice. I thought to myself, "Well they got me, and they got me again but good!" I said screw it and walked down to the front desk wearing only what God gave me at birth. The good thing was that the front desk girl was hot as hell. The bad thing was that she called security. Well, to say the least, I was able to talk my way out of it, God knows how, and got another key to get back into my room.

Todd came by our room at about noon laughing his ass off and said, "We're meeting in Tom's room in a half an hour; don't get locked out again."

I sneered and said, "Ha fucking ha."

When we got into Tom's room, the LT asked Scout to stand outside the door. He shut the door, turned around and said, "Ok, guys, we are a go. We're flying out tomorrow afternoon. Get your gear ready and pack as light as you can, just dump what you don't need. Also, we have been granted an afternoon to walk around Colorado Springs. No drinking! Got it?" We all replied, "Yes sir!"

"0430 hours ready to go tomorrow," the LT finished.

About fifteen minutes later, we were in the Air Force van headed into Colorado Springs. When we got there, we couldn't find anything to do, that didn't involve drinking. We went to an Army Surplus store and raised a little hell with the people working there. We actually found some good deals on some "Gerber" leathermans and some insect hoods. Then we went to this little square called the Adobe Walls Antique Mall where we took some crazy pictures in one of those large board cut outs where you put your head in the holes with a huge saguaro cactus coming out of the middle of it and a western theme. We spent the rest of the time running in and out of the little stores looking for some local woman to hustle. In which there were none, even for Rodge, who didn't have exactly the highest standards. So, we set back to the hotel to get our gear together and head in for an early night sleep.

One thing I do, no matter what, every time, if time allows, is get an ear washing kit for wax and wash my ears out. When you're in a combat zone, you have to survive mainly on your discreteness and your finely honed senses. And one of those senses is that of hearing. So, I always wash out my ears. I took the bulb and sucked up the hot water and squeezed it into my ear.

I repeated this numerous times when Trout sat straight up in the bed and screamed, "What the fuck are you doing? All I can hear is burrrgy, burrrgy, burrrgy! You're fucken driving me crazy, go to bed!"

All I could do was laugh my ass off as he pulled the pillow over his head. "See you in the morning," I yelled.

"Whatever, go to fucken bed!"

2

OFF WE GO

AT 0400 HOURS, WE MET IN THE PARKING LOT OF THE HOTEL WHERE there was an Air Force 44 passenger bus waiting for us. That morning was cold as hell. Every one of us was under dressed. We took our gear to the rear of the bus where there was an Air Force sergeant packing in the bags. I handed my bags up to him somewhat reluctantly because I didn't know this guy from Sam, but did what I was told nevertheless. We were getting into the bus in sort of a single file line, rubbing our hands together and blowing the steam from our mouths on our hands, when I looked up and saw the colonel we had met the other night at the Air Force Academy.

The driver looked to the colonel and asked, "What are the weapons?" He looked to the driver and said, "As you were, sergeant!"

He didn't say another word the entire trip; he just sat with his back to the window and his right leg propped up on the seat. At least the bus had a good heater.

We drove to the airport in downtown Colorado Springs where we had originally arrived. It strangely felt like we had been here for a couple of weeks, considering that it had only been a couple of days. The bus didn't stop at the front terminal loading area where we had originally got into the vans; it went down to the east side of the terminal where there was an MP and an Airport Police Officer standing on the inside of a sliding gate, which gave access to the aircraft and the runways. The MP boarded the bus, talked to the colonel, and gave the police officer the thumbs up okay. He sat next to the colonel, where they sifted through some paperwork. The MP then handed the colonel a two-way radio to the tower. The colonel got on the radio and said, "Strawberry three awaiting clearance."

The tower replied, "Copy Strawberry three, standby." About half an hour went by and the tower called on the radio saying, "Strawberry three, you are cleared to spot four taxi four bravo." The bus then went straight out to the aircraft parking area and stopped in front of about ten Air Force personnel and "Sky Cops" on the ground level outside of the terminal. We got out and got in a single file line in the back of the bus to get our gear. They opened the back hatch to the bus, and we passed all of our bags from person to person in a line up to an empty, shiny stainless-steel aircraft pallet. The Air Force guys packed the pallet and strapped it down with a huge desert camouflage net as we basically stood by and watched. I thought to myself that we were probably headed off to the desert by the looks of things.

The colonel yelled, "Stand fast," as he held the two-way up to his ear. We just kind of stood there, considering that we were already basically standing fast. He then called out, "Why don't you guys cop a squat, we're going to be here for a while." About an hour had passed by when we saw the MC-130 Combat Talon fly overhead.

"Well, I guess that's our ride," I said aloud.

The colonel stood up from where he was leaning which was against the packed pallet of our gear.

"Get your men ready, lieutenant," barked out the colonel. Finally, it seemed like our LT was back in the game.

"Let's go, guys," called the LT. An end loader huffed and puffed as it came from across the runway, belching diesel exhaust into the air, and loaded up our pallet. The MC-130E taxied in and pulled right up to where we were. The rear of the plane, now facing us, started to lower. If you haven't ever been behind a C-130 when its props are running, it is as windy as hell and you better grab your cover because there is no way you are going to be able to keep it on your head. It has the appearance of a Popsicle stick strapped to the top of a beer can. A C-130 just roars as these powerful props suck in the air and blow it back. The Crew Chief jumped out, chalked the tires on the plane, and hooked his headphone wire up on the right front of the aircraft to talk to the pilot. He gave a few hand and arm signals, and the engines slowed to an idle, which isn't much better as far as having to stand behind these things.

He motioned to the lieutenant and he yelled, "Let's go!" We went in a single file line right up the middle of the back lowered ramp of the aircraft. When you get inside past the wind, you automatically surge forward a little because you do not have to fight the prop wash. As we filed inside, we grabbed a spot in our nice red net seating. I would rather sleep or ride on top of the bags than sit in these fuckin' seats. After a few hours, you can't feel your ass and your feet just about freeze off your body.

The end-loader loaded the pallet onto the back of the aircraft and pulled away with a thumbs up and the Crew Chief disconnected his hearing apparatus and piled into the aircraft. Another Air Force crew member secured the pallet as he hooked the massive clamps to the floor of the aircraft. The Crew Chief then connected his head phones to a spot on the inside right rear of the rear of the aircraft, and as he started to raise the back door, the aircraft started to pull out for taxi. The LT casually saluted the colonel and then sat down. I thought to myself, 'Sweet we're not going to sit around all day waiting to get this thing off the ground." The Crew Chief handed around a box of foam ear plugs as we taxied out to the runway. Next thing you know, the engines roared and the plane started to shake.

"Here we go," I said, falling back into my net-like seat, ready for a little, but hopefully, long nap depending on the destination and how long I could stay in these seats.

I awoke to the landing gear going down. I got up, stretched, and took a look out of the small porthole windows of the aircraft. The air in the cabin was cold. At first, it looked kind of like Hawaii.

I turned to Trout and asked, "Where the fuck are we?" He was still half asleep with his black knit watch cap on and lowered over his eyes with his hands tucked into the sleeves of his field jacket to keep warm.

I saw the almost highlighter yellow fire extinguisher hanging right above his head and smiled when the LT shouted out, "Doc, don't you even fucken think about it!"

Well, it's the thought that counts, I guess. One thing, given the right circumstances, we would wake each other up with the fire extinguisher blasting the CO2 and foam all over your BDUs. Everyone in the team called me Doc, because I was the medic, and because I was working towards being a civilian doctor one day.

The captain called out on the speakers, "Well, guys, welcome to Puerto fuck'n Rico." Where in the hell are we, and more so, what in the hell are we doing in Puerto Rico? This thing was starting to get worse by the minute. I couldn't tell if we were in San Juan or Mayaguez. I had been to Puerto Rico several times before and, for some reason, none of this looked familiar.

The Crew Chief was already standing in the rear door with his headphones on as the plane was coming to a stop. The rear hatch started to go down right away, even as we were taxing. We were all in full BDUs and I had the feeling that this wasn't good. The warm humid air was welcome as it flowed into the cabin as the door went down. It was great outside, but all of the fumes that were rushing in were strong enough to make your eyes water.

The aircraft came to a halt and the LT yelled over the noise from the props, "Un-strap the packs and unload them off of the aircraft."

We jumped up and started to undo the mesh straps holding the pallet and packs together. We unloaded all of the bags onto the ground, once again in a single file line, and departed the aircraft. We all took a knee as the aircraft pulled ahead about a hundred feet or so and idled. Okay, now what is the plan, I thought. Are we going to have a full-scale aggression on Puerto Rico? Then, out of nowhere, a Pave Low helicopter came screaming in to land. I'm glad we were already down to one knee because of the C-130, because the wash from the helicopter's rotors was almost worse than the plane's engine wash.

The LT yelled, "As soon as we get the all clear, load the choppers." Once the Pave Low touched down, the back hatch was open. "We're getting a lift from the 20th Special Operation Squadron out of Hurlburt Field. We have spent a lot of time with these guys, and they have been good to us." The LT looked up with a smile and said, "So remember, be good to them, they've saved our ass plenty."

We had sat on the helicopter paddock not more than a minute when the first of two Pave Lows landed. The Pave Low's technical name is a MH-53J, and is by far one of the United States' most sophisticated helicopters and one of the best in the world. This huge 21-ton steel horse has a range of about 600 miles with a full combat team and gear. I always felt more than safe flying in one of these birds; mainly because it had top secret countermeasure devices really to no end, flare and chaff dispensers, radar warning devices, and all sorts of jammers to deceive anti-aircraft missiles. This thing wasn't one of the "Vanilla" planes; it could almost get us out of anything and, from past experience, these were by far the best helicopter pilots in the world. We were in good hands. I wasn't exactly sure where we were going, but nevertheless, these guys were the best and we were going to get wherever we had to go. Half of us loaded in the first chopper and right behind her was the second. These guys had to be flying around waiting for us. I've never seen such great timing. My question was, where in the hell were we going if we're loading up in the middle of Puerto Rico?

Well, as far as Trout and Ron were concerned, it was back to sleep and we would hear from them again at the next junction. And, likewise, I was ready to go back to my cat nap myself. The G-force in a helicopter was totally different than a plane, so we instinctively leaned against one another for stability on the drops and turns. Next, I was awakened by some turbulence, as it seemed, in association with a loud clunk. I stood straight up and thought that we either hit something or we are taking on fire. As I leaned forward and looked out the front cockpit window, I saw a huge Air Force KC-135 Stratotanker giving us a refill on some petro. I always loved to see mid-air refueling. It was so cool to think that we could really go anywhere and fly forever, as long as we kept getting refueled by the Air Force and the helicopter or aircraft held together. After the air refueling drogue detached from the Pave Low, I looked out the window and saw nothing but water, which meant we were going to be airborne for a while. I looked over at Trout and I'll tell you, when he is in a deep sleep, the reaper himself couldn't wake him up. I took part of a piece of tissue and twisted it up into a little point. I took it and, really lightly, put it in Trout's right nostril. His nose twitched a few times, he slapped his own face and, as always, he came up swinging.

"What the fuck are you doing Dave? You, asshole, leave me alone!" Trout yelled as he tried to hit me. We all started to laugh when Trout held up his middle finger as to say "fuck you" to everyone.

I sat back and thought about this Japanese girl I met at this sushi bar called "Ginza of Tokyo" before we left. I really liked her, even though she told me that because of our different cultures that a relationship would be impossible. I had never had anyone tell me that before. It kinda hurt. I don't know if it was because of the fact that I really liked her or if it was the fact that she shot me down. Anyway, I couldn't stop thinking of it or maybe her. God, she was so hot and her complexion was so perfect. She had such a soft voice and her every move was so graceful that it was like she was floating. Or shit, maybe I'm just horny as hell and need to get some. But to this day, I still think it was her. I was never able to find her again.

It wasn't before long and we got a red light with the buzzer. We were getting close to wherever we were going. The Crew Chief held his hand out with all fingers spread wide and yelled, "Five minutes!"

All of us then repeated down the line, "Five minutes." We grabbed our Load Bearing Equipment (LBEs) and our gear and started to suit up. An LBE is like a vest that conforms to your chest that holds your gear to include weapons magazines, grenades, radio equipment, knives, maps, and anything else that you needed to carry on your person. It is also referred to as a tac-vest. We grabbed our weapons and stood by ready for a combat drop from the aircraft.

The Crew Chief said, "Take it easy, guys; we're coming down to friendlies, it's a United States occupied area."

I didn't know about anyone else, but I was going to be ready for the shit to hit the fan considering it was in the middle of the night and the pilots were using Night Vision Goggles (NVGs).

When the rear door of the Pave Low went down, the air that came in the cabin was hot and very humid. And I can say, to this day, that I really had no idea where we were. It was a comfortable temperature and even though it was extremely dark, the ground appeared to be very plush and green.

We deployed out of the back of the Pave Low in readiness formation. We didn't give a shit what the Crew Chief said; we were going to be ready. You could tell that we were at some kind of makeshift airport out in the middle of nowhere. The grass had some morning dew on it and was green and healthy. There were two helicopters sitting out on the paddock. One was an A/M/TH-6 Little Bird. I was very familiar with this copter, as I have flown many missions with this aircraft. We used it frequently because of its undetectable size and because it can be fitted as a utility or attack helicopter. It has 7.62 (same caliber as the M-60 and AK-47) mini-guns, 70mm (millimeter) rocket pods, Hellfire air-to-ground missiles, or .50-caliber machine guns as well as AAQ-16 FLIR, ALQ-144 IR jammer and radar warning receivers. The other looked like an old news crew helicopter that had definitely seen better days because the tail was gone and it looked like it had been strafed by an F-16. The Pave Low helicopters took off and we were ready to start to raise some serious hell when we saw the shadow of a Hummer and a five-ton truck coming in our direction from the north with their "blackout lights" illuminated.

Koz yelled, "Three-sixty and Rodge, get up the SATCOM (satellite communications link)."

This was a portable radio with a small fan dish we used in order to have direct contact with Joint Special Operations Command (JSOC). The one thing that Rodge had was a LST-5, which was a high-tech transmitter for satellite communications. We set up a 360-degree circle, with equipment and packs in the middle and started to wonder where in the hell these guys dropped us off. Whenever we have to do this, you can't help but think about Custer's final stand. We heard a voice from about fifty yards away yell, "Lieutenant Randie!" The LT told us to stand down, but to keep vigilant. That fuckin' colonel from the Air Force Academy pulled up in the Hummer. I guess he took a fuckin' plane ride straight here and couldn't bear to either take us with him or take a little helicopter ride. I was losing some serious respect for this guy. He pulled up and said, "Lieutenant, you'll ride with me and I'll brief you on the way in." That was just great; who in the hell was this guy and where in the hell were we? We loaded our gear onto the five-ton and climbed in the back. A five-ton had eight very large tires, with a long bed, and the spare mounted behind the passenger side. The front four tires moved simultaneously to steer the vehicle. It was really a kick ass piece of machinery. It was set up much like a deuce and a half but much larger and newer. You could tell the newer military vehicles by the Central Tire Inflation System (CTIS) mounted on the rims of the vehicles. This system was controlled from in the cab with the compressor mounted in-between the truck's frame and hidden in the middle of the vehicle's undercarriage. The operator could either deflate the tires for sandy conditions, inflate them for normal driving, or keep regenerating a punctured or shot out tire. We were definitely experiencing a slight pucker factor on the ride to the building. The ride itself was nice, but we felt like we were out in the middle of nowhere with limited defenses if something were to happen.

When we arrived, this huge black guy pulled the rear gate to the truck down. He said, "Welcome to El Pongo, El Salvador."

I thought, "El Salvador, what in the hell are we doing here? This is a different regiment of 7th SFG country, not ours." 7th SFG, along with 20th SFG, controlled this part of Latin and Central America, to include the Caribbean. They were headquartered out of Fort Bragg, as well, but had different missions. We were in a sister country, not our primary mission focus. The guy who met us at the back of the truck turned out to be a fucking reservist from 20th SFG out of Pittsburgh, Pennsylvania. He said, "Grab your gear and follow me."

During the ride, I noticed a long, brick-like structure that looked like hog pens but constructed out of brick with corrugated roofing, no windows or openings, with one huge telephone pole with a light dangling and swinging in the very small night breeze positioned at the end of the building. It gave me chills and I wasn't sure quite why. I don't know if it was the way that the light was swinging or just the shadows by the wall. The rest of the way in, I was thinking of the revolt and war that had been here a few years earlier because of that soccer game and when the nuns were killed; the US had then intervened. Every briefing we were given about it made it sound like the entire country was nothing but a free-for-all slaughter. We were parked in front of a series of long, hangar-like buildings. You could tell that this was a very controlled environment.

The buildings were painted two-thirds from the top down lime green to a very light green teal and the bottom third was a charcoal gray. All of the paint was very much worn and peeling off the structures. The building windows were all horizontal slats, with bars over them, all without glass. The buildings looked more like a gigantic pill box than a hangar. On the outside wall, to the right of the corrugated loading door on the structure, we pulled up in front where there was a huge logo painted which said, "3d BATERIA ANTIAEREA, VALIENTES HASTA EL FINAL," (3d Anti-Aircraft Battery, Brave Until the End). With a skull and snakes coming out of the eyes and nose, two cannons crossed underneath the skull with the letters "F.A.S."

There were US military vehicles parked all over the place and even some old ass US aircraft parked only a hundred feet in front of these buildings. The aircraft looked almost to be an old C-126s, which were really old US planes. I had never seen one in person, but these things were like fuckin' relics. What, were we in the movie "Land of the Lost?" Had we gone back in time? Did we go through one of those funky clouds you see on TV where there is a Special Ops Team taken back in time? This was definitely some crazy shit! There were communication box trucks, medical Hummers, communication boxed Hummers, canvas topped Hummers, old deuces, cranes, fork-lifts, five-tons, mobile bridge emplacements, hard top up-armed Hummers, and a variety of other vehicles, to include civilian. Whatever this place was, they sure had the vehicles to do almost anything. Even in the Gulf, we didn't have this many vehicles.

The staff sergeant we were following turned to us and said, "This is their best building in the area and try to keep quiet as we have a full house tonight."

A full house? What in the hell was that supposed to mean and what in the hell is going on? This had to be some kind of shit ass joke set up for the LT, but there was no way that Uncle Sam was going to foot this type of bill for a joke. This was serious.

We went up a short jaunt of exterior stairs that had to have been at least five feet wide, into what appeared to be a loading area where trucks would off load their cargo. Instead, there was a GP-Medium (approximately a 15x15 heavy canvas tent) loaded with communication equipment and obviously one of the main comm areas for whatever was going on here and extremely active to boot. We went up another ten steps to what looked like an inclusive high school basketball court with a stage for drama. The outside doors were made up of sliding corrugated tin. The floors were all nice oak or maple-like boards, much like that of a school basketball court! The only difference was that there had to have been at least 100 fully occupied cots. The sergeant took us up to the higher level which I had called the drama area. It was like a stage used for formal speeches or for a play. We set our gear down and Koz said, "Scout, you take the first watch and Todd you pick up after three then Ron."

This meant that we were going to be in three-hour intervals on watch. If you have ever heard that rank has its privileges, this was a prime example. I had to piss like a racehorse. The latrine was behind where we had set all of our stuff. Therefore, everyone in the building would have to pass by us to get to the latrine. The latrine wasn't what I had suspected. There was about half an inch of water/urine/feces on the floor and I had definitely smelled better things. The walls and the stalls were painted in a mid-blue oil base paint. There was a long, basin-like structure that was about 20 feet long, three feet high, and made with light blue half inch tiles. You could see that there were small holes where water should, or did, come out of at one time because of the rust stains. Across from that, there was what looked like a small walk-in shower, but only eighteen or so inches deep, four feet tall, made with the same little, light blue tiles. This had the same type holes, but there was water constantly flowing out of them. I later found out that the El Salvadorian soldiers also drank this water.

I started to take a piss in this thing when a marine walked up behind me and said, "You don't piss in that one. You wash your hands and brush your teeth in that one. You piss over there," pointing at the thing that was about twenty feet long. "It used to be the other way around, but the water won't flow over there anymore."

Okay, so we brush our teeth where we used to piss! I can handle that. The entire bathroom area was lined with concertina wire (c-wire) along the ceiling. It looked like if the shit was going to hit the fan, this was going to be their final line of defense. The LT got us up at about 0400 hours local, which was about one o'clock am our time back home. He said he would be briefing us later and to get some sleep until he figured out some more specifics as to our mission. He told Tom to take watch. I figured he did this because he had the longest time in grade, making him third in command to the LT and Koz.

I woke up to a bunch of loud arguing. As I squinted to see what was going on, I saw a Marine gunnery sergeant yelling at Tom.

He looked over at me and yelled, "That's right pretty boy, it's time to get up."

I did my best to try to shake off the sleep considering that I was really exhausted and had a little bit of jet lag.

Danny said, "Who in the fuck are you?"

I was like, aw shit, here it goes.

The gunny leaned over and yelled, "I'm a higher pay grade than you, how about that fuck head? It's time for your ass to clean the fuckin' head."

Okay, now the buttons had been pushed! We all got out of our bags and stood up ready for a fight.

Tom stepped up and said, "Listen, you fuckin' jarhead, you're out of your league!"

And for Tom to come right out and start swearing, you knew it was serious. When the gunny stepped forward, all of us started toward him. In the background, you could see 50 Marines coming to his defense. But as usual, all of a sudden, the room was called to attention.

"Atten-hut!" One of the Marines in the building called out. And, to no avail, here came the LT, Koz, and that damn colonel.

"You will stand down, gunny!" yelled the colonel.

The gunny yelled out, "I don't think that we have been properly introduced there, Mr. Somebody!"

The colonel ran up and got in his face yelling, "I'm Colonel 'your worst fuckin' nightmare,' asshole, where is your God damn CO!?"

The gunny then stated that he was in the Headquarters (HQ).

"Well, sergeant, why don't you show me the way?"

The colonel and the gunny walked out of the building, with all of us still ready to take these jarheads down and them ready and willing.

Talk about odds. Let's see, 150 to 7? I could deal with that. Might not turn out so good, but we would give it one hell of a shot.

The LT looked down to them, because they were a few feet below us since we were up on this stage, and yelled, "As you were, Marines, as you were!"

The Marines went back to what they were doing, mumbling under their breath, and we tried to settle down a little ourselves. Clean the head? Well, I guess that was our welcome.

3

MEET JESUS

L ATER THAT SAME AFTERNOON, WE MOVED TWO BUILDINGS NORTH OF the previous hanger. The building that we moved to once served as the brig (jail). Today was hot and the ground was very dry and dusty. The sun was beating down, but really didn't feel too hot to the skin. There was a mild breeze coming from the west and it smelled like the ocean coastline. The mountains and the trees in the background were beautiful. We grabbed our gear and went outside to meet with the sergeant from 20th. Our new home was about 50 feet deep and 35 feet wide with 10 feet of clearance to each side of the building. It was used either for a walkway, or room for the inmates to get some sunlight or move around, before the first inner fence topped with c-wire, standing about 10 feet tall. The ground inside the fence looked like crushed grey granite in two and a half inch pieces. Outside of that, there was about five feet of clearance, then another fence that had to be around 15 feet in height with coiled c-wire wire atop of it as well. You could tell that between the outside and inner fences was a dog run used as a deterrent or another form of security because of the feces still in piles between the fences and the hair caught in the fence links. We had two porta-potties delivered to the outer gate of the facility while we were standing out there. I didn't know if this was going to be better than what we had earlier or not, considering the heat and the potential for horrific stench. But this was obviously going to be home for a while.

As we carried the gear up to the front gate to enter the building, there were four Policia Militar (PM), basically, the same as our MPs, but El Salvadorian.

They stood there and refused to let us inside the fence until the colonel came up to vouch for us. This time, he was accompanied by the South American officer that we had seen in Colorado Springs sitting behind the table by the blackboard. I thought to myself that at least the players in this were starting to come out of their shells and make their presence known. As he approached, the PMs snapped to attention and saluted our colonel; the other officer stood there as if we were supposed to say something to him or salute him ourselves. United States soldiers don't salute in a combat area because of the risk of snipers. I wasn't sure if this guy knew that or not. But he didn't say a word. He didn't even seem to blink; he just looked at us like we were from outer space.

The PMs were armed with old, rusty MP-5s, a web-belt without anything on it, and their BDUs. They were seriously skinny and dark from the sun, but did have some muscular definition in their arms. Their name tapes were on above their right breast pockets, as ours would usually be, and the other tape above their left breast pocket displayed the letters B.E.S.M., which I would guess stood for Bateria El Salvador Militar (El Salvador Military Battery). They had a patch on their right shoulders that resembled a police patch of civilian police officers. At the top, it was outlined in yellow with a band of dark blue, white, then dark blue again, with El Salvador written in black in the middle. The rest of the background was baby blue. It had a black bayonet standing up in the middle with two black muskets crossing through it. There were two black, old-fashioned flintlock pistols above the bayonet with brown handles, black hammers, trigger and trigger guard crossing one another. The pistol butt under the handles and the barrels were silver with black stitching through it, creating somewhat of a design. Directly under the bayonet was an outline of yellow with the letters B.E.S.M. stitched in black and the words SOBERANIA Y DISCIPLINA (Sovereignty and Discipline) outlining the bottom of the patch on the inside of the yellow border. On their other shoulder was a black leather arm strap with the letters PM in white. They wore a white helmet with a black brim, the letters PM in the front middle, with black lines going from the middle of the P and the M around to the back of the helmet and a black leather chinstrap that fit tight under their bottom lip. Under their BDUs, they had on US issued brown t-shirts with black US issued jungle combat boots.

When we got the okay to go in, they opened the padlock on the gate and the colonel and the LT led us inside. The very first thing you noticed was the condensation on the ground created from the cold masonry block and the hot air. It was truly humid as hell in there and even a little cold. The front room was 10 by 15 and appeared to be like a day room with a table and two chairs. This must have been where the guards were posted. Behind it, centered in the wall, was an iron jail door that was almost rusted off the hinges. There were eight cells in which the doors had been removed and a room in the back of the building that was either the shower room or the torture room. The floors and walls were blood stained and there were numerous bullet holes in the walls. We were told to stow our gear, that the area was secured, and that we could mosey around or do whatever until 2000 hours local. The LT, Koz, Tom, Petie, and Rodge were told to stand fast and that they were going to be doing a little decorating. As we walked out, we had to squint because of the sun and the difference from being in the cell area. I didn't realize that it was that dark in there. We were handed black laminated cards from the PMs as we passed through the front gate, each having a number and a type of animal on it. I got the rooster, which was ironic being that I was born under the sign of the cock in Chinese mythology, if that had any significance or not (I still to this day do not know). I never saw the other cards and really didn't care to see them; I guess I never thought about it.

We walked out to some of the old US aircraft that was parked down by the hanger where we were previously staying. It was riddled with bullet holes all over it. The exterior camouflage on the aircraft was terribly worn and it had the number 122 under the right cockpit window. This looked to be the only aircraft in the area that was intact. All the others were missing doors, engine covers, windows and, in some cases, the engines themselves. They used corrugated tin and rivets to patch some of the holes. It was obvious that this plane couldn't be pressurized or fly at any extreme heights. How in the hell did they get parts for this thing? I walked over and asked one of the native troops if they used this aircraft as a trailer to practice on aerial targets. He laughed his ass off at me and explained that the aircraft was their priority alert plane, that they also used it regularly for surveillance missions, and that they weren't able to stay at higher altitudes for any prolonged period of time. They hit their jumping altitude, jumped, and the aircraft quickly returned to a lower altitude where there were higher oxygen levels before the pilots passed out. "Well, all the power to 'em!" It was obvious that they were out manned as well as out gunned.

We started to walk toward the landing strip when, all of a sudden, there was a mass of gunfire that seemed to be coming from the tarmac area by the landing strip. We dispersed, hit the deck, and took up an aggressive posture. We looked to our right at the hanger we were previously in where two Marines and two PMs were laughing at us.

One of the Marines called out, "You're going to have to get used to that or you would think that you pretty boys would be by now. Just remember this isn't our country and that isn't our business."

Trout flipped them off and yelled, "Fuck you, jarhead."

Some officer, a Major Woods by his rank and name tape, rushed out of the hanger and walked out to us. He said, "I figured you guys would be out here.

They conduct executions here regularly; it definitely takes some getting used to, but remember we are a guest here, so don't intervene with their operations. Am I understood?"

We replied with an unsure, "Yes, sir." Considering he wasn't in our chain of command, I really didn't give a shit what Major Dip Shit had to say!

We started to walk out towards the area where we heard the gunfire and followed the taxiway out towards the tarmac. The grass and shrubbery were fairly high just off of the concrete taxiway, standing about four feet, or so, high. We circled around to the front of the long brick area that had given me the creeps when we first arrived. It was about 170 feet long and about 20 feet deep, with the roof gradually getting higher in two-foot increments as it went further down to the end, ending around 30 feet high. When we rounded the brick, to the front of it we saw five native soldiers, all with MP-5s and one with an M-60 propped up on some sand bags. They were all standing in front of the smoke-filled building as the smoke bellowed out and rolled up over the corrugated roof. It looked more like a Tombstone scene than an execution. They saw us immediately and turned, but we just kept walking towards them.

The stalls in the building were divided in different length segments, using ten-by-tens and chicken wire spanning the entire distance of the building, with one large stall at the end. As far as constructively and structurally, this was one of the most intact structures that I had seen yet in the area. Just as we got parallel to the front, you could smell death, the gunpowder from their weapons, and the stench of rotting flesh. The flies were everywhere and they covered your face and hands, stinging your flesh with every landing. The flies were nothing compared to what we were to see next.

We all instinctively ducked as we saw a large shadow appear above our heads. I looked up to see hundreds and hundreds of birds of all species, to include huge vultures. When the gunfire started, they must have all scattered, and were now returning for the feast. As I looked in the back of the building, I saw what had to be 40 or more people lying over one another and scattered within the stall. There was half of a brain on the ground; it was impossible to identify the owner due to the faces and skulls that were split everywhere within the slaughter. There were bone fragments, human tissue, clothing fragments, and smoke decorating the walls, the ground, and sporadically spread throughout the stall. The bricks on the inside back wall were all blown apart and replaced with concrete-filled cinder blocks. The blood saturated the dry soil and rolled across the ground as it pooled throughout the entire stall. The stench was so strong; you couldn't help but get a lump in your throat. You could even smell the feces as people shit and pissed themselves upon being shot, or maybe even before the slaughter. I think that I would have done so had I been in their place.

Todd gagged a couple times and Trout stood with wide eyes and said, "Shit on me," in a low, mellow tone.

I heard a muffled groan from within the pile; the only thing I could do was close my eyes and slowly turn my head from side to side. I had never seen nor heard of anything like this before. It was impossible to tell if the people had endured torture prior to this because of all of the entry and exit wounds from the gunfire. You couldn't tell the ages of some of the people, nor always determine their gender, because they were so seriously cut to pieces. They didn't appear to be malnourished and they all had on adequate clothing to suggest that they were not deprived of any. They looked like they were just taken out of their kitchens, eating their breakfast, and going through their normal daily routines. There were men and women amongst the dead; it was obvious that their executioners showed no prejudice, sympathy, or mercy. I had wondered why there were cinder blocks stacked behind this portion of the building. Now I knew it was a back stop so that the bullets wouldn't go astray throughout the compound.

It was explained to us that the people were given a one-day trial, interrogated, were all found guilty of being a sympathizer or an accomplice to the guerilla factions in the area, and were put to death by firing squad, all within the same morning. None of them appeared to have their feet, legs, or hands bound. They were probably pushed in there and executed. I have definitely had better days. I can't imagine how this could be allowed to take place, let alone that Uncle Sam's representatives were only a hundred or so yards away from this scene. By this time, the flies were stinging the shit out of us. The mere thought that they had probably just been eating on these poor people and now were landing on us told me that I had had enough of this. It was time to go back into the compound.

I turned to the guys and said, "Let's get back to the compound; this isn't our problem."

Todd walked up to me and said, "Isn't our problem? You're not going to do or say anything?"

"No, as far as I'm concerned, this didn't happen and we weren't here. Let's just walk away."

You could tell that none of us could believe what had just happened as we started to walk back. During the entire walk, we didn't have any interest in anything else around us and not one of us said anything for the next few hours. This is the first time that I have ever talked about that day that I know of and I am doing so more to clear my own conscious than to exploit the happenings. None of us ever talked of that day to each other or to anyone ever again that I know of, even though I think that the smell has followed us every day of our lives up to this point.

When we got back to the compound, there were about a hundred native soldiers dressed in tight blue shorts, white tennis shoes, and white t-shirts with a blue circle-like blue collar around their necks and arms, similar to the old baseball style shirts of the eighties in the US. They were in formation, preparing to do physical fitness training (PT). They are all very short, but fit. They did a lot of agility training, calisthenics, push-ups and sit-ups, but were incomparable in size, tone, shape, hardened look, and structure with much of our military forces, in general, let alone to our Special Forces soldiers. I would say that you could hang at least five of them on each one of us. To their credit, however, those little guys were fast as hell; they could run at a very fast pace for an extended period of time, without slowing. They were all termed as "combat veterans," since all of them had been involved in the previous war and multiple warfare missions.

We walked in a single file line behind them as they were doing their workout and went back to the "jail" facility where we were staying. We handed our "Black Card" back to the PM and filed into the building.

When we got in, Koz flew up and yelled, "What the hell happened out there?"

Trout shook his head and said, "Koz, you guys really don't want to know, trust me. But everything is fine and secure."

Koz took what he said with a nod and, by the look on all of our faces, knew not to push the subject. One thing about Special Forces soldiers was that after they had experienced enough combat, they became hardened to almost everything. They seldom talk about their experiences because once it was over, it was no longer important outside of a learning experience to help keep themselves alive for the next mission. Each of us made our ways to our individual "cells."

I sat with my back propped up on my rucksack in the third "cell" on the left. I just sat there, collecting my thoughts and going back to what we had seen earlier. Before I knew it, Koz walked by and said that it was 1930 hours and if we needed to take a piss, get a chew, shit or whatever, to do it now, because we would be starting the briefing in about half an hour. I walked out into the small courtyard, stepped into one of the porta-potties and took, I guess, what was a well-needed piss. I stepped out, stretched, looked up at the beautiful dusk sky that was setting in and looked at the stars, took a deep breath, and thought to myself that I felt a strong sense of security being in this jail. As I looked around at the ground in the little courtyard, I didn't look at it as if we were being held against our will in here, but more with a sense of being in full control of the area and safe. I gave a little shrug of the shoulders and went back in for the briefing.

The LT called us to attention in this small jail-like structure. The back room where we were sitting had very little elbow room when all of us were piled in there together. We quickly stood up as the colonel, the South American officer from Colorado Springs, and a somewhat deformed officer walked into the room. The deformed man appeared to have extreme, slash-like scars all over his face and was missing his right ear and a large chunk of his hair; it was just one huge scar that molded across the right side of his face. The colonel called out, "At ease," and most of us then leaned against the wall. He looked around the room and said, "Gentlemen, we are now entering operation readiness." This meant that we would now be starting a series of different stages to detach ourselves from anything and everything to ready ourselves for the mission.

At first, we were all very quiet and intense, trying to feel out our new guests. The colonel then introduced the men, saying, "This is Commander Rodriguez of the El Salvadorian Special Operations Division. He is here to be an advisor and be used at our discretion for intelligence. The gentleman to my left is Lieutenant Jesus (pronounced hey-suse), he will be your acting Executive Officer; he would prefer that you just call him Jesus." You could see all eyebrows go up with a questioning and uneasy look. "If any of you are questioning his appearance, he was captured and tortured by a group of banditos four years ago. He was struck countless times in the face and body with a machete and left for dead. We are grateful that he is here with us now. He speaks English fluently and will be one of your biggest assets on this mission. Lieutenant, we welcome you and thank you for being here." Jesus lowered his head with a slight nod of understanding and introduction.

Combat had its strains and one of those was the ability to keep the utmost mental discipline at all times while keeping the level of alertness always at an all-time peak. You had to learn how to disassociate and detach yourself from whatever elements were needed at that point in time. The problem was that everyone here had the emotional repercussions that came with that disassociation technique. The question was where Jesus was in this mix and what was his present state of mind considering the demons he had to be fighting? I knew that I was going to be watching him very closely for the next few days, if that meant looking for physical abilities, warfare knowledge, or current mental abilities and condition. The LT was looking at me silently saying the very same thing. The one thing that I noticed right away was that one of the machete cuts went directly through his left eyeball, eyelid, and separated the center bridge of his nose that had to be affecting his septum and sinus abilities, let alone his peripheral, night, and normal vision capabilities. But I would have to wait and see for myself through a systematic evaluation that we used primarily when training Airborne and Ranger units.

The colonel said, "From this time on, all of you will be quarantined together for the up-coming mission, with the exception of the commander and myself, within this small but sufficient compound." An A-team could be held in quarantine to prepare for a mission for up to a month, separating them from the outside to include news, interaction with other soldiers, especially if they weren't in Special

Forces, and most of all, loved ones or significant others. If someone was going to hesitate about something or doing something very dangerous, their hesitation is usually contributed to a loved one. This was designed to utilize total concentration on the mission and to alleviate the possibility of anything getting leaked. If you couldn't talk to anyone, you couldn't leak any information. Not that we have ever had that problem, but it was still protocol.

We were like Silverback apes, confined within a small cage, surrounded by barbed wire fencing. Having that much testosterone in one tiny building made us wind up even more, even to the point that I saw several of us bouncing a foot or leg up and down, leaking out some of the adrenaline rush. One thing that I hoped that the colonel had taken into perspective has when you get a specialized team like ours and confine us, we may walk around appearing to be very calm and collected on the outside, but on the inside, we are a pressure cooker ready to blow. Depending on the amount of time an A-team is bound up like this, and the longer in isolation, the more likely that the team will behave more violently. Those pent-up emotions, adrenaline, and aggression explode outward like a bomb during the mission more so than under normal circumstances. The colonel gave us the packets that we had looked at in the US, but this time all of the maps and intelligence guides were marked very specifically.

The maps were of El Salvador and a concentrated area between several mountain ranges and out closer to the ocean. There were also a few places marked in the country of Honduras. I got a bad feeling that we were going to be starting something big. The information that we were given was now headed by the words "Mission Analysis" and included infiltration plans, different types of terrain analysis, demographics, local politics and rulers, approximate meteorological surveys done from the previous year and for the next two months, terrorist threats, weapons loads, and drop zones. Also included were passwords and running passwords (running passwords were passwords that were pre-set for immediate friendlies in the area to call out in an emergency situation so we didn't blow them to pieces as they approach us, probably running); sign countersign (which was a running silent numerical password; for example, if the password was the number three, the person at the area of operations would hold up one finger and the guy running towards him would hold up two fingers, thus all fingers equaling three. You only get two chances, and if you fuck up, you're going to get lit up); and a list of contacts that we had to make during the mission. All of the information in the packet would include all the requirements that we used in the "Special Forces Detachment Mission Planning Guide," a guide that we used like it was our Bible. It was similar to an Operations (Op) plan. They would be approximately 19 to 20 pages long and held all of our specified contingencies and the requirements we would need for any mission, regardless of where or when the mission took place.

The colonel then said, "As of now, our deployment time and chalk time has us departing Thursday night at 2230 hours."

Wait a minute: today is Sunday. They are only giving us a few days to get this down? My gut was starting to give me a case of the "oh-shits." Not as much because of the timeline, but more so because someone put a lot of time, money, assets, and personnel into this, meaning it was probably going to be very big or very messy. I noticed out of the corner of my eye the two lights in the room were slightly swaying. They hung from a single tattered wire and had the appearance of the top of a wok, painted dark green with a light bulb in the middle. There was one in every cell, two in the front room, and two in the back room. It was just like the movies, how they sway just enough for you to notice.

My eyes then quickly went back to the colonel as he said, "You will be picked up and flown out by three AH-60 Blackhawks from the 160th." I knew these guys very well; it was like being picked up from school by an uncle or grandfather, a member of your distant family. These guys were part of us, our own brethren: The Night Stalkers. "Your Lieutenant and Jesus will take the briefing from here. I'll see you guys in a couple of days, good luck."

The commander and the colonel walked out of the room. Just about then, Todd let one fly. He had to have farted air as dead and as old as the fucking mummies in Egypt. We were in this little room of bloodstained walls and very little circulation and, as I remember, needed our Nuclear, Biological, Chemical Warfare (NBC) gear, because I swear nobody could breathe.

Tom yelled out, "Who in the hell did that?" Everyone pointed to Todd. "Okay, asshole (shaking his head and hand in front of his face), you can go out and stand guard and air out a little." Todd threw his hands up with his palms toward the ceiling and said, "Sorry," with a sneering look on his face.

Koz called out, "He should stay in here and melt the walls and paint in here with that! Not out there!" We all laughed and shook it off. Jesus never flinched one iota; I guess he didn't see the humor in it. I'm surprised he didn't puke. The timeline was going to be tight on this one and we had to get ready, all joking aside.

Special Operation Units, because of their more complex missions, were usually given numerous days, weeks, or even months to plan and rehearse operations pertaining to the specific mission. In this case, we were being given days for what looked like a very specified and complex mission. I just hoped it would be enough, considering that, as of right now, Jesus was "baggage." With the exception of Jesus, we were a special unit with a special way of doing things and a very dangerous and powerful collective group. The mission now depended on security of personnel and information, unit buildup, and target date.

Instinctively, the LT, Koz, Tom, and Jesus got into a group and started to discuss command information and tactics so they could report them to "SOCCE" (pronounced sock-see) which was the Special Operations Command and Control Element. Leadership always would distance themselves from the other troops because fraternization risked contempt. All the rest of us broke off as well and headed for the middle cell on the right that was being used as a temporary armory with weapons and specialized gear within black hard plastic containers. The cell was packed to the ceiling.

Danny was in charge of the armory and weapons dispensing. He, like the rest of us, was sort of a perfectionist. He did everything with precision and meaning, which was good, because he never left any open questions of why. He started unlocking the huge crate like boxes and handing out the contents as he called the soldier that it belonged to. This trip we were definitely packing heavy. Rodge was carrying an M-4 Carbine (which can fire a 5.56 caliber tracer, dummy, blank or ball round) with infrared laser scope and handle grip attached to the fore stock. Danny cleared it and made it weapon safe. He then took out his AN/PVS-7B night vision goggles (all NVGs used by the team were the same, as well as Global Positioning Systems (GPS)), and his GPS locator. As I sat there and waited for him to get all of his gear, I could hear the condensation dripping off of the ceiling, drop by drop. It was definitely a sobering sound. He grabbed his gear and moved into the day area rubbing the wall, leaving paint slowly floating to the jail floor.

Next was "Ron." He was handed the M-16 A2 that used the same ammo as the M-4. He then got his NVGs, GPS, and a RF 1 Laser Rangefinder, which is a highly precise optic-electronic measuring instrument. You can measure exact distances to objects inside of a large area. He grabbed all of his stuff and followed Rodge into the day room.

Danny called out, "Doc," and I walked into the cell and was handed my baby, an M-60 that carried the name "Mother." She was my baby and long-time friend. She got me out of more shit than I care to even talk about. I grabbed her, opened up the bipods, put them on the ground, turned the cover latch, and opened the cover.

I lifted up the feed tray and looked into that beautiful clean-as-a-whistle barrel, smiled, and said, "That's my girl." I flipped the firing selector switch to fire and pulled the cocking lever handle back to the rear, closed the cover, grabbed the cocking handle, pulled the trigger, and rode the bolt forward. There is no feeling in the world like a perfectly functioning and clean weapon ready to fire it up. Am I obsessed with this weapon? No, but we had a very close friendship and mutual understanding. Some people had kids; I had "Mother." She was 43.5 inches long, weighed 23 pounds, had a maximum effective range of 1100 meters, fired a 7.62 caliber ball round, had a tracer ratio of one to four, and had a cyclic rate of 550 rounds a minute. And that's my baby; where I go, the "Hog" goes with me. I got my nods, my other gear, and went to my cell.

Todd was next with his M3A1 .45-caliber Grease Gun and his sawed-off 12-gauge pump Ithaca Light shotgun, with a duckbill attached at the end of the barrel to disperse the shot in a horizontal pattern. This was one weapon you didn't want to be on the wrong end of at any time. He got the rest of his things and joined me in my cell as we prepared our gear and packs.

Trout carried an M-4 with an M-203 Grenade Launcher undercarriage. I swear he could hit a mosquito's dick in flight at a hundred yards with that thing. Not only was he proficient, he was downright deadly. He also toted a M72A2 LAW (Light Anti-Tank Weapon). He received the same gear as all of us, but also received a Laser Aiming Lighting Projector System (LALPS), which was an infrared laser targeting designator and a white or infrared lighting projector. With it, you could light and engage a target when you had your NVGs on or distinguish a target for aircraft support. He went down to the first cell on the right just up from ours. Petie got the M-249 Squad Automatic Weapon (SAW) that fired 5.56 caliber rounds and only weighed 22 pounds. This ole girl could fire 850 rounds per minute and was definitely one bad ass mamba jamba. Petie also got a LAW, then went to where Trout was.

Danny and Scout were taking care of some other weapons and gear we would receive within the next couple of days. Everyone was preoccupied with what they were doing when automatic gunfire started up. You could hear charging handles being pulled and released when Jesus yelled out, "They're doing more executions!" Well, this guy spoke and understood English well. We all stood fast, waited for the LT to give us the nod, and went back to what we were doing.

You could see the LT immediately asking Jesus if the executions were on a schedule or if they were always sporadic. Jesus said, "They do them as they see fit. It depends on how the Commandant is feeling that day and if their holding facility is getting crowded." The LT raised a brow and went back to analyzing the map they had put up on the wall. I was starting to get worried that we were getting caught up in a whole bunch of someone else's problems. Tom called out to wrap up what we were doing, grab a Meal Ready to Eat (MRE), and meet outside in the courtyard in five minutes.

Rodge opened the MRE case and started throwing one to each of us. Sweet, I got menu #12, "Escalloped Potatoes with Ham and accessory packet A." They came in a dark brown, thick plastic bag with all the contents in their own individual packet, with the exception of the coffee, sugar, salt, napkin, and all that stuff. They were high in calories and you couldn't beat it if you were out in the middle of nowhere and hungry. I didn't mind them at all; Rodge, on the other hand, was obsessed with them and would eat them every day until his dying day if it were up to him and never seemed to gain a pound. I never could understand that. Each of us laid or sat on the rocks outside eating, trying to pop in slight questions to the LT and Koz as to what more specifically was going on.

They were vague with every question, even down to if they had seen the new mural on the wall of one of the hangers further down. I could tell that the LT was getting the game plan together and was going to tell us things in his own time, and at a psychologically fitting pace. That way, our questions that would be repeating through our minds would arise and be answered at the final briefing so that we were all in understanding and on the same page.

We traded the contents of our MREs, as soldiers always do, then grabbed a chew, and talked for about an hour amongst each other. The LT walked inside for a minute, then walked back out saying, "Now would be a good breaking point. Hit the hay, if you want, while Koz and I work out a few bugs." Todd and I picked up our loose equipment, packed it up, grabbed our poncho liners (a thin camouflage blanket which felt like and was made of a silky parachute like material), and each took a different corner of the cell. For some reason or another, I was ready for bed.

4

THE LAY OF THE LAND

I WOKE UP TO WHAT SOUNDED LIKE A DEUCE OR FIVE-TON OUTSIDE revving its huge diesel engine. I shivered as the temperature in the cell couldn't have been more than 40 degrees. I lifted my left arm with my right because the left was asleep; I squinted down at my watch, rubbed the condensation off the crystal with my right thumb and read it being five to five local time. I was lying up against my rucksack (Alice pack) and, as I moved a little to my left side, I realized that not only was my ass asleep, but my pants were soaked. First thing to come to mind was, "Holy shit, I pissed myself in my sleep." I gritted my teeth together, lifted my head up, and closed my eyes; right at that moment, that fucking truck was revving and braking, revving and breaking. I stood up shivering, clinching my ass cheeks together with a good stretch and started to grab another set of BDUs and clothing out of my ruck.

To my right, I heard Todd saying, "I pissed my fucken pants, what in the hell, I didn't even drink last night! Son of a bitch!"

I laughed and looked to him and said, "Dude, it's the condensation from the concrete walls running down and soaking the floor. Either that or you pissed so much you soaked me and flooded the entire cell."

He turned his head from side to side and gave another, "Son of a bitch!" lifting his wet legs and hands. Well, it was good for him and, I guess, all of us because it sure got us up in a hurry and ready to start this complex and important day. I changed and headed out to the courtyard to see what in the hell those trucks were doing. When I got out there, they had taken six or seven five-ton vehicles and surrounded the fenced-in jail compound with them. Well, I guess this was our added security and privacy barrier? Primitive, but who cared. I could hear a bunch of commotion coming from where the jarheads were.

"I wonder what's going on down there?" I asked Koz, as he stepped out into the courtyard.

He said, "I don't know, but there's only one way to find out." He pulled the two-way radio out of his cargo pocket and called in, "Sierra Foxtrot Alpha to Hotel."

"Hotel, go ahead."

"Is there a problem in Uncle Sam's House?"

"Negative, sir; there was another hit last night and you will be briefed at a later time."

"Copy, Sierra Foxtrot Alpha out." Koz held the radio at about chest level looking straight forward and said, "I don't know what is going on or who got hit, but I intend to find out." He turned around and went back into the day room. You could tell that the not knowing was getting to Koz and a lot of us. What were we doing here and exactly who put us here?

Then, from inside the compound, I heard, "Holy shit, Todd, you pissed your fucking pants again! Where did you get the booze from?"

"Fuck you, it's from the water on the floor, asshole!"

Todd wasn't always the brightest guy and had pissed himself many times, but he was good at what he did and was usually funny as hell. Everyone inside started laughing and it was well overdue. It certainly broke the monotony, even if it was at Todd's expense.

The LT walked by every cell and said, "Get your weapons ready. We have a ten o'clock hot chalk, pack light."

Sweet, I thought, we were finally going to do something. Todd looked at me and said, "I don't think I pissed my pants?"

I laughed and said, "Get over it man, everyone was wet."

I heard some trucks drive by the front of our building; I wondered what was going on now. I just wanted some of the blanks to get filled in, even if it was only a couple. I grabbed a pack of freeze-dried pears from my ruck for breakfast and readied my gear. We went back to the back room and looked over the maps on the wall. It looked like we were going to be moving through sectors to our objective.

Jesus was in the doorway, watching us. He said, "Everything will make a lot more sense after today."

I turned and said, "I sure as hell hope so, but for now I'll hurry up to wait." He let out a puff of air as his head lifted up slightly.

At 0930 hours, a canvas-covered deuce backed up in between the five-tons outside of the front gate. The LT called out, "Teams one, six, and five in the deuce; four, three, and two on the next; wait for them to back in before mounting." We were on the second chalk with Rodge and Koz's teams. We grabbed our LBEs (suspenders with vest), our weapons, and waited for the first group to leave. After the first truck pulled out and ours backed in, we started to mount up in the deuce. As I walked outside, there had to have been at least 20 PMs on the sides of the deuce and they also filled in behind us, prior to us leaving. An additional four rode outside, along the back, and up by the driver and passenger side doors. So much for not drawing any unnecessary attention! By the time we got out to the paddock, the LT's Blackhawk was taking off and ours was coming in. We loaded in our Blackhawk and immediately took off.

Koz was armed with his usual M-4 Carbine. Jesus had his AK-47, which used a 7.62 caliber round, same as mine. The only difference between our weapons was that he could use any of my ammo if needed, but his would not cycle through mine. I would have a stove pipe (where the brass doesn't properly eject out of the ejection port) or jam on the first shot. Looking down at the camp, I couldn't believe my eyes how many vehicles were actually there. We shortly joined up with four other Blackhawks dividing our group and with one more on our tail.

The ground throughout the countryside was light brown to tan, for the most part, with small patches or speckles of green trees scattered throughout. The country was fairly mountainous and had quite a number of waterways and/or lakes in the region. Land plots seemed to be divided by hedgerows or rows of trees in the lower plain areas. We flew over several little towns and a couple of large encampments, one of which was operated by the Marine Corps. Jesus explained how they have been using the Marines to fly daily over the countryside, frequenting the position where we would set up our base camp and that for the last few months, many of their flights were decoy helicopters conducting false insertions to confuse guerilla patrols. The sky had very few clouds and went from a light hazy blue up to a clear darker blue the higher you looked up. The country was actually very beautiful from our present position. When we got out to the coastline of the Pacific, it looked like a straight line of sand along the water that curved slightly to the southeast as we flew further south.

As we zigzagged across the countryside, we started to see sporadic clouds of black smoke rising through the jungle canopy. Koz touched the sleeve of Jesus and asked what the smoke was. Jesus leaned toward him looking dead into Koz's eyes and said, "Banditos, guerilla sanctions. That's why we're here." He then leaned back in his seat and looked back down onto the landscape. The rest of the ride was more to familiarize us with the layout of the area than to get into specific places or factions.

When we got back to the paddock, the command chopper was already down and loading up in the deuce. Meanwhile, we circled around for another 15 minutes before landing and loading up to go back to the base camp. I couldn't help but think about what Jesus said on the chopper and the look he had in his eyes. When we were coming in for our landing, I noticed a UH-53 helicopter parked just outside of the camp on the vehicle tarmac. I was wondering if that was going to be one of our birds or someone else's. As we loaded up in the deuce for the short ride back, everyone seemed to notice the UH-53 and commented on it at the same time.

When we were finished backing up to the jail compound, they pulled the canvas tarp on the back of the deuce back to reveal four US MPs and two big guys who looked to be Mercs (US hired mercenaries) with black tac-vests on, one carrying a CAR-15 with laser scope and the other carrying a 9mm Smith & Wesson M79 submachine gun, which lead me to believe that they were probably ex-SEALs. We dismounted the deuce and walked through the compound into the day room. You could see the two civilians in the back room; considering they were wearing khaki pants, polos and blue windbreakers, they kind of stood out. Tom stood in the dayroom to the right with his arms folded across his chest. He was a model picture as he stood there with his high and tight streaked with gray and white, his legs exactly shoulder width apart and his huge forearms bulging across his chest. He had a hardly pleasant smile on his face when I asked him if everything was alright; he told me to safe my weapon and meet in the back room.

When Todd and I walked back there, we could see the walls were covered in reconnaissance photos, some black and white, others in color. The LT told us to quiet up as he told us that these men were here from the NSA in Washington to brief us on mission details. Every one of us trusted the NSA about as far as we could throw it. These guys always had their dicks in someone else's ass.

They started out like they always do, saying, "This briefing is Secret, non-foreign, and is to be held in the utmost of secrecy." I rolled my eyes and mumbled, "yah, yah, yah." He pointed to some of the photos on the wall stating that they were satellite photos taken a few days ago, southwest of the city of Jiquilisco. The photos were of a mass slaughter of everyone in the area, with huts and surrounding buildings on fire.

He then pointed to another set of photographs, that only showed the dead lying around this small village. He said, "These were taken yesterday by a U2." The U2 spy plane was a strange looking aircraft, the center fuselage and cockpit looked like a huge black cigar with enormous wings across the top. The wings were so huge compared to the center of the plane that each wing had a wheel under it because the wings sagged to the ground on takeoff then the wheels dropped off as it became airborne. When it landed, it would taxi into the hanger where the wheels were re-applied to support the wings while in the hanger or sitting on the tarmac.

He started telling us about the band of guerillas that came together after the revolt and how they were on a free-for-all killing spree, seeking vengeance for their lost families and friends. This is why we were here: to dismember and destroy this faction of guerillas.

Scout said, "We got that in the back of here, you sure you got your photos straight?"

The man looked at Scout and said, "You are here to neutralize these factions with extreme prejudice, you got that?" When I heard that, I could feel the heat and tingle on top of my head, down the back of my neck, and in the tips of my fingers from the growing anxiety of what the future might hold.

The LT said, "The United States has an interest in this area because they will be erecting a submarine radar sight not too far off the coast."

One of the guys in civvies said, "That is correct. You will secure the sight and take care of our friends and we will take care of the rest. You will be meeting with several contacts throughout the mission and they will further advise you of any changes in plans." They also said that the guerillas used anything they could get their hands on, as far as weapons were concerned.

So, we were going to be acting as chess pieces throughout a drawn-out game of chance. We asked very few questions and at the end of the briefing, one of the men said, "We will be following your movements and progress through aerial recon, ground observance and guerilla movements. I would like you to all keep this in the back of your heads through this entire mission: you are being ordered to do this with extreme prejudice." He clearly clinched his teeth together after saying that as his cheeks bulged out two or three times.

The two guys grabbed their bags, thanked us, told us good luck, and walked out to their awaiting Hummer. We all stood there in silence for a couple minutes looking at the photos when the LT called, "Atten-hut!" The colonel and the El Salvadorian Commandant walked in. The Commandant told the LT that calling the room to attention wasn't necessary anymore for any of the officers. He then went on to explain that the people of his country have been suffering for years because of these "soulless murderers" and that he, as well as his country, would be grateful to us.

Then a PM called in from outside to the Commandant. He walked to the front room and said for us to come out to the courtyard. In the courtyard, they brought us a hot meal from the Marine mess down the way. Of course, it was based with potatoes, as were all military meals. There were boiled potatoes, with beef stroganoff and corn. This was a great surprise, to say the least.

As we sat there eating, I looked down the hall to the back room and saw Jesus studying the photographs. Jesus was a good guy and, to my amazement, was well accepted amongst the men. He didn't have anything to prove to anyone, but he did walk around like a man without a heart, a conscience, or a soul. He was a machine that had been trained and programmed for revenge for his past and the pasts of his fallen comrades. You could tell that he didn't care about anything, except whatever it was he had to do. Oddly enough, when you were around him, you didn't feel a threat of any kind but also kept a sense of his capabilities. He was definitely dangerous, but kept his hate at a minimum and maintained his composure to the point that he would never talk unless spoken to or if there was a need to say something in an act of safety (like when they were conducting more executions.) The one thing that I did notice that bothered me was that he didn't seem to disassociate himself from his past; instead, he used it as fuel. This was a warning to me and the others, because we didn't know enough about him to measure up his actions and we didn't know when or if this guy was going to go postal. I kept a watch on him every chance I got.

We were later asked to go over to the Commandant's building later that night for dinner. We went over, had another good hot Marine meal, and went back to the jail to turn in for the night. We were kept under constant guard, 24/7 by numerous PMs, joined now by US MPs, that were ordered not to talk to us or acknowledge anything about us other than our security.

For the next few days, we were up at 0430 hours and did some calisthenics in the courtyard, which was hard on the feet and the hands. The LT later got us into their gym facility. We flew out shortly after that every day, but with earlier take off times each day. The goals were to keep up the constant inbound and outbound activities of the flights and to familiarize us with specific landing zones, areas that had been hit, and any evidence of local resistance. We were eating two hot meals a day in the Commandant's building and were able to talk a couple of the PMs into getting a coffee maker and a fan for us. We were grateful and paid them in cigarettes and American currency.

Tom was the one to watch if you were trying to be conscious of the food you ate, because he ate very wisely and healthy. Danny, on the other hand, was the God of salt. He drenched everything in salt no matter what it was. It was truly a wonder how he didn't have a stroke or a heart attack every day and the funny thing was, all of us would leave salt stains on our t-shirts every day but he never did.

Their gym facility was nice, considering. The Commandant had the area cleared until our departure, so we were able to use anything in the facility to our liking. We used their free weights, even though one of us could lift every one they had. We used the wall peg board and the three ropes they had hanging from the ceiling. We stretched three times a day, did push-ups, sit ups, cardinals, jumping jacks, and ran circles around the floor of the gym. We also practiced non-contact martial arts training. It was all non-contact because we didn't need anyone to get hurt this close to deploying for the mission which was interesting because most of us used different styles and would choose the one that worked best for that individual. I used Aikido; my father got me into it when I was young because one of his friends told him that it would help me with discipline, self-control, sports, and it would help me do better in school. Best thing about it was that it eventually helped me protect myself against him. In doing this, we all found a way to vent and to have an exit for the adrenaline that all of us had growing in us every day.

The Commandant had a hose brought over for us to use for showering and hygiene. He also had about fifty cases of Evian water brought to us for drinking and brushing our teeth and a bottomless box of apples and oranges, which we all knew that Ron enjoyed, because he got a plug from the pulp in the oranges. We were afraid that he was going to need surgery. But we heard him pass every little bit of that plug as he sat in the porta-potty, grunting and groaning with every explosive burst, which we all had front row seats to witness that night because the LT, Koz, and Tom were going over some things in the back room so we were told to stay outside. If Ron had had an embarrassing moment in his life, you would have to chalk this one up in the top ten, but nevertheless, it was funny as hell listening to him in there. That is one thing I always laugh about to this day every time I think about it.

After that, we all headed in for the night knowing tomorrow was going to be our departure day. I checked Ron out and gave him an IV so that he didn't become dehydrated in the night. Koz walked through the center of the jail and leaned into each cell quietly saying, "Our chalk has been moved up, we're leaving this morning, not tonight. Suit up." This was better because we all worked better instinctively rather than playing a waiting game.

5

CHALKS UP

I DON'T THINK THAT ANY OF US GOT ANY SLEEP THAT NIGHT. WE WERE ALL too wired up and ready to get the hell out of this place and out of quarantine, or sitting in jail, even though all of us had experienced the inside of a jail cell in the States at least once. It was about 0100 hours and I finished getting my Alice pack ready. I had two med kits; one I carried on the outside of my Alice pack that I can get to quickly and/or take it off and carry it on my tac vest. I also carried a surgical kit that has more specific medical equipment that I carried in a waterproof sealed and sterilized carrying pouch.

I grabbed my laminated checklist I always carried and started to go down it, checking each individual item: wood dowel and belt to make a tourniquet, morphine, syringes loaded and empty, three bags lacerated ringers (IV bags), sutures, anti-venom kit (for snake or scorpion bites), sterilized scalpel/scissors/needles/forceps/tweezers, nitroglycerine tablets (cardiac), quinine (intravenous infection), Benzedrine (amphetamine sulfate), antiseptic cream, iodine, elastic bandages, corks (to take burning ashes and cauterize the wound to prevent infection), wadding and trauma bandages, rolls of gauze, 10 cravats (triangular bandages for splints, slings, and a million other things) with safety pins included, epinephrine (for allergic reactions), penicillin (for infection), Omeprazole (for acid indigestion), Meclizine HCL (for dizziness/nausea), Pyridoxine HCL (assist in cell regeneration), Chlorpheniramine Maleate (as an antihistamine), Therapeut tabs (dietary supplement and vitamin), salt tablets, iodine tablets (for drinking water), chocolate bars, chewing gum, two logs of "Grizzly" straight long cut chewing tobacco, and just some plain old generic aspirin.

After going through the checklist, I took all of my MREs that we previously took apart to save on weight and space, got my ammo, water (2 two-quart canteens), a machete on my back, a double-edged knife that I called "The Widow Maker," and a series of different explosives to include M67 fragmentation grenades and "Willy Pete" (White Phosphorous), AN/M14, TH3 incendiary grenades, smoke, M-127A1 slap flares, and a few M18A1 anti-personnel mines, also known as claymores.

I picked up "Mother" and said, "We're going to the dance, baby." Danny called us in one at a time and handed out our side arms with a thigh holster/magazine holder and two wrist magazine holders. Tom's holster was attached to his tac vest on his lower chest. Tom, Danny, Scout, Petie, Todd, Rodge, and I were all carrying a 45-Ruger P90 DC with 230 grain jacketed "Black Talons" (hollow points) with explosive silicone tips. If we were going to be close enough to have to use it, we were sure as hell going to blow the shit out of it. The LT, Koz, Trout, and Ron were given their weapon of choice, which was a 9mm Beretta with similar loads, I'm sure.

Our packs were evenly distributed weight wise throughout the team, at about a hundred pounds each, and were now lugging around "The Big Green Wart," which was a phrase we used to describe our Alice packs. It was 0300 hours and the deuces were here. We all bowed our heads and took a knee as we offered our prayer:

> "Almighty God, who art the Author of liberty and the Champion of the oppressed, hear our prayer. We, the men of Special Forces, acknowledge our dependence upon Thee in the preservation of human freedom. Go with us as we seek to defend the defenseless and to free the enslaved. May we ever remember that our nation, whose motto is "In God We Trust", expects that we shall acquit ourselves with honor, that we may never bring shame upon our faith, our families, or our fellow men. Grant us wisdom from thy mind, courage from Thine heart, strength from Thine arm, and protection from Thine hand. It is for Thee that we do battle, and to Thee belongs the victor's crown. For Thine is the kingdom, and the power and the glory, are yours now and forever. Amen."

As we got up, the LT then called out the mounting order: "First and third in the first deuce, second and sixth in the second deuce, and fourth and fifth in the third — you got Jesus. See you guys at the AO, keep sharp." The LT and Rodge's team stepped out and mounted up into the deuce. The second deuce backed in, waited about ten minutes, then had Koz and Danny's team mount up. I noticed that Koz was carrying his Heckler and Koch MP-5 with infrared sights and a sawed-off Ithaca light 12-gauge pump with six shot and topped with a spherical slug; he planned on doing some very personal hunting. He gave the M-4 to Jesus to carry. We finally mounted up as well, then went out to the landing paddocks out in the middle of the field with what sounded like numerous helicopters sitting in wait, as you could hear all of the rotors screaming in the early morning air.

It was dark as hell out there when they pulled the canvas back at the rear of the truck. We started to load into our MH-60 Black Hawk when I looked out in the field and saw at least six or seven AH-60 Black Hawks. My brows definitely went up and the only thing I could get to come out of my mouth was "holy shit." An AH-60 Black Hawk is a mean and brutal war machine; it has a variety of weapons to include, 7.62 caliber mini-guns, 70mm rocket pods, .50 caliber machine guns, or Hellfire air-to-ground missiles, as well as a 30mm canon and Stinger air-to-air missiles. This was one bad bitch that could slap the smile off of anyone's face permanently!

We took off in sporadic order and took to the skies in a hurry. We had one hell of a roller coaster ride, zigzagging in and out of tree pockets, to avoid enemy patrols or outposts, I'm sure. We were skimming 20 feet off the tree tops at about a hundred miles per hour — what a fucking ride! I'll never know how those guys could fly so proficiently with their NVGs on in total darkness.

When we were in flight, you could see that there were a lot of patches of water around, which was odd because the ground itself was so hard and dry. There were lakes, ponds, and a lot of marshland. There were millions of stars; I don't think I have ever to this day seen as many stars in the sky as I did while serving in El Salvador. I looked over to Jesus, who was looking directly forward, never blinking, never making any kind of expression, which I wasn't sure he could. I know that he could squint his eyes, frown with his eyebrows, and when he talked, he couldn't move the left side of his mouth or lips. The scars on his face seemed to reflect all light. They were shiny against any light and because they were so pronounced, in the dark, they gave an extremely grotesque contrast to his face.

When we were in the base camp at dinner one night with the Commandant, he spoke briefly about our teammate, Jesus, in a nonchalant manner, and was talking almost like he was telling a fairytale from generations past. He looked into dead space when he shared with us that "He had stood with El Diablo (The Devil) and stared into his eyes. Some say that he saw Hell's gates and escaped with his scars as a reminder. He now walks the Earth as a hollowed soul, seeking eternal revenge." One thing I knew of Jesus was that he didn't care about life or death and that he was looked at as a patriot of his people. He always seemed to look into the abyss as a hardened shell with nothing inside and glassed eyes. Sometimes even now when I think of him, I get chills and am kind of embarrassed because when you were with him you couldn't help but stare and I would catch myself doing that so often. I had never seen a living man with such disfigurement. Now he was our guide, and we were his revenge; with us, he realized the opportunity to dispense something Jesus' people hadn't had in years. We would carry him through Hell's gates, tools he would use to seek his revenge.

On the ground, we could see small campfires burning in the night air. Some would try to put them out as the helicopters approached, spreading cinders into the air like scattered fireflies. We got our red light and the crew chief yelled out "five minutes," which passed throughout the cabin. We nodded our heads, then locked and loaded. We set down in a clearing in the middle of nowhere and deployed into a 360 formation, close to the tree line. I saw several choppers continue on to give the illusion that no helicopters stopped or touched down. We waited there for about four or five minutes until the choppers went over the mountain pass and our hearing and sight became accustomed to this new environment.

The immediate area was very quiet, with the exception of some roosters. It was like the fucking internet of roosters out there; one would sound off, then another on the horizon, and another somewhere else. It went all throughout the entire countryside. We were briefed that sometimes the guerillas would shine flashlights in the faces of the roosters to send a signal across the country, which, by the sound of things, would travel very quickly and proficiently better than any radio. Meanwhile, Rodge was on the horn with a Marine post that was to be our first rendezvous.

Tom called out, "Wedge heavy right by two." This meant that we were going to be in wedge formation, bounding over-watch, heavy weapons on the right side, and two squads. We instinctively took our position based on Tom and started walking to the east for a couple of miles. The ground was covered in eight-inch, sun-burned grass and very hard, dry soil. There were rows of aloe and yucca plants, both having quills and burs, and a great deal of small shrubbery. Palm, bamboo, and mango trees were plentiful in this area. As we walked into higher elevations, the ground got very rocky and there were fewer trees. The ground was covered in volcanic ash, from what I suspected, was from many years ago.

We stopped to shoot our azimuth and determine our exact position when we saw a series of flares go up. We hit the deck and waited for them to either extinguish or fall to the earth. I don't think that the flares were intended for us as they were too far to the northwest. Someone was out here with us. We moved into a tree line and stood fast.

Within a couple of minutes, there was a group of small arms fire coming from in front of us and in back of us. It appeared that we had walked into a cross fire and I don't think anyone knew we were there. Tracer rounds were flying three feet above our heads and to our left, some of the tracers were orange and some were green. I never did like the sound of bullets flying over my head. I could handle ones flying next to me, maybe, but not over my head; they were too unpredictable. I knew that the green ones were NATO rounds. I suspected we had just found us a few jarheads, even though they should have known when and where we were coming into the AO.

Time started to go against us immediately, because some of the tracer rounds had started several fires in the immediate area, which were spreading rapidly. If this thing didn't end soon, we were going to finish it. The fire behind us grew into the trees and we knew that we had to get down to the waterline. Petie said that he saw a small stream just to the south of our position. Meanwhile, the fire that was in the grass was only a few feet off the ground but was hot as hell, nevertheless.

Not only was the heat intensifying, the smoke started to thicken and it became harder to breathe. The LT then ordered, "Hit the stream, in twos, and bound over each other." We broke off in our teams of two, with Todd and I taking off behind Petie and Trout. We found the stream and every one of us fell in it due to the overgrowth along the shore. After all of us landed in the stream, we readied ourselves on the shoreline thinking that we must have been heard or seen by someone. The fire didn't continue down towards our position but spread off to the northeast and died behind it almost as fast as it started.

The ground was hot and smoldering. The individuals involved in the firefight must have dispersed when the fire broke out or took off to regroup later. I checked with everyone to see if there were any injuries and everyone, with the exception of Ron who singed his leg, was unscathed. Who would have thought that we would be in the middle of a firefight and a fire within the first several hours of the mission and still remain undetected? I thought about all of the explosives we were carrying after the fact and was relieved that the fire wasn't worse. Rodge got the Marine camp on the SATCOM and after an hour of sitting in the water, we headed east to the camp.

You could feel the ground crunch under your feet with every step thanks to the now smoldering grass. The smoke lightened quickly, allowing us to breathe, as well as see more proficiently. We stopped about a hundred yards from where we were in the trees and found 7.62 and 5.56 caliber brass all over the place. Are these the remnants from the firefight and possibly from the Marines we were supposed to meet up with at this location? I hoped not, for their sake and ours.

We followed a well-worn path, sticking to our azimuth and traveling in what we called "linear in-depth formation," which put us in a single file line, 20 yards apart, and muzzle direction alternating every other person. Jesus leaned over on the way and picked up a fried dead iguana that he said he was going to eat for lunch. I personally hoped that he was going to share it amongst the crowd. We walked for about 30 miles stopping every five for a 15-minute break. It was strange that we didn't see any life around except a few birds flying from tree to tree. The other thing we found strange was that the roosters didn't call out as the sun came up as you would think that they would. It was light out now and the sky was as blue as ever.

The heat started to set in just about the time we reached the Marine camp. Our packs were getting heavy as we walked toward the fenced-in camp. There were four Marines in the back of a deuce that had been parked in front of a cattle-style gate. One got on a two-way radio and another stood up and said, "What took you guys so long?"

The LT answered, "We had to stop and get a haircut and a burger on the way." We all smiled and laughed under our breath. The Marine looked puzzled and in disbelief.

As we stood at the gate, a couple of the Marines said, "Boy, we're glad to see you guys!"

Koz looked up at them and said in a sarcastic manner, punctuated with a sneer, "Gee, we're glad to see you, too. Do ya think that you could move the truck and open the gate?"

The sergeant replied, "Yes, sir, the CO is on his way down."

The LT then told us to drop our packs and catch a breather. I noticed that the deuce had bullet holes scattered all over it and looked like it had seen a lot of recent action. Obviously, our new foreign and unknown "friends" weren't shy about giving the Marine base a good time, which led me to believe that they were not only heavily armed, but large enough in size and organized enough that they weren't intimidated by the Marines' presence whatsoever. We would have to get more intel from the Marine CO as to what these guerrillas were after and what they had to gain by attacking the camp.

The supposed CO that came down to the gate to meet us was a major and looked like he was fresh out of college with the pimples to boot. We grabbed our gear along with an apology from the major for keeping us waiting out there. The staff sergeant moved the deuce and opened the cattle gate; I call it that because the frame was constructed out of two-inch aluminum pipe crossed in the middle with taut fence throughout to seal the holes, much like you would see at any standard small-town American farm.

As we walked into the camp, I couldn't believe how huge it was. There were 27 General Purpose (GP)-Large tents up, all with wood platform floors. There were about six conex (these look like the box or back on a semi-truck, but without the bottom frame or wheels) boxes that were dark orange, tan, and even white, which told me these guys obviously weren't too concerned with camouflage or concealment, even though it would be impossible to keep something this size a secret. They had bulldozers, end loaders, five-ton trucks, fuel trucks, semi-trucks (tractor and rear), deuces, hummers, and miscellaneous grading vehicles, to include backhoes. This place was huge, especially for being out in the middle of absolute nowhere.

The major led us into an empty GP-Large and told us we could stow our things in there. The wood floor looked like it just came out of the Home Depot parking lot. Petie, Danny, and Rodge's teams stayed in the tent while we went out for a quick recon and also so I could find their medical tent to get a few more things I needed, as well as some cream for Ron's leg. There was a pile of lumber that had to have been at least 200 feet long, 30 feet high, and 50 feet deep. These guys had enough materials to make a small town. It didn't make any sense why all of this was out here. These were obviously the materials that were needed for creating the radar site, but why were they stockpiled here?

As we were walking around, we noticed that there were some Marines, probably engineers, working on the wood base floors for the GP-Larges. Perhaps this place was going to get even bigger than it already was. We noticed a small, box-like structure about a hundred feet out that said "The Head" painted on the side. I told Todd, "I gotta see this." As we headed in the direction of "The Head," I noticed several scorpions running about on the rocks. This was something I needed to pass on to the team, so none of us would get stung or put our foot into a scorpion occupied boot. There was about a foot of clearance at the base of "The Head" and several four-by-eight boards nailed to two-by-fours that were set in the ground. They had four three-inch PVC pipes that were planted into the ground with approximately three feet standing above the ground with duct tape mesh netting over the hole to keep the insects out. I was impressed and felt much obliged to take a good healthy piss in their pretty little pisser.

We soon found our way to the medical tent and got the IVs and materials I needed after a long, drawn out argument with the corpsman, because he needed me to sign for this and have authorization for that, but we got it worked out. We went to the tent where the rest of us were only to see everyone, to include several Marines, standing outside watching scorpion fights. Of course, it was Danny and Ron and, by the look of it, Danny was winning. The LT, Koz, Jesus, and Tom went to the HQ to talk with the major and got brought up to speed on our mission. Now, I wish that I would have grabbed that big, fat, black scorpion that Todd and I passed; he was a winner for sure. The majority of us went into the tent, cleared our weapons, and took a nap. I cleaned and dressed Ron's leg, which wasn't that bad, but needed to be dressed nonetheless, and took a nap as he went back out to have the "world's best scorpion fights."

When the LT got back, it was already nightfall. He informed us that there was a "meals on wheels" (mobile canteen also known as an MKT mobile kitchen tent) serving "hots" (hot meals), that they were showing a movie in the middle of the camp if anyone wanted to go, and we would be meeting at 0400 hours the next day. All of us stayed in the tent, most going back to sleep while a couple went through their gear and cleaned their weapons. So far, this trip wasn't so bad at all. Actually, it was getting kind of soft, which was worrying me, but I soon fell into a deep, comfortable sleep, listening to the soft night sounds of El Salvador.

It was 0245 when we heard the roosters start sounding off. We all grabbed our weapons and were prepared for the worst. We got dressed and waited while Koz headed outside of the tent and took a knee. We could hear him talking to one of the Marine sentries and was told that the roosters were unreliable as far as the guerrillas hitting their camp, but were definitely a very good warning that something was going down somewhere. Not long after, we heard gunfire from at least 20 or so miles away. I'm not sure whose side the roosters were on, but we would use them to our advantage. We rested lightly for the rest of the night.

By 0400, we were up and most of us had shaved and brushed our teeth already. We followed Tom to the canteen for some eggs and a couple awesome cups of java. One thing about the military is it's hard to fuck up coffee, because the stronger the better, and I would be just as happy if you could stand the spoon straight up and down in it. Trout and I were known on many occasions to take the coffee packs out of the MRE and stick it between our lip and gum, just like chewing tobacco.

We brought back the LT, Danny, and Scout some food and made sure we got a handful of salt packets so Danny could kill everything we brought him. Jesus and Koz pulled out a laminated map and showed us our exact location and where we were going to be moving to tonight. It was about 20 miles to the south and we were expecting heavy resistance around the eighteenth mile, where intelligence had marked a guerrilla camp known to be at least 60 strong. This was to be the lesser half of the faction that we would have to exterminate at a later time. They were known to be extremely aggressive, fought very tough, were well trained, and were known through the neighboring countries as being merciless. Even though they seemed renowned in their warfare skills, they were still conventional fighters. Our biggest worry about guerrillas such as these was the unpredictability of their actions, even to our advanced reconnaissance and satellite imaging. The LT went on to say that the Marines had been here over two years already and that while the guerrillas' tactics were undisciplined, they were cruel and brutal. So, this thing has been in the making for a long time and Uncle Sam says it's time to move.

The Marines had told the locals that they would be erecting a school for them and asked for patience. The code name for the "school" was "Operation New Horizons." Now, I'm sure they would be putting up a school, but clearly the main focus for the Army Corp of Engineers and the Marines was to put up the radar sight. At the same time, a small group of engineers from the El Salvadorian military and the Army would put up the school to placate the locals. Clearly, we were here to get rid of the mice. The United States frequently used humanitarian missions to cover up more important strategical operations somewhere else, but close enough that they could use the troops from either operation to complete the higher priority mission. The LT told us where the showers were and to get cleaned up immediately.

6

SLOW AND EASY

Y TEAM AND PETIE'S TEAM WENT DOWN TO THE SHOWERS TO RINSE off and clean our uniforms from the night before. The smell from the smoky fire was strong enough that someone could pick it up in the breeze and give away our position or worse, give us away if we were within feet of them and going to take them out. We couldn't take any chances. When we got down there, the construction of the shower was very similar to the "Head" they had made across the camp, but it was just above a small group of trees that were in a forty-foot ravine. Everything on the base was flat except for this point, which was ideal because the entire runoff from the shower went into the ravine helping the base utilize better hygiene and the natural disposal of the water. There was a wooden pallet on the ground for you to stand on and a black water bag hanging from a two-by-four several feet above your head, putting the spigot not but a foot above your head, which I found to be just perfect. There was a picnic table over to the left that had several bags of water in the sun to heat them for the shower. There were two shower stalls, each four by four feet, with a mirror hanging on the outside of the door for shaving and a tray inside for your soap, shampoo, and toiletries. They had a really nice setup here.

Behind us, I noticed that there were at least 300 office size bottles of water for the Marines to use for drinking, cooking, and personal hygiene all stacked neatly in a steel containment rack much like a wine rack. Trout and Petie got in first, while Todd and I checked out the landscape. After a couple minutes, they were done and Todd and I stepped into our individual shower. There was a science to taking a shower with a bag. You spread around the water just enough to get your head a little wet, soap up fully, and then rinse off. All of us had it down to a tee. I was drying off my head when I heard a fairly loud "Doc!"

I pulled my towel down and looked around when I heard someone yell again, "Dave!" I twisted around to my right to see Danny walking over to us with only his combat boots, boxer shorts, and a t-shirt, looking like something off of the TV show "Mash." He was taking very slow steps and stopped dead in his tracks and yelled, "Don't move, Doc, and don't you move either, Todd." I saw Scout, not 15 feet behind him, also stopped. Danny slowly picked up his right arm, spread his two fingers, and pulled them up to his eyes, then pointed down slowly, moving his head from side to side as to say no. I froze where I was and looked down slowly to hear a hiss.

At first, I thought that they were playing another prank on me with the shower thing, but when I looked down, there was at least an eight-foot Bushmaster snake, ranked in the top five deadliest snakes in the world. It was dark brown and had the same type pattern as a boa constrictor. I couldn't believe the size of this thing. I had only seen a boa constrictor in the zoo that was this big and he wasn't four inches from my left foot. Danny called out, "Just don't move Doc. Let him get his drink and let's hope he moves on, just don't move," pausing between each word. I didn't have to worry about moving because my legs were as stiff and as heavy as concrete. An edge of my towel fell and the snake's head moved slightly to its left and turned towards me. I closed my eyes, not that it was going to help, but when the towel slipped down, I thought for sure he would strike. The only thing I kept thinking was we got all the way down here and were almost guaranteed to get in the shit tonight and I was going to be killed by a fucking snake. If, by chance, someone was to get bit by this snake, it wouldn't have mattered if you were a hundred yards from the hospital, the venom was so powerful that the person would go into neurotic shock seconds after the bite and they would be dead within two minutes.

I stood there frozen in time, waiting, and watching. I tried to look if there was any way I could pull myself up on the top edges of this makeshift shower without moving any part of my body. The snake was as frozen as I was, but I definitely think I was more scared than he was. Time stopped and this became the waiting game of my life. Danny calmly said, "Don't think of any crazy shit, Doc. He's gonna leave, just let him do what he needs to. He doesn't want to bite you." His head moved slightly and I took a long, slow blink with my eyes again. Sure as shit, he was drinking the water off of the pallet. After what seemed an eternity, the snake slithered off the pallet and moved down into the ravine. Danny yelled, "Yeh now, that was fucking cool. That was some serious Steve Irwin type shit!

Whooo, you can move now, Doc, he's gone."

I let out a slow, but relieving, sigh. I turned to Danny, who was now outside of the shower and said, "Thanks, man, I owe you one."

"No big deal, Doc, anytime — just make sure you wash the shit off of the pallet before I get in there." He was laughing and I smiled and nodded as I got out of the shower stall. That was one great thing about Danny; he was as cool as anyone could get under the worst circumstances and the only time I ever saw him get upset about anything was when he lost a hockey game when we were playing Nintendo.

As Todd and I walked back towards the tent, Todd said, "I think I'm the one who needs to take a shit." I laughed and he said, "No seriously." We turned back and walked over to the far south side of the base where they had the outhouse. It was a big box with four toilet seats next to one another and each seat went into its own 50-gallon drum that had been cut in half. I walked around to the back to look for snakes only to see the lower four doors to pull out the barrels. The first thing that came to mind was trying to take a shit and getting bit on the ass by whatever. I said forget it, "I'll hold it," and went back to the tent and got dressed.

Tom and Koz were going over some last-minute plans and the LT and Jesus were cleaning their weapons. When I walked into the tent, Koz looked up and said, "Hey Doc, how was their makeshift shower?"

I rolled my eyes, sat on the floor, and said to Koz and Tom, "I had a little run in with a Bushmaster."

Tom immediately turned and said, "The snake?" I nodded my head yes and Tom stood up and said, "I'm getting a bad feeling! We are getting soft sitting around here; we're losing our vigilance and need to go into another quarantine to get our head back in the game. We're already starting to make small careless mistakes." I told them that it was a fluke and the snake just kind of appeared. Tom said, "Bullshit, it kind of appeared? Where the hell was Todd and where the hell is he now? Where is the rest of the team? This isn't a field trip where you get to ditch the teacher! I'm telling ya, LT, I'm getting a bad feeling." The LT lifted his brow, looked at Tom, and continued what he was doing. I told Tom that Todd was in the shitter, Danny and Scout were in the shower, and Petie and Trout went up to the meals on wheels. I didn't have the slightest idea where Rodge and Ron were at that moment.

Koz scratched the top of his head and said, "Tom, this is no different than a lot of missions. Don't let a few tiny things get you wired up. Rodge and Ron are in the comm tent finding out the latest on the guerrilla movements." Tom sat back down and I put my blouse on and saw Todd step in the tent. Tom shot him a look. Todd sat down next to me and said, "What the hell did I do?" I told him that Tom was pissed about the snake thing and that he was getting a bad feeling about some things. It wasn't long after that that Trout and Petie returned.

Trout came over to me and said, "Hey Doc howsss wassssss your sssssssssshower?" I got the joke that he was elongating his S's in reference to the snake.

I said, "I had a little pucker factor, but it felt good to get cleaned up." Trout laughed and got dressed.

Tom stood up, walked towards the tent door, and turned around calling out, "All right guys listen up. This is our current location at the Marine base (pointing to the map) and this is where we are going to be aggressing tonight (pointing southwest of our current position). We are anticipating at least 60 to a hundred strong." You could tell by the expression on everyone's face that he clearly had our attention now. He went into specifics as to their weaponry and their living quarters within their camp. He said that we would be surrounding the camp and hitting it in sectors, taking out everything in a grid format, leaving nothing or no one around that we would need to get into a face-to-face or small arms battle. We were going to hit them hard enough that they would be at Saint Peters Gates before they even knew that they were hit. We were going to position the claymores in a star like pattern, all exploding inward, then firing the LAWs in a tighter circle in the middle of the camp, taking out anything that didn't get hit initially by the claymores. While all of this was going on, Trout was going to be lobbing in some high explosive (HE) rounds with his 203.

The plan was very similar to a strike tactic that the Sioux Indians used to use when attacking cavalry camps on the open range. They would hit the outside with small arms and set the camp on fire from the inside out, burning the occupants out of their cover and positions. I know that each of us had studied those tactics when we were at Bragg and continued to do so, knowing that if history repeated itself, we needed to understand historical tactics to better apply them and defend from them.

The study of tactics employed by the Sioux and other tribes always fascinated me. I think that one thing that piqued my interest into Special Forces was my respect and admiration of Native Americans. When I was younger, we used to visit my uncle's house in Kalamazoo, Michigan. His house was actually an old horse ranch built directly on top of an Indian burial ground. My cousin and I used to find arrowheads, pottery shards, and several other artifacts on the property. We used to hear things at night while staying in their house that my uncle called "ghosts of the warriors that walked nightly, protecting their ancestors." I know that there were many times when we were there that you would have unexplained feelings of remorse and sorrow, which my aunt said were the saddened souls of the Indians that were wrongfully stripped of their land and rights. The ranch was built there by my aunt's grandfather and no one ever knew if he was aware that it was on holy ground. She later inherited it and did some ghost hunting, finding out the background of the land. They found out who the chief was and hung his picture above their mantle. After doing this, they never had any more problems from the ghosts. But I will always remember when I witnessed the man on the painted horse in the middle of the field when I was about ten. He sat there, for what seemed to be forever, as his horse danced back and forth on its front feet then rode off into nowhere, just disappearing. Many family members claimed to have seen similar things, but I know, regardless of age, that it was real. The sense of no forgiveness and never-ending sorrow will stay with me until my dying day, in part because of my experiences on that farm in Michigan, but also because of the tragic stories of the people who fell and died there.

Returning my thoughts to the briefing at hand, Tom described a lake that we would move along that presented some problems because it was totally covered in lilies and would not have a defined water line. We would follow it for a few miles until we hit a gravel roadway. I found that to be somewhat comedic: we would be traveling until we hit a gravel road, but from what I understood, there were very few gravel roads in this country. We would cross the road and then enter into a heavily occupied guerrilla township. There would be many civilians in this town and we were told to skirt it and, under no circumstances, confront anyone in the area. The town was known to be one of the more prominent drug depots that the guerrillas used to move cocaine and sell small arms out of to fund their war.

The plan had us following a small stream coming out of the town that would lead us directly into the guerrilla encampment. We were told of a specific area in the stream that we were to destroy. It was merely a few chicken wire fences across the stream that the guerillas used to catch boxes of arms caches and drugs sent from further upstream. The area would be guarded and resistance was a sure thing, considering this was their homemade Pony Express for delivering expensive and important commodities. It sure seemed that it was going to be a very busy and dangerous night.

All of us checked our weapons by doing function tests and having one another look it over. "Mother" was ready and willing and Todd's grease gun was in perfect condition. We then checked out the explosives, to make sure we had what we needed, and made sure who had what, specifically. We went down to the "meals on wheels" and got a couple cups of coffee after having the LT talk to the gunny because the jarheads said that it was closed and we would have to wait. I don't know if it's a jarhead thing or what, but it seemed like they gave us as much bullshit resistance whenever they possibly could. After a little coercion, we sat around with our coffees, a big fat chew, and talked about how Ron couldn't wait for his estimated time of service (ETS) to come so he could sit down and smoke a fat one and watch a porn with his girlfriend. He was always funny as hell with everything and it was hard to know when you should take him seriously with some things.

Dusk was setting in and we headed back to our tent to get camoed up and check our gear one last time. As we sat in the tent applying camo to our faces, you could hear a pin drop as everyone concentrated on the task at hand. The ritual allowed us to get in "ready for anything" mode and to do anything we had to ensure the success of the mission. Out of nowhere, Trout started humming and getting restless, as his foot bounced up and down on the floor. You could smell the old canvas of the GP Large as it mixed with the hot humid air. That is a smell I can still recall to this day, and will love it forever more, as it holds millions of memories.

Trout got done with his face camo and looked toward me and fairly quietly started humming a riff. "Dwaree Di Dom Done, Dwaree Di Dom Done, Dwaree Di Dom Done," then in a soft voice said, "Keep on pushin, baby, like I've never known before, Dwaree Di Dom Done, Dwaree Di Dom Done." Ron, Danny, Scout, Todd, and Petie started bouncing their heads up and down, tapping their feet to the beat.

I leaned up where I was sitting, with, I'm sure, a terrifying look on my face, and took off after Trout, singing louder, pounding my feet: "You keep on pushin' babe, like I've never known before... You know you drive me crazy child, I just wanna to see you on the floor, Dwaree Di Dom Done, Dwaree Di Dom Done."

Danny chimed in after me, singing even louder, almost yelling, "I want a superstitious woman, she's got a superstitious mind!"

Trout immediately matched Danny's singing: "Dwaree Di Dom Done, Dwaree Di Dom Done. I can't see you baby, I can't see you anymore, no more. Keep on lovin me, like I've never known before. I want a superstitious woman, with a superstitious," boom, boom, boom, as Trout's right foot pounded the floor. "A superstitious mind and I don't mind. Dwaree Di Dom Done, Dwaree Di Dom Done, baby, look out! Da, Da, Da, Da, Da, Da, Da, Da; Da, Da, Da, Da, Da."

And then all of us at once started singing, "So take me down, slow and easy!" Boom, boom, boom, as our feet hit the wood floor. "Make love to me slow and easy, another hard luck an' trouble is comin' my way, so rock me 'til I'm burned to the bone, so rock me 'til I'm burned to the bone!" We kept singing for another ten minutes or so and then slowed to a steady boil with our feet tapping the beat on the floor quiet enough that you couldn't hear anyone else's feet, but you could see the movement of their feet going up and down. Now our blood was pumping and something was going to die tonight. Not another word was said as we finished with our gear.

Tom stood up and said, "Ok, saddle up, girls," in a low and concentrated voice. We helped one another put on our Alice packs because of the weight and help make adjustments moving the pack up, down, or side to side, to assure the pack didn't rub or sit wrong on your back, which could possibly lead to a future injury. We had to put the pad where we needed it and to get the shoulder straps on meat rather than bone. Then, we attached each other's Camelbaks to the back of our Alice. They were a small bladder of water that had a rubber tube which went to your mouth so you didn't need to open a canteen, you just pressed your teeth on the end of the tube and you could suck the water from the bladder; so in positioning the pack, you needed to have the tube brought around to the front so you could drink on the move. As soon as we got the Alice packs as comfortable as we could, we stood ready and psyched ourselves for the hike ahead of us, not only rehearsing the song "Slow and Easy," by Whitesnake, over and over again in our heads, but also visualizing our impending mission with deadly precision. Tom, Koz, and the LT knew that we would have to get moving quickly before we psyched ourselves into physical exhaustion. A couple of minutes later, a few Marines came to the tent and guided us out the back of the compound through a small opening they used to move in and out of when they had choppers come in for re-supply or to move reconnaissance groups out.

We moved out and headed southeast. The ground seemed even harder with this pack load on than it had when we arrived at the Marine base camp. The air was cooling and the sky was darkening with every minute. The underbrush gave us some trouble; it was so entwined that you needed to pick your feet up much higher than a normal walk. The land was silent, without any immediate noise in the area or in the distant mountains. After a couple hours of walking, we came to the lake. Tom and Jesus weren't kidding that it would be hard to find the water line. From a small distance, it looked like a huge open field covered in high overgrown crabgrass, with different large patches of varying shades of green. There were a few spots in the lake that almost looked like putting greens because of their light green color and they stood out clearly from the paddies around it. We tried to stay closer to the trees to keep us out of the water but we kept walking into the muck, nonetheless. The air down by the lake was wretched and had the smell of sewage, decay, and sour cabbage.

We had only walked for a few minutes along the lake when we ran into a six to seven-man century with a small fire and a lot of talking. They were so into what they were doing that they wouldn't have noticed anything around them even if it was to come straight up out of the water like the "Creature from the Black Lagoon." They were laughing and drinking on the shore line, but were still armed and in our way. Koz had us put our packs down for a rest and give our friends a little time for us to get to know them. If we were to go around them, we would lose valuable time. We weren't able to go through the water because of the noise and also because of our heavy loads which would cause us to sink in the mud, leaving us vulnerable in the middle of an open area. It would allow them to take us out like ducks in the tub.

We sat there, enjoying the break of taking our packs off, but knew that we needed to get back to moving or we would start to fatigue and lose our original momentum. Koz and Tom came up with a plan to have Jesus go off 50 yards to the south and act like he was in a drunken stupor to see if we could lure some of them away from the fire. The plan was thought to be a hit, so Danny, Scout, and Tom went with Jesus to take out the banditos before they got to Jesus. Meanwhile, the rest of us (besides Rodge, the LT, and Petie, who would stay with the gear) would take out the remaining guards down on the water line. Tom took his group to the south and we readied ourselves for when we received the signal.

The men were making all sorts of noise while their silhouettes moved, shadowed by the fire. The gleam of the fire highlighted their drunken features. Jesus started yelling and singing out in the darkness and talking about how he was in love. Several men sitting by the fire immediately started stumbling around, trying to find their weapons, and respond to all the noise coming from behind them. They called out to him telling him that this was private land and they would shoot him if they found him. Jesus responded by asking them if they had any beer or liquor and assured them, he would leave them alone to their fiesta. He explained that he was getting married and was out celebrating when he got separated from the group he was with, but just needed a couple more beers and he could find his own way home. The banditos said that they would be more than glad to give him some beers and he could even sit with them at their camp fire. I saw one of the men pick up a machete in front of the fire pit and then all I could hear was Dwaree Di Dom Done, Dwaree Di Dom Done, ringing in my ears as I reached down to my right thigh and pulled out my side arm. Trout, Todd, and I very calmly and directly walked down to where they were sitting, without hesitating or taking any cover, and very nonchalantly walked straight to them with our side arms drawn.

It was like a scene from Tombstone, out in the middle of the jungle, instead of at the O.K. Corral. I was in the middle, Trout was to my left, and Todd to my right. I heard a weapon discharge to my far right; we raised our side arms and started firing at the men as they stood around the fire pit. I fired at the short little fat man in the middle and worked my way to the right, Trout and Todd worked from the outside in. The very first man I shot flipped over backwards as his head snapped back from the entry wound. I had forgotten that a short man will do a backward somersault with a high caliber headshot. In the same vein, a taller man will move in a larger arc, falling sideways, to one side or the other. The gunfire couldn't have lasted more than five seconds and they were all dead. Still, my ears were ringing because of Todd's gunfire. He was just to my right and he had his side arm not three feet from my head. I was impressed by Trout's first shot, as his target was facing him and the impact caused his arms to come together, his head to snap down, and picked his feet a good foot off the ground. Center of mass shots can be very interesting as to the effect of the impact and the target's response.

Jesus came from our right, holding what looked to be a bowling ball or a log in his right hand. I saw Tom, Danny, and Scout in the background, walking back towards our packs. Jesus came up to the fire, where we were stripping the banditos of their possessions to make it look as if they were attacked by another guerrilla faction, when he hit the light from the fire and exposed the head of one of the banditos he killed. I looked at him and asked him what in the hell he was doing, he answered that he recognized that man, and beheaded him so that he would never see anyone or anything he ever loved in his afterlife. He then told me that the fact of us being there had robbed him of the chance to dispense the true pain that the banditos deserved and that only Satan himself could understand what he was going to do to them. The first thing that I thought of when he said that was that this guy was a genuine fucking nut job! But I then saw his features as the light from the fire reflected the grotesque scars on his face and I felt sympathy for him and better understood his position because of his pain.

We took all of the possessions of the dead and threw it far into the lake to further the suggestion that they were victims of a robbery. We searched for any maps or intel that would be on their persons. We then took several of their weapons and fired them into the air to simulate a fiesta. All of their weapons and ammunition were then thrown into the lake as well. We rolled over Trout's first target and looked at the eight-inch diameter hole that his hollow point caused. He smiled and said, "Fuckin' a, they don't call 'em hollow points for nothing." As we looked into the hole in his back, we noticed that the round literally blew all of his backbone and spinal cord out. I looked over to the fatter man I had shot and noticed that it split his head open like a canoe. As weird as it may seem, whenever I have dealt with head shots, I have found it interesting to see the brain matter as shortly as possible after the wound was made. Sometimes, if it is right after the kill, you can still see the brain pulsating within the skull. However, my victim was as dead as dead can get. We removed the boots of two of the men, who seemed to have gotten them fairly recently, again to throw off any assessment of the slaughter.

After setting the scene to our liking, we grabbed our rucks, got them fitted again, and moved in a linear, in depth formation along the shore of the lake. The travel was difficult, but the rush from our earlier confrontation fueled us to our next potential point of extermination or bloodbath. We needed to move at a faster pace now because the firefight we had earlier could prompt the banditos to send someone to check the status of the century, checkpoint, or whatever that position was deemed. We moved as fast as we could until we hit the gravel road. Koz and Ron went on a recon across the road as we hung out not but 30 feet from the gravel road. I was starting to worry about the time, because as soon as it started to get light, we would be exposed and our presence would potentially be compromised. If that happened, this could turn into a very bad day. I was somewhat confused as we sat there, because I felt this very weird, sick yearning to kill as many people in this country as I could. I shook my head to try and gain some sanity back and ask myself what in the hell was wrong with me? This place was starting to get to many of us, in an unexplained manor. I had to wonder what it was about this place that was making me lose my very well-trained composure. I was quickly being sucked into a war that was not mine, nor any of ours, and was yearning for things I had never thought of before. What the hell was happening to me?

7

CAPTAIN F'N AMERICA

K OZ AND RON RETURNED TO OUR POSITION AFTER ABOUT 45 MINUTES, stating that we were not far from the stream. Koz took the lead and led us across the road in two-man increments. We were all across, except for Danny, Trout, Scout, and Petie, when a small transport truck approached down the road. The grinding gears, sputtering engine, and headlights gave the approach away with just enough time for us to stop crossing. You would think that something so loud could have been heard from half a country away, but the mountains and the foliage muffled the sound so well that we didn't hear them until they were almost on top of us. The rest of our team still left across the road had taken cover, as we readied ourselves to engage the vehicle. It was a small, canary yellow cargo truck with side fences on the back, loaded with at least ten armed men. They slowed as they approached our position and all of us tensed up for that second or two, only to hear the grinding of gears as they neared the curve. The truck loudly sputtered as the driver accelerated and the occupants in the back fought to keep their balance. After the truck passed, we all let out a sigh of relief, not knowing if we had to have aggressed the vehicle, what side would have engaged, would we have caught ourselves in a nasty crossfire, or would they have hesitated knowing that the rest of our team wasn't 30 yards across the road from us. Koz motioned for the rest of us to cross and led us in the best direction towards where he and Ron had found the stream.

When we got to the stream, we couldn't believe how small it was and how slow the current was. The water was clear and presented a relaxing image and sound as the water trickled in the stream. I found it hard to believe that they used this stream to float weapons and drugs down. There wasn't enough depth or force to float anything of any size. I couldn't imagine or grasp how they were doing it.

Danny and Scout took the lead as we followed the stream up to what we hoped to be the fenced-in area where the guerillas intercepted their cargo. As we approached a widened spot in the stream, we noticed that there was a nest on our ten o'clock with at least two occupants and both of them were smoking. Danny and Trout went up towards the nest, dropping their packs and low crawling, making sure not to make any noise. They were about 20 feet away by now when Tom made a bird like noise with his lips. Trout and Danny immediately took cover and looked back towards us as Tom put his middle and pointer finger to his eyes and pointed to a second nest on our twelve o'clock. This was definitely not in the briefing we had received a few days earlier. We now had two nests with at least two occupants each, let alone the fence, which was sure to be near. This was turning into a bad fucking dream with all of the surprises from hell to boot.

The jungle was dark and very quiet, only lit by the stars above. Tom observed that the first nest was at enough of an angle that if Trout and Danny could take them out without being heard or seen, the other nest wouldn't see. Tom put Scout on point with his "257 Roberts" so that he could hit the second nest if Trout and Danny's aggression compromised their position. Tom had Todd and I cross the stream and circle around to the right to approach the second nest. We didn't make it 50 feet when we saw a small building with a 50 cal on the roof, with reinforced sandbags and four guards standing in front of the building and at least one on the fifty. The building was so covered in vines that it was impeccably camouflaged and the sandbags on top were old and worn, easily blending in with the surroundings. The window on the side of the small building had a flickering light from inside that looked like a television and shadows often crossed the windows. We were definitely getting into some deep and unexpected shit that none of us wanted to be in at that moment.

We determined that the town had to be very close, so we were unable to engage in a firefight without alerting nearby posts or having the town's populace descend down on our position. We had to do this the old-fashioned way, silently, and with extreme prejudice. Petie took a position where he could take his 249 (SAW) and light these fuckers up, if need be. This was a delicate moment in time where we would either do this right or start world war fuckin' three, because we were all prepared to light every one of these bastards up to the point that not one of their distant family members would ever see straight again. Damn it, this was not good, and was getting worse as we sat staring down this 50 cal that would for sure cut us in half, if given the chance. We had not even found the fence that we were supposed to take out and we were already in some deep shit. When I looked over towards the rest of our group, I saw Rodge on the SAT Comm link, which told me that whoever he was talking to knew now the horrific position we were in. As we sat there, I noticed that the starlight would periodically shine off of our camouflaged faces giving the appearance of ghosts in the darkness.

Todd and I were in a prone position, waiting to find out how we were going to do this, when I saw Koz, Jesus, and Ron crossing the stream coming towards us. They just got to the other side of the stream when another truck, similar to the one we saw earlier, pulled up to the back side of the building with its headlights shining right on Todd and me, loaded with at least ten more armed men. I laid there and shook my head from side to side, then laid my head on the ground in front of me. I love to take on crazy odds, but this was starting to spin out of control; now all of us were pinned down. The four men that were standing in front of the building put out their cigarettes and started to walk down towards Koz's group, missing us by only a few feet. As they walked, they turned just slightly to their left, alerting me to the empty nest that all of us missed while walking up here. All I could think was holy shit, we now have three nests and a fortified building.

Koz low crawled up to Todd and me and whispered, "We're going to have to take 'em all out at once, then diggy across the stream and stay to the north. Rodge called in a couple choppers to help us out. I need you to set charges as close to that building as you can get, then fall back and meet up with Ron down by the stream where we crossed. Danny and Trout are going to take out the two nests on our ten and 12. Soon as they do, you light that building up! I think we're going to have a barbeque tonight, what do you think?" I nodded with approval and with, I'm sure, a huge shit eatin' grin on my face. Well, so much for doing this the old-fashioned way. Koz crawled off to our rear right, while Todd and I crawled up towards the building, finding it difficult to be silent while everything on the ground was so dry and dead.

As we got closer, we noticed that there were at least ten guards to the rear of the building all talking and enjoying a smoke. I thought to myself that this had to be one of the best reasons in life not to smoke or need that half-hour smoke break. In this case, you are going to die sooner than later because of that smoke. I kept looking up at the guy on the 50 cal, he seemed to be trying to overhear the conversation below much more than hugging that fifty yearning for an opportunity. Returning my attention to my task at hand, I couldn't get the blasting cap into the detonator well on my last claymore. I took a small stick and carefully tried to get the grass, or whatever was in the well, out. I got it so the cap went down about a half an inch and decided that was going to have to do before I either blew myself to smithereens or caused a premature misfire (detonation). Todd and I set all of our charges with electric M4 blasting caps, grouped the wires, and pulled them back towards the stream. The building couldn't have been more than ten-by-ten and a little higher than 15 feet tall, but it was made with reinforced rebar, as you could see the rust stains that ran down the sides of the building where the pins were.

As I was crawling backwards, I ran out of wire and I had to send Todd down to Ron and tell him that we were going to have to set them off a lot closer than we had wanted. This was truly my definition of "danger close," as I could smell their cigarettes perfectly like I was standing amongst them. I could see Ron give me a hesitant "thumbs up" and nod. I hooked up the charging "clackers" as fast as I could and laid there waiting for good ole Danny and Trout to start off the fireworks. An hour passed and I was getting worried that the posts were going to shift or change out altogether. If they did, they would surely see the lines we set coming from the sides of the building and see myself or Ron and Todd down by the stream. All I could hear was the same guys out in the back smoking their lives away, literally, because when the shit hit the fan, I would be roasting their asses.

I heard a mumble or groan coming from behind us. I carefully bent over to see Jesus and Koz taking out the nest behind us. I looked up to see if anyone had heard it as well. The men out for their smoke were talking loud enough that they couldn't have heard. I was lying in the undergrowth, sweating my ass off, when I heard the roosters in the distant background, I closed my eyes and thought, oh shit, here it comes. Because every time I heard those damn roosters, something bad happened. And sure as shit, all of a sudden, I heard Danny and Trout light up their LAWs, hopefully taking out the two nests that they were supposed to eliminate. I pulled my head down towards my knees to help block some of the concussion and started squeezing the M57 electrical firing device "clackers" as fast as I could, setting off enough claymores to take out a small village. I could feel debris hitting my back like little small needles, then increasing in size, feeling like large dirt clogs. I saw debris and destroyed trees flying over me as the concussion pushed my entire body further away with every blast.

I turned to start crawling towards the stream when I felt a sharp burning in my back. I clenched my fists for a split second then started pulling myself in the direction I thought I needed to go. There was so much debris raining down and weapons fire flying in every direction that I found myself disoriented and confused as to my present position. I kept pulling myself away from the large fire behind me that I figured had to be the building, when I heard what seemed to be endless rockets firing off above my head. The concussion from them picked my legs and lower torso off of the ground and sent me flying head first into the brush.

When I woke up, I was disoriented and started to fight, not knowing if I had been taken captive or not. Tom jumped on top of me putting his hand over my mouth to quiet me, saying in a forceful and angry manner, "Doc, you're fine! Calm down! You need to calm down!" I nodded my head in understanding, then felt the excruciating pain from my back go racing through my body, causing my eyes to squeeze shut. My ears screamed with a roaring buzz and every sound seemed muffled. I realized that the concussion damaged my ears, causing a slight case of vertigo.

Todd crawled over to me and said, "Well, good morning, Captain fuckin' America. Holy shit, man, I wish you could have seen yourself flying through the air. It was fucking awesome and you don't have any broken bones or anything. That pain you feel in your back was a piece of bamboo that fragmented and stuck in your back." Todd started quietly laughing, "Dude, that was fuckin' awesome."

"Okay, Todd, I think he's got the point," Tom snarled. "I cauterized the puncture wound on your back so it's going to be sore for a while. Let me know if you need some more Ranger Candy," as he handed me two 800mg Motrin tablets. I swallowed them as fast as I could get them down, then slowly started to sit up, asking Todd how long I had been out for, assessing my condition. My head was now swimming in pain.

Koz turned and said, "About an hour, man, talk about luck. I thought we had lost you for sure, the way you went flying through the air." He shook his head back and forth, laughed, then turned again towards what looked to be a small house or shack.

"Where the hell are we?" I asked, rubbing the top of my head.

Koz turned again and said, "Shhhhhh, we're on the north side of the village. We got here just in time when they started sending every last reinforcement down to their fortification by the stream." As I was getting my focus back, I could now see the team positioned in a fan-like wedge, with a small rock cliff to our rear. I guess they moved us to a higher elevation for observation. Trout looked over to me and picked his head up for a quick and silent "What's up." I returned the nod then remembered my pack, frantically looking around. Rodge said, "Yeah, I got your pack, Doc. I'm always having to pick up after you, ya cheap bastard." I laid back down with a smile on my face. Rodge was right to an extent; we did pick up after one another and, from our training, acted without hesitation to make this fine machine hum.

Dawn was approaching quickly and the LT told us to get some rest while he had Todd dress Tom's arm. I quickly looked up, trying to see where Tom was and if he was ok. I saw him slide through the grass slowly moving towards Todd. I asked him what happened and he said that there was another nest just beyond the building that had gotten off a few rounds at us and our choppers before being sent back to the "stone age." I couldn't believe it; how in the hell could the intel be so off? Even more so, how in the hell did we make it out of there without being compromised or followed? Trout would later explain that the choppers took everything out and did a minor strike on the village. He said that it was the most awesome display of power that he had ever seen at that range. He also added that "not even a colony of ants could have lived through that and you missed it. What a fuckin' shame." The LT said that the DEA tried something similar, years before, with absolutely no success and a 100% casualty ratio, so we hoped that the guerillas would see this as the DEA's second attempt and free us of any association with this matter so we could move towards our objective without too much resistance. I must have fallen asleep quickly after listening to the LT, because I don't even remember closing my eyes.

I awoke to the sounds of distant commotion coming from below us. I slowly rose up and crawled to the top of the small berm I was sleeping behind and carefully looked over the top to see what was going on down below. There were trucks coming in and out as fast as they could, considering the small road they had to travel into and out of the compound. They reminded me of a riot of ants, spilling out everywhere after someone had kicked the top of their mound. There were people running every which way and all seemed to be yelling about something; it was truly chaos.

As I inched back down, I felt the stinging in my back that I had momentarily forgot about. Everyone was cleaning and preparing their weapons and gear. The LT, Koz, and Jesus were having a little powwow above me to my right. I grabbed my weapon, held the charging handle to the rear, and opened the cover letting the belt of 7.62 fall to the ground. My head was feeling slightly better as I started to take it apart, removing the rear stock, and ran a rod down her and cleaned all of her vital organs with a little break free, carefully, just like you should do when you caress a woman. As I was cleaning my weapon, I watched the LT's facial expressions as he was looking worried and somewhat distraught. Once I finished with my weapon, I grabbed the belt of ammo off of the ground, wiped it off, and inserted it into the belt feed tray under the cover until hearing and feeling a click as the feed caught the belt. Now all I had to do was pull the bolt to the rear and the belt would automatically feed the round into the chamber, ready to rock and roll.

Ron was in a defensive position just to the left of the LT when he leaned over to his left side and hissed, "Pssst, Psssst." I turned to look at him and he whispered, "Either you are the luckiest son of a bitch I have ever known or the stupidest."

He shook his head from side to side and I said, "Thanks, I love you, too." He shrugged his shoulders and rolled back over.

Koz crawled over to us and said that we would be moving in a couple of hours and that because of our small, but discrete, "War of The Worlds" that we had, we were way behind on time and needed to do some catching up. We waited until the sun started to go down because we needed to go up and over the other side of this mountain and we were sure to have resistance when we went down. The LT asked how I was and if I was going to be all right to move and I quickly answered,

"Well, hell yes, LT, it's just a little scrape." He nodded and went over to his gear. I turned my rucksack with the straps up and did what I like to call "the reverse Rucksack Roll," putting my arms through the straps and rolling it over onto my back. I laid there for a few moments quite comfortably, actually, because the weight on my wound felt good.

Tom took the lead, as all of us suited up and came to a low crouch, readying ourselves to move out. As we moved to higher elevations, the ground got harder with increasingly jagged rocks that made it hard to get your footing, especially with a heavy pack on your back. All of us would slip from time to time, causing all of us to hit the ground and take cover, in case anyone was in the area or looked up to see what the noise might have been. We were supposed to be making up time, not losing it, but walking in this terrain meant we were actually falling further behind our timeline. Jesus put his fist in the air to motion for us to halt and take cover. He then walked over to the LT and must have told him that we would make better time if we would get to a lower elevation and walk through the jungle instead of battling the rocky terrain. Jesus, Koz, and Ron then walked straight down the mountain, motioning for us to follow. We went down about 150 feet by pace into the thick jungle that would now allow us to make better time, as well as give us better cover in the event that we ran into hostiles. Danny and Scout were bringing up the rear and were only about 70 feet behind us when Scout passed up the line to halt. We all took a knee and waited as Tom fell back to the rear to talk to them.

When he worked his way up the line of us, he stopped and briefed us all the way to the front with Koz and Jesus. Tom said that Scout spotted a couple of sentries walking about a hundred feet in front of our position, which was down to the far left of theirs allowing them to have a better bird's eye view. Tom had us take cover until we got the all clear. Ex-jarhead or not, that son of a bitch had some of the best eyesight of anyone I had ever known and, in this case, most likely saved our lives, let alone ensuring we avoided another firefight.

While we held, I couldn't help but look all around me to see the beauty of this country. I actually enjoyed listening to the very few birds that were singing in the near distance as the sun went down. The air was still hot and humid, while the ground was hard and dry. We had waited about 20 minutes when I heard some rustling in the jungle ahead of us. I took "Mother" and held her just to the right-hand side of my stomach, pulling the charging handle to the rear and pushing the now very free moving handle all the way to the front and locking it as quietly as I could. Anyone who has ever fired an M-60 can tell you that it doesn't take long to seriously mess up someone's day. It is highly effective and one of the deadliest weapons in Uncle Sam's arsenal. And this one was mine.

We waited for what seemed to be an eternity for whatever was in the bush ahead either to reach us or divert in another direction. Scout finally emerged and quickly jerked his head to the left, giving us the all clear and to follow him. We got up and started to move again. The sky had darkened quickly when Scout and Danny went out to take care of whatever or whoever was out there in front of us and left us to move out into the pitch-black night. I was glad that we had moved down to the more vegetative level than the jagged rocks. We would have been falling all over the place by now if we had not come down lower. We were now moving at a much faster pace when we came upon Scout and Danny going through the pockets and the belongings of the two deceased guerillas who, by the looks of things, were out looking for a little privacy with one another as both of their pants were down and the man in the front was still in the fetal position with his head literally bashed in. They both smelled like ass and would die hiding that one little thing that they obviously couldn't let others know about. As we moved out, Danny and Scout once again brought up the rear.

We walked along the lower edge of the mountain, bringing us to the other side and connecting us to the trail where we were supposed to have been on in the first place. We walked all night in utter silence. The night was so quiet here. If you stopped and listened carefully enough, you could hear a fiesta in the background, with people shooting into the midnight sky and yelling out the other end of the bottle, but in our immediate vicinity, time stopped, and there was just silence. We stopped every four hours, with our second 15-minute break just before dawn. It was hard to understand all the violence in such a wonderful place. Everything at this moment seemed so calm, almost like the calm you would feel in your backyard as you sat in your lawn chair, sipping back a cold one, enjoying a fresh summer day. But on the back of your neck, the hairs would stand up for no apparent reason, leaving you to question the surroundings and the fear you were unable to see. There was definitely something here in the air or in the landscape that made me very uneasy.

As I was staring into the dark, Petie nudged me and said, "Are you ready to move out there, Mr. Captain America?" laughing with every word.

I quickly jerked my head over towards where he was and gave him a quick, "Fuck You!" He laughed even harder. Petie had one of those contagious laughs and personalities that everyone loved. His laugh helped put me at ease with whatever I was feeling or thinking at that moment. We got up and started heading out towards the southeast, watching and feeling the sun come up over the tops of the mountains. Our toes in our boots and thighs were soaked from the morning dew stuck on the foliage. Even though we were wet, we were still comfortable due to the warm, pleasant climate.

As the sun hit us, it felt brilliant and pleasing. We walked out in the middle of nowhere, without a worry in the world. The first thing to come to mind was a bunch of Boy Scouts walking in their single file line, carrying their packs, on their way to a new adventure and to where the Scout Master would deem a good place to set camp. We walked until we hit the Lempa River in the early afternoon. We set our packs down as Rodge got on the SAT Comm to tell JSOC where our position was. All of us got out our MREs and ate a good military meal for the day. Those of us who used tobacco took out a chew or a cigarette and enjoyed the flavor of the moment. Todd came over to me and asked to look at the wound I sustained earlier. He lifted my blouse and t-shirt and in doing so tore open the scab that had adhered to my t-shirt, throwing a lightning-like pain throughout my body, even shooting down my legs. He put some antibacterial ointment on it with some gauze and tape, handed me a couple more "Ranger candies," and told me I'd be fine for now and to "call him in the morning if anything worsens." He then walked over to Tom and checked his bandages, only spending a very brief moment to look over him, as he was intimidated by and unsure of Tom. I would have to compare Tom to a tiger. He had the calm essence of a cozy little cat, but had the capability to tear any man apart limb by limb, so you always gave Tom that small, but respected, space just in case he chose to turn and bite.

We shot an azimuth and found we were only a couple hundred feet off course; we would be able to get to our camp by tomorrow afternoon. Jesus explained that after we crossed the river, we would be entering no-man's land: houses and townships would be somewhat scarce. After our break, we went south about a half a mile to a makeshift bridge that crossed the river. Petie turned to Jesus and said, "How in the hell are we supposed to get across this thing? Those ropes won't support our weight, let alone the weight of our packs! This is not good… that thing looks like it was made before Christ."

Jesus took a couple of steps forward and squinted looking at the bridge. "It will hold us! We have used this bridge for the last 20 years, it will hold!"

"Alright Trout, you're the lightest of the group, let me know how things look on the other side. Mr. Jesus here says you can make it and I know if any of us are going to make it, it will be you, so please be my guest," exclaimed Petie.

"I'm on it," Trout said, just after spitting a huge mouthful of Copenhagen on the ground just in front of Scout.

Scout quickly pulled his feet back, called Trout a dick, and then said, "I hope you fall in."

"I hope I do, too," Trout whispered as he stretched his neck out, making his eyes go every which way. We all started to laugh as Trout turned and walked in the direction of the bridge. He squeezed the frayed, braided ropes and gave them a good tug and then stepped out on the rotting wooden planks that held the two sides of the bridge together. We could all hear the wood splinter as it absorbed his weight and the weight of his pack. Trout turned and said, "I'll see you beeotches on the other side." Petie and I went prone on each side of the bridge ready to light up the other side if Trout ran into any opposition. Scout went to the far left and stood ready with his "Roberts," scanning the opposite shoreline. The bridge started to sway, pulling Trout's planted feet up to each side. You could see the strain in his forearms as he gripped the braided guide ropes to retain his balance and not let the huge pack pull him over. After a good 10 to 15 minutes, he made it to the other side, giving us the thumbs up and taking a defensive posture, being alone on the other side in unknown territory.

Todd, then Ron, then Tom, and so forth, all took turns as they crossed. Only Petie and I were left now and it was my turn. I started off gripping the ropes almost as hard as I could to keep my balance. It wasn't before too long that I could start to feel some fatigue. The pack on my back was causing so much counter weight that I was afraid I would invert the bridge. I could feel the pack ripping the gauze off of my wound and could feel the sticky trickle of puss or blood run down my back and under my pants. I stopped for a second and repositioned my pack and loosened my grip a little to conserve my energy in case I needed to catch myself. The tight grip I had was already causing my thumb and forearm to cramp. I looked to the other side and just calmly walked over, realizing that it wouldn't have been so bad if I had started out that way in the first place.

Petie started across after I got to the other side and within a couple minutes, Scout snapped the "Roberts" up to his eye and started to lean in for a shot. I quickly turned to look to the other side of the river when Jesus yelled, "No, don't shoot; it's just a little boy." Scout kept the scope up to his eye, but relaxed his position slightly. I looked over and saw a boy that couldn't have been more than four or five, standing at the other side of the bridge. Petie turned quickly trying to keep his balance with a nervous look on his face. The little boy was wearing a blue striped polo with red cotton shorts and no shoes. His hair was well groomed, and the first thing I worried was how long had he been following us? Jesus yelled across the river and told him to go home, but he just stood there watching us. When Petie got all the way across, the little boy picked his hand up about chest high and waved to us, then turned around and disappeared into the jungle. I think a strange feeling went through all of us as we watched the boy fade into the brush. Maybe he showed us how vulnerable we really were in this terrain. I think he was a sign from God knows where or what.

We shook it off and started walking to the southeast. The landscape changed from thick jungle to open fields in 50-foot increments. We stopped after a couple hours of walking to shoot another azimuth and for a drink of water. Due to the heat, we were going to have to drink water more often, which we could do through our Camelbaks, so we wouldn't have to stop. Tom said we had a contact point just to the south to gather intel about the exact position of the radar site and what kind of opposition we would be dealing with there. We adjusted each other's packs and took off towards our next point of contact. The temperature was pleasant, with a slight breeze, and no humidity. We were gaining momentum and time with every stride.

We ran into a small road that was cut out only by the tire tracks of a vehicle leading to a house. There was a fence made out of tree limbs and woven barbed wire about a hundred feet long along the side of the road, up to the house, used for cattle or horses, as you could see the animal hair stuck on the wire. The house was by far one of the largest I had seen in this country, comparable to a small ranch-style in the States, but constructed of cinder blocks and a thatched roof. There was a small garden just below the back of the house that was weeded and well taken care of by someone. The house was quiet, almost too quiet. To our right, there were about 20 dead fruit trees in an enclosed field with high, brown grass resembling wheat. Just above that, at the top of a hill, were fields of sugarcane as far as you could see.

As we neared the house, we caught the odor of death. The stench was so terrible that it made your eyes squint and wrinkle your nose up to try to block off some of the smell. We readied our weapons as we approached the carport area of the house where there was an old rust colored Chevy truck. The vehicle was parked with the bed facing us. As we got closer, we tried with every step to see into the bed and make sure there wasn't anyone in there, but when you entered the carport, the stench was so putrid that you couldn't breathe. After clearing the rear of the truck, we backed out to take a breath.

We went down to the side of the carport and took off our packs. Koz had Trout and I go through the other end of the carport to clear it and see what in the hell was making that smell. It was obvious that it was the smell of death, but we didn't know what to expect or if there was anyone inside. I took a couple of cravats out of my bag and handed one to Trout to wrap across our faces to dull the stench and filter our breathing. Trout took the lead as we inched around the front of the carport to see two dogs that had been shot and slashed into several pieces resembling a greyhound or mutt similar to a greyhound. The flies were so thick that they almost seemed to blend into the air we were trying to breath.

As we went around further, we saw the front of the truck, which had a naked man tied to the hood cut in such a grotesque manner that it resembled beef strips lying out to dry. The man's genitals had been cut off; his throat was slit like a Columbian necktie, meaning his tongue was pulled out through the slit in his throat. It was very evident that this man had been tortured for an extended period of time and that he probably bled out instead of dying from the wounds he sustained. His eyeballs had been burned out, leaving a black pit where they had been, and you could see where the vitreous fluid from inside the eyes had run down the sides of his face. He had a gaping hole in his chest, from which his heart had been removed. The flies were so thick that they discolored his skin in places where they swarmed to the point that you couldn't tell if a spot was severely bruising or if it was the flies. You honestly couldn't tell what race the man was because of all the different colors and lack of skin. The air in there was so thick that you could feel it on your forehead and hands. Trout and I walked up to the passenger side of the truck, towards the open door into the house, stepping carefully, to avoid stepping on the flesh and body parts that had fallen off of the hood. Large cut marks were evident on the hood where the knife, or probably machete, missed the body, striking the metal and leaving a very distinct impact mark.

Trout and I backed out of the carport and went over to where the rest of the team was to tell Koz what was in there. The dirt on the floor of the carport was like powder. It was so dry that every step created a tiny puff of dirt. The pieces of meat from the man's body that were on the ground fell into the dirt just like a piece of dough would fall into powdered sugar, covering it the same. We had also told Koz that there was a door going into the house from the inside middle of the carport. Danny and Ron went along the back of the dwelling while Jesus and Petie went around the front to create a 360 perimeter, sealing off any possible escape routes. Trout and I put our heavy weapons down with Koz and the LT and took out our side arms to enter the house. I took the lead as we went up the side of the truck again, watching our step, and trying not to look over at the body.

I rounded the door and went inside the house with my pistol raised and ready. We had entered the kitchen that was connected to the living area. The floor in the kitchen was linoleum that had to have been from the sixties. We couldn't have walked five feet when I saw the legs of a child lying in a pool of dried blood off to my left. From this viewpoint, all I could see was the legs and the rest was blocked by the back of a broken chair. There was a slight breeze raising the plain white curtains over the open window. I could feel and hear my heart beating as I walked closer towards the child to find it slashed and mutilated as well. It couldn't have been more than four. I have to refer to the child as "it" because you couldn't make out the sex, being that it was so badly torn apart. I then looked to the right, away from the child, to see a dead infant partially buried in broken furniture.

I tried to say "clear" to Trout, but my voice squeaked, sounding more like a moan than a word. The lump in my throat was so big that I could barely breathe, let alone speak. I then walked straight across the blood-soaked floor, towards a hallway that I was sure led to the bedrooms. My arms felt like they were as heavy as sandbags as the tip of my pistol started to shake almost violently. There was a room to our immediate right that was the children's room, which was empty, other than that all of the furniture in there was broken. Six feet in front of that was another room on the left.

As I rounded the corner, I saw an adult woman, lying on a queen size bed, naked, and disfigured. Her breasts had been cut off, her throat was slashed, and it appeared that a large knife, machete, or other sharp object had been inserted into her privates, tearing her wide open. Her face had been beaten so badly that you couldn't tell where her eyes or nose would have been in proportion to her head. Both of her arms had sustained compound fractures, almost giving her arms the appearance of being bent backwards, like that of a dog. The bed was totally saturated with her blood and had even started to drip through onto the floor in certain places. It was very evident that she had been raped repeatedly. The semen had discharged out of her in large clumps and oozed significantly between her legs. Oddly enough, the window that was on the same wall as the kitchen's was open as well, but nothing moved; not the curtains, not even the flies.

We cleared the room and I turned to Trout and said, "We have to get the fuck out of here!" He was already starting to gag as he nodded. We went out through the living room again, through the carport, and ran out into the backyard. I pulled the cravat off of my face and leaned over, propping my hands on my knees. The sweat was stinging in my eyes and I couldn't for the life of me catch my breath. I squeezed my eyes shut as hard as I could and at that moment in time, I never wanted to open them again. I took in deep breaths and tried to gather some composure. The entire world was now moving in slow motion and there was utter silence. I was alone trying to breathe through the heat, fumes, and carnage at the edge of hell.

8

LOSS OF AN OLD FRIEND

I FELT A HAND SQUEEZE MY LEFT UPPER ARM AND I RESPONDED VIOLENTLY, flinging it off, and making a fist with my right, preparing to strike. I stopped as I heard, "Doc, Doc, pull yourself together! Sergeant, what in the hell is wrong with you?"

I blinked my eyes several times and squinted in confusion, questioning, "Tom?" I stood up straight and bowed my chest taking in a deep breath. I let it out slowly to see Tom standing by me and to see Koz over to my right with Trout. I shook my head from side to side and took a step closer to Tom and said, "You don't want to go in there! I'm serious Tom; you don't want to go in there!"

Tom nodded with a sense of understanding and replied, "I believe you. Take a second and let's pull ourselves together." Tom backed up and walked over to where Koz was placing his hand on Trout's back in comfort. I looked over towards the back of the house to see Danny and Ron on one knee in a defensive position, looking over at us with a confused look on their faces. Danny held up his right hand and pulled his head down slightly, trying to get me to give them some sort of response as to what had happened.

I looked at the ground and took in another deep breath and turned to Tom and said, "We need to bury these people."

Koz looked into Tom's eyes, then looked back over towards me, and agreed with a very low and quiet, "Okay," and slightly nodded his head.

I walked over to my rucksack, opened it, and pulled out several pairs of latex gloves and my e-tool. I walked down to the garden without saying another word and started digging a place for these poor people to finally lay to rest. I heard some bags being moved around behind me and I took a quick glance to see Rodge taking out his e-tool as well. He didn't need an explanation or a reason, he just knew. That was only one of the many moments in my life when Rodge really stood out to me and made all the difference in the world.

After a few moments, Tom and Trout came down to the garden and helped dig the graves. The only thing that was ever said while we were digging was when I said, "We need four," in a broken and scratchy voice. Other than that, there wasn't even a noise from the wildlife or jungle in the area; time seemed to stop as we dug in utter silence. Todd and Koz got out their ponchos and went into the house. Rodge and I took off our shirts and continued to dig. Todd came out within a minute and Koz was right behind him, both holding their sleeves on their biceps over their noses and mouth to muffle the stench. They bent over, putting their weight on their lower thighs as I did earlier, trying to catch their breath. After I finished digging the hole for the man, making sure that it would be deep enough so animals wouldn't dig him up, I threw down my e-tool at the head of the hole and pulled the latex surgical gloves out of my pocket. I started to put them on while I was walking towards the house. I stopped just to the right of Todd on my way up and handed him a pair of gloves and said, "Let's get this over with already."

As I approached, Todd rose up straight and bent his head all the way back looking straight up into the sky, then lowered it and twisted his head, bringing his chin up from side to side, cracking his neck. He lowered his head, then looked at my hands as I extended them to give him a pair of gloves. He took them out of my hand and let out a long sigh, then turned around, putting them on his hands and started walking towards the house. We laid out the poncho on the ground in the front of the truck. I took the driver's side and Todd took the passenger side, both of us grabbing the dead man's wrist and calf to slide him down onto the poncho. On my side, his leg from the knee down came off as I pulled, as there was so little tissue holding it there.

As I picked the foot up higher, I noticed that this man had a tattoo on the inside of his left ankle. I tried twisting it back and forth to make out the words on it and what the main part of the tattoo was, while turning it and looking at it from every angle and perspective. Part of it did resemble a skull, but I wasn't sure. I don't know why I was so interested in the tattoo. Maybe I felt that it could help explain who this man was and what happened to these people, but there was so much dried blood and disfigurement. I laid the leg on the poncho and then grasped his thigh and wrist to pull him off of the truck.

As soon as we got all of the body parts from within the carport onto the poncho, Todd and I dragged it down to one of the graves and rolled him over into it. His back was not as damaged as the front, actually giving him some color outside of the lividity (the pooling of blood at the lowest part of a deceased body). The man's backside made him look white, so I called the LT and Koz over to question them as to who this person was that we were supposed to meet with for our mission. They walked over to the grave; Koz squatted down on the side and the LT kept a safer distance, remaining standing with his hand over his mouth and nose. Koz turned and twisted his head from side to side looking for some kind of evidence of who this man was. "I can't tell much of anything from the corpse's remains, but, yes, he does look white. The only problem is that he probably bled out, so naturally the body would look whiter. I just can't tell," Koz exclaimed, as he squinted his eyes and wrinkled up his nose due to the stench. Koz then stood up slowly and shook his head saying, "Who or what could have done this to a man?"

I looked at him and said, "I wouldn't have a clue, and as of right now, I don't think I would want to know."

Tom walked over to me and asked for a cravat to put over his face while he went into the house and started looking through things to find out what this person had to pass onto us. I took another one out of my pack and handed it to him and said, "It's not good in there." He nodded, took it out of my hand, and placed it over his face. He then walked up to the house with Todd and me. Todd and I walked through the carport into the kitchen and over to the child to the left. Tom walked in and gave a "Whoooey!" as Todd and I slid the child onto the poncho.

Tom looked over towards us and said, "Oh my God, what in the hell?" After moving the child, I picked up the infant and placed it on the poncho as well. Todd took one end and I took the other as we carried them down to the garden. Rodge had already started to bury the man when we put the infant and child each into their own grave.

Rodge turned his head and said, "Holy shit, what the hell happened in there?"

I looked at him and said, "It was an all-out slaughter. The woman is the only one left and we're going up to get her now."

When I walked back into the house, the first thing I saw were the drapes rising up from the breeze. I went straight back to the woman's room to find that the drapes were still stiff, even though the window was open. I found that to be almost creepy. We placed the poncho on the bed and started to roll her over when she gave a moan. Todd and I jumped back, and I yelled, "What the fuck!" I immediately jammed my finger on her carotid artery. She was definitely dead; there must have been some air in her lungs and when we turned her over, it escaped, causing a noise as it crept past her voice box. By now, I was shaking a little and stood back to get some composure, and I noticed Todd doing so as well. We rolled her onto the poncho and started to carry her out of the room when Todd's hands slipped and her head fell and thumped on the floor. Todd and I could feel the difference in weight between her and the man. She was much heavier, making us realize how very little of the man was left.

As we adjusted our grip on the poncho, we carried her through the bedroom door into the hallway where we saw Tom sitting on the remains of the hutch looking through a heap of papers. He looked up and over to me and asked, "Hey Doc, do you remember Bill Ledbetter from Bragg?"

As Todd and I shuffled down the hallway, I said, "Yeah, that crazy son of a bitch still owes Scout some money from that 48-hour poker game we had."

Tom turned and opened a passport, holding it up in the air facing me, saying, "I think that (pointing out towards the garden) is Bill Ledbetter. Remember how he dropped off the face of the Earth and how he was talking about retiring? I think we just found him." Tom's head dropped down, looking through the papers. "Have Koz come in here when you take her down." I nodded affirmative, as Todd and I shuffled through the mess, trying to keep the woman and the poncho off of the floor. We took her down to the garden and placed her in the last grave, with the poncho covering her. Koz was helping Rodge and Trout push the dirt over the corpses when I told him that Tom needed to see him inside. Koz wiped his brow and headed up into the house. Todd and I grabbed a couple of e-tools to help to finish burying the family. Koz and Tom were in the house for at least an hour before coming out with a handful of papers and smoke starting to bellow out of the house. They walked over to the LT and were showing him something as the house became engulfed in flames.

Everyone from in front and in back of the house walked over to the garden as Tom took a knee. With a lowered head, Tom said, "Our contact was Bill Ledbetter from fifth (meaning 5th SFG.) We couldn't find anything that would suggest what he needed to talk to us about, but then again, I wouldn't expect to, knowing Bill. It looks like he had found some peace in this world, even though it was short lived. I vow right now that I'm gonna kill every one of those mother fuckers right to the end!" Trout and I looked at one another at the same time, because this was way out of character for Tom to react like this.

After saying the Special Forces Prayer and our own prayers for the deceased, we gathered our weapons and gear and moved out towards this supposed future radar site. As we walked off, I could hear the burning wood and debris crackling behind us. I was confused by Tom's fury. I had never seen him like that nor had I ever heard him talk like that. He was always so quiet and reserved, not enraged and vengeful. I felt that our mission had now changed from securing a radar site into a glorified hunting party. We had now become more dangerous than anything walking the face of this Earth; we were out for justice for a fellow comrade without barriers and with extreme prejudice.

We had walked, for what seemed to be only an hour, before the sun started to go down. Not one of us had spoken a word since we left the house. We had walked down a gravel road with thick brush on our left and right sides, when we caught up to two cows and an ox walking, in single file, down the road. If these were from Bill's house, we didn't know or care. The ox was white and had a good ten-inch laceration across its side, with dried blood almost covering its entire left side. It walked with a distinct limp and I was tempted to have a look at the cut and see if I could remedy some of its pain, but I could tell in the mood of things, that wasn't going to happen. Time was moving in slow motion and I felt a need to help the ox for some kind of closure to what we had experienced at the house. At the house, I was helpless in my position of healing; there wasn't anything alive in any direction to heal, only death.

As we walked down the road a little further, we saw a large blue sign with the word "malaria" across the top. Jesus said that the entire village was laced with malaria and that they hung these signs up as a warning to others not to enter. There were at least 30 small makeshift huts scattered around this small area, with two small buildings constructed of corrugated tin, painted navy blue and teal. One had a small open sitting area to eat and the other only had a few chairs that were occupied by men drinking and smoking, as they talked their days away. All of the people stared at us, terrified and cornered, as they had not seen or heard us approach. There were food items hanging in front, along with several bags of potato chips. They had oranges, mangos, limes, and dried meat. There were several jars containing things like eggs, which I assumed were pickled, beans, peas, and corn on the front counter. They also had two cases of Coke that I think had caught all of our eyes.

We walked up to the small store and bought Cokes for all of us as Jesus questioned the elder man about any guerrilla movements in the area. He asked that we didn't kill him and that he would give us anything we wanted, if we would spare all of their lives. Jesus explained to him that we were not there to kill any of them, that we only wanted the guerrillas because they were in need of cleansing. We paid him well to tell us that the guerrillas knew we were coming for them and that they called us "The Chupacabra." Jesus later explained that "The Chupacabra" was a monster that was part goat and part man. It had the reputation with the locals similar to how Americans looked at "Big Foot." But everyone here believed this creature to be true and very much a part of the jungle. It was feared to be a descendant of Satan and that there were only a few elders that had ever seen it and lived to tell about it. The people were scared out of their minds at the mere mention of the word. And now we were regarded as this mythical creature and were glad for it, because we were going to hunt these guerrillas; down to every last one of them.

The people around the stores had stopped everything that they were doing, staring at us as if we would start burning them at the stake at any minute. Their dress wasn't as primitive as I would have thought. All of the men were in jeans, with fairly nice shirts, and the women were in very colorful dresses, some even bright white. The old man told us to go over to the other end of town, where there was a hospital that had several Americans in it. We thanked them and walked through the middle of the town like we owned it. Several women walked out of their huts to look at us and every one of them stood with their arms crossed with a stern look on their face. For a moment it seemed that we were on a different planet and we were very unwanted. I felt the hair on the back of my neck standing up as if something bad were going to happen.

As we got to the other side of the town, there was, in fact, a hospital. There was a Toyota Land Cruiser parked under a detached carport, with an orange yellow cross on the doors and on the passenger rear door. There was a fence surrounding the hospital that had to be at least 15 feet high, topped with c-wire. It was odd to see a hospital with such an enclosure. The building was painted white, with four windows on the front of the hospital, all with slatted glass. The front door was made of steel and painted the same color as the crosses on the vehicle doors. The building itself was very small and it was questionable if there was even anyone in there.

We walked into the small courtyard just in front of the main door, as Koz took off his pack and asked me to do the same. We secured our heavy weapons with the rest of the group and took out our side arms as we approached the door. Koz turned the doorknob softly and quietly, then inched the door open. The aroma of a well disinfected hospital crept out of the door as he cracked it open. We walked in quietly so as to not alert anyone to our presence. There wasn't a sound anywhere inside.

As we rounded out of the front room, we walked into a waiting area where there was a woman lying on her back on the floor, wearing a long lime green and purple dress with a white washcloth over her face. I could see her chest rise and fall with her every breath and she seemed oblivious to our presence in the room. A nurse came in the doorway and we raised our weapons to her head. Her hands went up in the air, her head went down, and she fell to the floor screaming, "Please don't kill me, this is a hospital for God's sakes!" Her accent clearly identified her as an American.

I yelled to her, "Who else is in this building with you?" Her hands were now shaking as they were stretched out inches above the floor with her face firmly planted on the floor.

"There is one doctor, a nurse, three patients, and myself!" she said frantically. The woman lying on the floor had pulled the washcloth off of her face, looked at us, and fainted. The nurse then yelled, "The Geneva Convention prohibits weapons in a hospital!"

Koz said in return, "Well, that's all fine and dandy, but we are in need of some medical supplies and some information. You can get up off the floor now; we aren't here to hurt anyone."

The nurse stood up dusting her uniform off and said, "I will have to ask you to leave this hospital." I walked past the nurse into the next room to see a doctor taking the vitals of a patient lying on an observation table. I told the doctor that we were Americans and I needed a few medical items from their storage and then we would leave. The doctor pointed to a closet door across the room. I walked over to it and started to open it when the nurse stuck her foot in front of the door preventing me from opening it.

She gently pushed me aside and said, "We are very low on supplies ourselves. How are we supposed to replenish what you take?" I holstered my pistol as I pushed her aside, taking several IV bags and a bottle of penicillin, telling her that we would be back to help them and bring in more supplies in a few weeks, but at that moment, we needed the supplies. She put her hands on her hips and yelled at me, "A few weeks? A lot of good that's going to do us now! I want the both of you out of here right now!" I have to say, I love American women and this one was a frisky one to boot. She had the looks of a ten-year old basset hound, but she was all American. The entire time she was yelling at us, the doctor, who had to have been a native, had wide eyes and looked like he was going to shit his pants.

I turned to the nurse as we were walking out and said, "I promise that I will come back and bring more supplies."

She gritted her teeth together and said, "Please leave!"

As Koz and I walked out of the hospital, you could hear the door slam and latch shut. Rodge yelled out to me, "Make a new friend, Doc?"

I replied, "Oh, ya, and if we ever make it back this way again, she is all yours." Rodge stood up, as his expression changed with a smile, "What, a hottie?"

I nodded and said, "Oh yeah, trust me, she's a keeper."

Koz shook his head laughing and said, "Let's get out of here."

Rodge then looked at Koz and asked, "Was she a hottie? Come on, Koz, tell me straight up, was she a hottie?"

Koz lifted his enormous pack onto his back, looked at Tom and said, "Let's move out."

Rodge was still trying to get me to say anything about her, saying, "Come on Doc, what was she like? Don't leave me hangin! Oh, okay, it's gonna be like that, huh? I'll remember that next time we're out on the prowl and you need something from me."

9

THE FIELD CAME TO LIFE

As we walked away from the town, I had a morbid feeling run through me like I was never going to see any of it again, even though I was being truthful when I said that I would be back with supplies. At the time, I feared the worst. I worried that maybe we had been seen and the villagers would suffer at our expense. Nevertheless, I still couldn't understand why I was feeling this way. Koz turned around, walking backwards, and said that we would hoof it for a couple of hours then break. He just as quickly turned back towards the front, once again, leading the line. I could still feel a little vertigo as we were walking, even though the ringing had gone down considerably. For some reason, my body wanted to go to the left as the spinning increased. I did remember that I had some Meclizine HCL in my pack that I would have to get out when we stopped. I thought that it might help my head and slow down the spinning.

As we walked, you couldn't help but look up at the mountains in the distance. Some were rounded like a perfect hump, and others came to a small peak, making them look similar to a small volcano. There were a few small clouds that stood still between some of the crests, looking just like a frayed cotton ball. You could also see the humidity as it hovered above the mountains, looking similar to very light smog. As we walked, I caught myself staring at the backs of some of the guys that were ahead of me. I wondered what they might be thinking at that same moment. I was enjoying our march and looking at the scenery, but I never forgot that every step we took could be our last. Every once in a while, we would walk past a batch of bamboo; the bright yellow stalks stood out against the brown and green background. Aside from the guerrilla factions that we were now hunting down, this country was truly beautiful, for the most part, but hidden beneath that beauty was an evil and grotesque reality that the scenery disguised very well.

We stopped at a group of mango trees for a brief break. After lying my pack and weapons down, I took off my boots to inspect the wear on them from the last few days. They were starting to fray slightly and the leather was cracking and was in desperate need of a coat of mink oil or polish. While taking out a tin of mink oil that I had brought, I started to feel the spinning return and remembered to take a couple Meclizine HCL tablets to help steady my head. I tossed back the medicine with a swig of water and then coated my boots with a good thick layer of mink oil. After I was done with my boots, I called out to Rodge and threw the tin to him. He replied with a quick nod and a good catch.

I continued my inspection of my uniform, noticing that my socks were literally falling apart, showing huge gaping holes where they had rubbed themselves away from a mixture of friction and moisture. Koz looked over to me as he was doing the same thing and said, "Give any destroyed clothing to Doc to bury before we leave." Next thing I knew, I had several retched pairs of socks flying over toward me and on me, except for Rodge; he balled his up and threw them at me with a little grease behind it. Instinctively, I raised my left hand and caught them before I had even known what they were. It surprised me, but also brought me back in the game. I quickly looked over to Rodge to see him give me a grin and thumbs up. By throwing the socks at me, he checked my response time, reflexes, and instincts within a second, with just that one throw. Deep inside, I appreciated it. He had subtly given me a test that could have been the difference between life and death. A Special Forces Soldier must have impeccable reflexes and reaction times. I believe that all of us embodied a gift that allowed us to slow time down so that everything moves in slow motion except for us; we are able to sort out possibilities and decisions at an incredible rate. We always have more time than the enemy or others, because we move in regular time while they are stuck moving in slow motion. That is just one of a million things that makes us the deadliest living creatures to walk this Earth.

I checked on Ron's leg and Tom's arm to see if they needed anything. They both quickly said they were fine and that their wounds had healed. I could tell that we were nearing our destination because the mood was changing quickly and I think every one of us knew that the miles to come were going to be the hardest we'd had to endure throughout the mission thus far. I handed everyone a glucose pack and instructed them to put the first half under their tongue and they could slam the rest if they wanted. Jesus was a little skeptical at first, and hesitant, until he saw the rest of us squeezing the tube under our tongues. He then followed and within a minute you could see the relief he and everyone else got from the sudden boost of energy and the ability to rejuvenate themselves. We pinned our uniforms where they needed mending and most importantly, changed our socks out. A bad or worn pair of socks can cause blisters and unforgiving rub marks that could cripple an un-rested man. Bad foot wounds could slow or stop a soldier faster than a gunshot wound. Our clothing was our protection from the environment and the elements; it had to be cared for just as much as a weapon.

I personally felt great and recharged after this break, almost better than the day we had left El Pongo. By the looks of everyone else, they seemed to feel the same. The journey had a few hard spots at first, but now it felt like our pace and overall wellbeing had created a positive inertia that would certainly propel us through anything. We were now losing daylight fast and needed to move out quickly because we had to go through one more known village before the radar sight. You could see the jump in everyone's footsteps and the confidence with every step. My pack felt lighter or I felt stronger; regardless of whichever was more accurate, I was back in the game.

Suddenly, I had Bill Ledbetter on my mind and what Tom had said earlier. An image of him at Bragg, when he pulled up alongside a couple of us in his Jeep, popped into my mind. You could pick his Jeep out of a million, because he had painted our crest on the leather cover that went over the spare tire at the back of the Jeep. He had that Jeep jacked up and decked out like no Jeep I had ever seen before or to this day. In recalling those memories, I desperately wanted revenge for what they did to him and his family. My mind was becoming very eager and imaginative about how I was going to seek my revenge. Payback was coming and everybody could feel it; I was not alone in my thirst for revenge for Bill. You kill a fellow Green Beret and, regardless of who you are or where you are, you're gonna die. It's that simple.

The jungle was silent and every star in the sky was out; the only noise was the rubbing of canvas as our packs slid from side to side on our backs and the periodic sound of plastic when our slings or a stick hit the stocks on our weapons. We had walked for about an hour when we broke out of the jungle and came to a large clearing. The grass was about chest high and swayed in the night breeze. Tom held his right fist up, so we all stopped and took a knee, altering sides with our weapons. He quietly took his Night Observation Device (similar to NVGs) out and scanned the field very carefully, knowing well that we would be out in the open for at least 20 minutes at a good pace. He held up his hands making an upside-down V, which meant wedge and chopped at his left arm with his right hand meaning travel strong or heavy left. I was the last man on the far left with my 60 at the ready pointing left with Todd, Trout, and Petie in front of me, staggering in a wedge formation to the right. We needed to move across this thing as furtively as we could.

We walked at a very slow pace, minding to pick up our feet so they didn't get caught up in the grass. Ron had the lead and was about halfway across when the field seemingly and violently, came to life. There were bullets and tracers flying in every direction. I had taken several steps forward to set down cover fire, when I fell into a large hole. I landed right on top of a guy; it was evident that everyone out in the field was asleep in a series of foxholes when one of us had stumbled into one of them.

The guy I landed on started to scream. I raised the butt of my weapon and started to butt stroke him as fast as I could, trying to get past his flailing arms. I hit the side of the foxhole with the butt and a round went off in my sixty. The noise was deafening and the muzzle flash was so blinding that I fell to the back of the foxhole over my pack. The man kicked me in the nuts, so I grabbed my crotch and clawed my way towards him as he was trying to get out of the hole. I grabbed his pant leg and pulled him back down; he now fell on top of me and was hitting me in an uncontrolled panic. I grabbed him by the throat with my left hand and punched him square with my right. Blood seemed to explode all over me when I split his nose in half. He raised his hands towards his face for only a second and that was all I needed. I still had his throat with my left hand and I pushed him down to the other side of the foxhole. I literally started to beat his brains in once I had command of the situation. As I was punching him, I felt the left side of his face cave in as the bones gave way. I reached down and unsheathed my knife from my right side and drove it through the left side of his throat, ripping upwards, towards me, as his carotid arteries sprayed the inside of the hole.

As I put my knife back, my eyes were stinging from the blood and sweat running into them and could smell the body odor of the now dead man; I grabbed my pack and threw it out of the hole. I grabbed my weapon in the darkness and raised myself to the edge of the foxhole. The grass was too high to see what was going on, but I could see the tracers flying over the top of the hole that brought my head down in a hurry. I was desperately trying to catch my breath. There was screaming and yelling, coming from all directions, and in several different languages. I crawled out of the hole and went in the direction towards where Ron was on point. I pushed the grass to each side as I high crawled toward what seemed to be the middle of the scurry. I had the sling of my weapon hooked on my right thumb as I pulled the earth and grass to my sides and underneath me, as I tried frantically to reach the rest of the team. As I pushed aside a patch of grass in front of me, my hand hit the bottom of a boot. I stopped and looked up the leg for any movement; I could see the head of the man silhouetted from the flashes in front of him.

I slowly and carefully pulled my hand free of the weapon sling and again drew my knife out of its canvas sheath, never allowing my eyes to leave the man's head.

After I pulled my knife out, I turned it around so that I could easily stab the man in the back. I studied his pant leg for a pattern or to see if they were US issue BDUs and then looked down to his boot where I noticed the word "Wolverine" in yellow stitch on the side. That was all I needed. I jumped on top of him and drove my knife deep through his back and out through his chest. The man didn't move at all; when I looked up, I noticed that most of the right side of his face and head were gone. The man was already dead and now my knife was stuck in his chest cavity.

I drew my side arm knowing well that things were too up close and personal to fire a 60, especially without knowing where the rest of the team was. I didn't have the time, or the energy, to pull my knife out of the man's back. I was going to have to leave it or come back for it later. I hated to leave it behind due to the history, proficiency, and relationship I had with this tool that had saved my life more than once, but I was spending valuable time worrying about something that could be replaced, which was something I couldn't say about the rest of the team.

I slid off the man to the left and inched up his side, trying to get a better view of the action in front of us. I tried wiping off some of the sweat with my thumb that was now streaming into my eyes, when I heard Danny, in front and to the right yell, "Whoooaaa, come get some, you mother fucker, yah you want some?" I then heard his SAW spit out at least 50 to 70 rounds as he strafed from left to right. The muzzle flash lit the entire area where he had exposed a guerrilla quickly rising up out of the grass to my immediate right. I couldn't believe that we had been lying in the grass so close to one another without noticing any movement or sound from one another. I pushed my hands up like a pushup, with my pistol in my right hand, quickly rising up to an immediate kneel position. I raised my pistol and inflicted a headshot to the guerrilla next to me that spewed a strawberry mist into the night air. My weapon's fire also caused Danny to turn in my direction and put a couple of rounds only inches above my head, as I immediately flattened back down as quick as I could, hitting my face on the dead man's arm below me.

I yelled, "Danny, I'm on your nine, Goddamn it!"

He in turn yelled, "You mother fuckers!" and started firing off to his right, hopefully understanding where I was.

I rose up out of the tall grass at ready pistol to see people running everywhere; it reminded me of flashlight tag as a kid, with guys running every which way, with the flashlight trying to tag all of us. I could see Danny perfectly in front of me, when I heard someone yell, "Doc!" followed by the international "I'm fucked" sound of a shotgun pump going, "Chick, Chick!" I turned slightly to my left, when the shotgun went off, spraying flesh, bone, and gristle all over my entire upper torso and face, knocking me back down to the ground. I can remember seeing the muzzle flash through the approaching man's body, as it liquefied his side, sending his body matter covering me, and spinning him to the ground. As I hit the ground, I curled up with my hands on my face yelling, "Son of a bitch!" as I had felt some of the bone matter slice into my face.

Todd ran over to me yelling, "Holy shit, Doc, are you alright?" as he knelt by my side.

I looked up to him and yelled back, "I keep getting knocked down on this mother fucker and still can't get my knife out of his back! Where the hell is everybody?"

Todd's head ducked down from another shotgun blast on our left and yelled, "We're everywhere; it's a total cluster fuck!"

I wiped some of the debris off my face with my left hand, in a similar manner that you would wipe off a pie after it just hit you in the face and yelled, "Shit!" Todd and I stood back up, both of us bringing our weapons up to the ready. I again started off towards where Ron should have been and saw Danny send a guerrilla flying out of the corner of my eye. I heard another SAW machine gun go off behind me and as I turned, I saw four guerrillas coming up from our rear position as Petie engaged them. They were all firing their weapons, in a jerky and overcompensating manner, as the fear rushed through their veins. I took the third to the right out with a headshot and watched the other three fly backwards, one even somersaulting, as Petie sent a barrage of bullets in their direction. Petie looked over towards me and we both turned around to hear some of the final shots going off.

There was so much smoke from all of the gunfire, it settled on top of what grass was left, much like a thick fog. Petie, Todd, Danny, and I were now all down to one knee as we all swept the muzzles of our weapons from left to right, in front and behind, looking for any movement or survivors, as small fires burned the grass to our every side. Tom yelled out blindly from in front of us and through the smoke, "Koz! Scout, Doc?" Scout and I called off at the same time, "Here!"

I rose up once again at ready pistol, and Petie yelled out, "I've got Danny, Doc, Todd, Scout, and myself at the rear!"

Koz then called out, "Doc, I need you over here!"

I yelled out, "Hang tight, I'm coming from your five." I slowly brought myself up hunched over and inched my way towards the general direction where Koz's voice came from, looking at the small fires surrounding me and hearing groans coming from everywhere. The grass had been beaten down as if a herd of deer hunkered down for a night of rest, leaving only a few spots untouched. As I slowly slid my feet across the flattened grass, totally blind to anything more than a few feet in front of me. I ran into numerous bodies that had literally been cut in half. Thankfully, I hadn't run into any of our guys yet. The smoke from all the gunpowder was so thick that it was burning my eyes.

I heard Tom call out, "Ron and I are on point."

Then Rodge called out from our far right, "Doc, Jesus and I are over here and he's got a pretty bad leg wound."

Todd then yelled out, "Rodge, I'm coming from your nine. I don't know how many of them are left or where they are, but cover my ass."

I had walked at least 15 yards by now, and in a half whisper, called out to Koz, "Where are you guys?"

All of a sudden, only three feet to my left, I heard, "I'm right here," in a calm and controlled voice, as I flinched to see Koz slowly lower the muzzle of his Ithaca.

I closed my eyes for a split second to allow the blood to flow back in my head and after a large swallow said, "Fuck! God! This is fucked!" I slid over to Koz, observing the foxhole behind him. I took a knee and asked, "You all right?"

He nodded and said, "Yeah, but the LT isn't."

"Where is he?"

"He's down there," as his right hand left the trigger of the Ithaca and pointed in the direction of the foxhole behind him.

I put my pistol in the holster on the side of my right thigh and got down on all fours and slid into the foxhole. The LT appeared to be sitting on his heels, with his head and chest bowed all the way back, resting on the back of the hole. His eyes and mouth were open as I slowly reached for his carotid and saw that his chest was fully saturated with blood. As the fires in the background flickered, they illuminated parts of the foxhole differently with each turning second. I slowly started picking my head up in Koz's direction and said, "He's dead."

Koz looked out across the field as he had been when I arrived, biting his lower lip and said, "Yeah, that's what I figured."

At that very second, Danny yelled out, "Got two on our nine!" Koz stood up and turned around in a single movement and fired off three shots with his Ithaca in addition to an arsenal of bullets that hailed from Danny and Petie's position.

As the barrage of bullets came to a halt, Tom yelled out, "Stand fast, everyone, stand fast. There are more of them in here and we are all spread out in too much of a cluster. Verify your shots and stand fast!" Koz lowered himself back down and asked if I was okay as he now noticed the body matter that was still falling off of the front of my shirt.

I answered, "Yeah, I'm alright," and started to flick some of the chunks off of the front of me. The saturated blood in my shirt was slowly starting to dry, which gave the feeling similar to that of a heavy starch. I didn't have to worry about the smell of anything anymore: my nose was totally blocked by the smoke and the dust that had incrusted both nostrils.

Koz slid into the foxhole with me and yelled out to Tom, "We're going to have to wait this one out, Tom, and then we can clear this field without risking crossfire."

Tom yelled back, "Copy that, everyone stand fast!"

The field now grew silent, outside of the slight popping of burning grass and insects, now praying on the dead, and from within the jungle. Koz was keeping watch out of the front of the foxhole and I looked out more to the right and behind us to where most of the team was. After a few minutes of waiting, we heard a voice coming from behind us with a slight accent, but still positioned between where Koz and I hunkered down and Petie's group. "I need help, please help me." I tried to see exactly where it was coming from, but between the smoke burning the hell out of my eyes and the fires constantly shifting shadows, it was impossible to see. The man pleaded for help for at least an hour before falling silent.

45 minutes later, the sun started coming up. Each minute that followed revealed the absolute carnage that was spread in every direction. There were blades of grass in pockets that were so saturated with blood that it was still dripping off the ends. There was what seemed like ten feet of intestines that had been dragged out of a man as he tried crawling away. The entire area looked like someone had stuffed live humans into a hopper and sprayed the aftermath out, projecting body parts, fatty tissue, gristle, and bone fragments into the air, showering the ground as they fell. Koz stuffed shell after shell into the port of his Ithaca, never moving his eyes, not even a blink. There was a guy that was laying ten feet to our right and something had opened his face from just above the bottom jaw line through the mid back of his skull, yet he still seemed to have an expression on his face. He looked at peace, staring aimlessly into the sky, awaiting his next destination; one had to wonder if he would be set free or if he was to burn in the forever damnation of hell fires.

10

LICK OUR WOUNDS AND PRESS ON

THE SMOKE DIDN'T RISE WITH THE SUN; IT HOVERED OVER THE CARNAGE, like a blanket of evil. All of us held our positions and waited to see what this new day would reveal to us, as God lit the sky slowly, declaring his judgments, making us wait to reveal Satan's henchmen. As everything came into focus, with all of us lying in wait, there were at least sixty men hovering on the edge of the jungle, leaving us fully surrounded. The only thing that we had going for us was that they didn't know how many of us there were, nor how many of us were left. The men on the edge of the jungle started to talk to each other, shifting their weight from leg to leg and rising up on their toes, trying to see through the remaining grass and smoke what was in the middle of this small field of death. After an hour of them contemplating if they should go into the field or not, they took all of us for dead and started to tighten the circle they had around us.

At first, they stepped carefully with every inch. I noticed several of the men making the sign of the cross on their chests as they looked upon the gore and blood. After they had moved between 15 and 20 feet towards the middle, you could see them relax in their approach, with some of them resting the barrels of their weapons on their shoulders, assuming that because there wasn't any movement or sound, that the field was only one of carnage, free from any life at all.

You could read the state of awe on the faces of every one of these men as they walked into the field. I felt my muscles tighten and all the exhaustion from the night's terrors left my body, as energy and hate surged through my veins. I very slowly looked to my left and saw Koz smiling; he turned to me and said in a hushed tone, "Let's rock," with a wink of his eye. Like in slow motion, he then turned and rose out of the grass while I stood, with "Mother" at my hip, ready to pour hell into them. I pulled her in tight, squeezing the handgrip and the hand guard like a rope that held my destiny: life or death.

As Koz brought the Ithaca to his shoulder, his first shot liquefied a man's head that now stood only feet in front of him. His entire head disintegrated instantly; everything happening around us, once again, seemed to move in slow motion. The man's body stood there for what seemed to be an eternity, headless, until his knees buckled and collapsed to the ground with his body still erect and motionless, his jugular arteries bursting a fountain of blood into the air with every heartbeat. Then slowly, the upper torso fell to the earth, spewing out what seemed to be every last drop of blood that his body once possessed.

I felt my teeth clinch together as my finger squeezed the trigger and my body immediately prepared for the recoil of my M-60. I heard firing start to my rear as my hog split the bodies of the men in front of me in half. I swear you could see light through their chest for a fraction of a second as the bullet passed through them and blew out their back. The concussion was breathtaking as the belt slowly dissipated off of my left forearm as it unraveled itself. The guerillas had been much closer than I had thought when I popped up out of the grass. Each round that I fired seemed to explode on impact as it penetrated the target's chest cavity, throwing body matter into the air, decorating the background like a Monet tapestry. Every hit had a distinct thump to it, seemingly louder than even the firing pin hitting the primer. The guerillas didn't have a chance; they let their guard down for only a fraction of a second and felt the wrath of some pissed off Green Berets.

As the sounds of the firing came to a halt, I looked around me to see every one of us standing motionless, like Greek statues, holding their weapons at ready. All of the guerillas were dead or were running fast as hell. As I looked at the rest of the team, I couldn't tell if anyone was hit or not because we were all covered in blood. It was like blood poured from the sky, drenching us from head to toe as body matter fell off of our uniforms. I had never witnessed anything so grotesque in my life. A Hollywood movie could never portray such rampant destruction of human life. The fires burned in the background as we just stood there, waiting for our next kill.

I turned and walked over to the foxhole I had been in with the LT. The LT's eyes stared into the heavens and his mouth lay open, seemingly trying to either ask for forgiveness, confess his sins, or to cuss the heavens for taking the only thing that he ever loved. Koz sent Trout, Ron, Scout, and Danny into the jungle to set up a 360 perimeter while the rest of us gathered all of the bags and weapons. Petie would bring up the rear as he set up all of his remaining claymores, hoping to buy us a little more time. Koz stood hovering over the corpse of the LT, staring into the foxhole. I asked him if he wanted help burying him and he turned and in a monotone voice said, "He thought this was the break he needed to command a team of his own. He was going to tell me about something he heard back at SOCOM. I really have no idea what it was that he wanted to tell me. But one thing that I do know is that, he always said that wherever he falls is where he will lay and I do owe him that. So, thanks, Doc, but I'll do it myself," as he slid into the foxhole and laid Randie (LT) down on his back.

Koz removed the LT's dog tags with care and said goodbye in his own way, as he jumped out of the foxhole and knelt on the edge. He made the sign of the cross on his chest and then over the deceased First Lieutenant. Randie had never fraternized with us. He always kept to himself and only talked amongst other officers. I couldn't understand all of the actions that led up to this moment. It was like he was a part of us, but at the same time, he existed in a completely different and separate entity from the rest of the team. After watching Koz at the edge of the foxhole, I thought about how, in combat, religion is a funny thing; some can draw closer to God or find their personal religion. Some alienate themselves from their faith, living solely off of hate or fear, disbelieving that anything could reign over all of the death and destruction that combat produces. I think for most of us, it changed from mission to mission, relating specifically to how close the individual actually came to meeting his creator. I readily admit that sometimes it's hard to look to faith for protection or support for men like us. Especially when we walk the Earth as one of the most proficient forms of death and destruction that this planet has ever known.

Following the moments spent honoring the LT, the jungle started to come to life again with a sort of harmony as the birds started to chirp, oddly enough, and then a gentle breeze lifted into the air. My arms and legs felt like rubber; my ears were ringing so loud that I found myself tilting my head from side to side trying to make out certain noises that were or were not there. I was having a hard time deciphering them. Danny came out of the jungle and told us that there were more men on the way and that we needed to diggy out of here quickly to avoid another slaughter, where the aftermath may have a very different ending. We certainly would not have the advantage if another skirmish occurred, as we were all exhausted and in desperate need of hydration. We had been lucky by every definition of the word. With the exception of the LT, for a team to endure that big of a bloodbath and come out, for the most part, unscathed, was truly unreal. We were trained to a tee in how we engaged with the enemy and a free-for-all like we just had experienced was unheard of in our line of business. It was utter chaos and undisciplined, but we made it out okay; I recall at that moment being very worried about the time when our luck was going to run out.

I quickly walked over to the guerilla I had stabbed in the back and manipulated "The Widow Maker" out of his back and chest cavity. In attempting to pull it out, I realized how tired my muscles were; the physical combat and adrenaline had sucked all of the energy out of me. Pushing through my extreme fatigue, I pulled the knife out and once it finally gave way, it tore chunks of flesh. The knife pulled layers of skin up and down, separating from the muscle tissue and skin platelets, as the serrated edge worked its way out. It gave a hollowed suction sound as it passed through his lungs. I felt my left foot slide slightly on his chest as I looked down. The light morning dew had added to the already blood-soaked ground.

Those of us that remained in the field carried two rucksacks each in order to free up the rest of the team patrolling out in the jungle. Koz dragged a few of the dead guerillas into the foxhole with the LT, enough to cover his body so that the other guerillas wouldn't see him. They would leave their dead in the hole and make it their final resting place. As tragic as it was, the LT was to spend the rest of eternity in an unmarked hole in the middle of nowhere and only our team would ever know where he was in this beautiful, damned place called El Salvador. Koz had stripped the LT of all objects that could associate him with the United States. We never went into missions like this with name tapes or rank anywhere on our uniforms, but he did have a wallet and a couple other items we intended on bringing back to post so they could be given to any family he had to be disposed of properly.

Knowing how the military works, the items would be destroyed and his DD214 would state that he died in a training exercise. He would have a closed casket burial and the full 21-gun salute ceremony at Arlington Cemetery. He deserved at least that, as he did die for his country, with honor. He was an Army brat and the only thing in life that he knew or wanted to know was the military. He had all the family he needed right there on post amongst our tight family within Special Forces. There were many like him within the Green Berets and almost all of them wanted to stay where they fell to spend the rest of eternity in the place where they made the ultimate sacrifice, even though Uncle Sam often had big problems with those wishes. While many consider burial at Arlington as a sign of heroism and patriotism, SF soldiers are a different breed. Many are comfortable with just simply being put to rest where we fell. I personally felt that if I wasn't coming back alive, let the ones I loved the most remember the memories we shared and remember me in their hearts, not by a gravestone.

We needed to move out as fast as we could and put as much distance and time between us and the upcoming guerilla party, knowing well that they had to be closing in on us. The weight of the additional packs was almost unbearable, making it difficult to pick up our feet as we entered back into the jungle. Our first few steps into what had been the tree line, revealed how almost all of the trees had been cut down or damaged by all of the bullets barraging in and out of the jungle. Every tree seemed to be affected for at least the first 50 feet and the ground was now totally littered with fallen branches, making our escape that much more difficult. Once we were in the former tree line, we realized we had to shift our course to the southwest to offset the guerillas. They had to have followed our path to the southeast, meaning we needed to go to the west and buy us some time. Danny, Trout, Petie, and the rest of the team caught up to us after about a half an hour. They cleared our tracks and added a few booby traps, on top of Petie's claymores in the field, to help slow our pursuers down. Our team had also attached a couple M119 whistlers to a few of the trees that the guerillas would have to pass through to follow us.

We stopped for a couple minutes and gave the extra packs back to their owners. The first thing I thought of when we took the second pack off was that it seemed I was going to float away. My pack was now so light compared to carrying two packs that I knew my body could easily make it for a couple more hours. When Trout and the guys caught up to us, they looked like something out of a Halloween movie. A couple of them had blood that either ran down from the top of their heads or was sprayed into their eyes, making their tear ducts overflow trying to flush out the foreign matter. The tears partially washed away some of the blood that was on their face, creating either a clown-like effect or an image that there was blood flowing from their eyes. It was creepy and morbid. We literally looked like the walking dead, which momentarily made me question if we were. Did we actually make it out of that firefight or not? Maybe we were the walking dead! I shook my head and realized that the heat and exhaustion were starting to play with my mind. I told Koz that we would need to break and recompose ourselves, which he quickly agreed with, but in the back of my mind, I had a hard time convincing myself of the realities of our outcome following that bloodbath.

We had walked a very short distance when we came upon a timber bridge that vaulted over a shallow, but somewhat lengthy, river that went straight across and butted up against an amazingly thick jungle. The current was flowing very slowly, so we all waded into the water in three-man intervals until we reached the other side. This way, we could cool down and wash off a little in a slow enough manner that it would be good for all of us. I certainly wasn't going to trust another one of these makeshift bridges we had crossed at the onset of this mission. Calling to mind that bridge, my attention turned to Jesus and I noticed him limping as he walked across the river. I had forgotten all about the leg wound that he had sustained in the field. I noticed a trauma bandage wrapped around his left leg that Todd had applied which was now saturated in blood, as well as, I'm sure, the cholera-infested water; well, I guess that would have to do for the time being. He had a lot of problems getting up the embankment on the other side, which made me question if we would have to leave him behind to keep up with our now very tight timeline. He was now part of our team to an extent, being involved with a mutual mission, but as far as being one of *us*, he simply wasn't. At this point, Jesus was simply becoming more and more expendable with every hour.

It was Todd's, Ron's, and my turn to cross the river. The water felt great on my sore and worn legs and feet. As we crossed, Todd explained to me that the wound Jesus got in the firefight was a six-inch laceration where a bullet skimmed across his leg. He followed up by mentioning how lucky we were and how he couldn't believe what this mission had turned into, as he removed two 100 round 7.62 ammo belts from around his neck for my hog. When we reached the other side of the river, the embankment looked a lot bigger than it did from the other side. It literally took everything I had to claw and scrape through the mud and dirt to bring myself up the 15-foot embankment. I had to give Jesus well-deserved credit for scaling that embankment with his injury.

Once all of us had made it to the other side of the river, we stashed our gear in the thick jungle and went back down to the river to clean up. We figured the river to be laced with cholera so we needed to mind not getting any of the water into our mouths. Tom had Todd, Ron, Petie, Danny, Scout, and Jesus go in first while the rest of us stood guard. They used the sand, silt, and a rock to scrub our BDUs as best as they could in the river. They all threw what was left of their uniforms up to us to lie in the sun to dry after an admirable attempt to clean off all of the human matter that covered every one of us. I only half broke down my M-60 to break some of the carbon and powder residue that was now blanketing all of her moving parts. The rest of the team did so as well with their weapons and when I glanced down at the guys in the river as they rinsed off, even though the current was very slow, the water flowing downstream from them turned a dark blood red as they washed off the remnants of the day.

They were in there a good 20 minutes, enjoying a much-needed break. As they got out, we had to cut the now blood-filled leeches off of them before they put on a clean pair of BDUs, shirt, socks, and boots that they retrieved from their rucks. We would have destroyed the old uniforms, but we didn't know how long it would be before we were to get a re-supply. I immediately worried about the leeches, because they could have very well infected any one of us with an unknown virus or disease.

As we set our bags down, Koz and Rodge immediately got on the radio to contact JSOC. As I rested on one knee, I could hear Rodge asking the radio operator on the other end what the hell he was talking about. JSOC was asking us to authenticate, which meant Rodge had to look on a predetermined card with numerous numbers and letters on a grid, similar to the game "Battleship," to create an authentication code. For example, they would call out "B-5" and you would go to the left-hand margin to B, across the top to 5, and scroll down the matrix to the appropriate number or word that intersected in the middle. It was rare that we would have to do this because we usually had a secure net where authentication codes were not required.

Rodge authenticated and started with what we call a SALUTE report: "S" was the size of the enemy force; "A" was the activity of what the enemy was doing; "L" was the location of the enemy; "U" was the unit in which we confronted, to include distinctive features, special equipment they had and or any markings on their uniforms. "T" was the time in which we observed or engaged with the enemy and "E" was the equipment the enemy wore, carried, or used. He then went into an ACE report which was a summary of our status: "A" represented our ammunition status within the team; "C" summarized our casualties, specifically, if there were any losses within the team; and "E" communicated any equipment needs we had following our engagement. Rodge gave all of this to JSOC in a coded message that most of us wouldn't understand let alone anyone who was listening in, but I did know that somewhere within the report notification of that our commanding officer was killed in action.

Rodge started to write down a large amount of information that JSOC communicated back to us on his notepad which piqued the curiosity in all of us that were standing guard in the immediate vicinity of the radio. From a bird's eye view, it looked like he was writing down eight-digit map coordinates which could mean a lot of things. As he was finishing up with JSOC, Koz was getting a map out of his Alice pack and started to find the location where we were being sent to. Rodge talked to Koz for a couple minutes, which led Koz to shake his head from side to side with a disgusted look on his face and swearing under his breath, "You've gotta be fuckin' kidding me!" He looked up in the air, gave a big sigh and closed his eyes for a moment, then lowered his head, clenched his fists, and stood up. One thing about Koz, when he was pissed, his bottom lip and jaw would shake uncontrollably.

As I was finishing up in clipping the last of the four hundred round belt of ammo together, it was our turn to get into the river to wash off. Tom, Trout, Rodge, and I went down to the stream and rinsed off the blood and aftermath that was now hardened and dry on our uniforms. I thought about the leeches and the risks we were taking, but at that moment, I didn't give a shit. I just wanted to get all of this shit off of me and all of us were taking malaria tabs, and had been vaccinated for every other disease known to man, so I said "fuck it." The water was cool and very refreshing. It reminded me of when I was young and would go skinny dipping in the pond by my house to cool off from the heat of the summer. I pulled my hands to my face and blew my nose only to see blood, dirt, snot, and powder resin fill my palms. It reminded me of when I had been in High Altitude

Low Opening (HALO) training in Indian Springs; we called our snot "Nellis nuggets," because the dust from the desert climate would harden into nuggets in your nose.

My nose wasn't the only thing clinging to recent events. I could still taste the gunpowder in the back of my throat with every breath. After about ten minutes of bathing, I felt the concussion of a claymore behind us. The river water slightly rippled as the claymore detonated. All of us in the river momentarily ducked our heads down and moved for the shore knowing full well that they weren't far behind us now. We scampered up the bank and got into a fresh pair of BDUs as we stuffed the wet ones into our rucks.

Within ten minutes of the first blast, they had obviously found the rest of the claymores which slowed them down considerably, but the guerillas were clearly now headed into the jungle because two whistlers went off almost simultaneously. Koz turned us around to go due south, which would eventually have us crossing back over the river again. He was the only one of us that didn't go into the river to wash off. I think that he needed to feel the stickiness and smell the raunchy iron of blood clinging to his skin and his uniform as a reminder of the LT. It fueled a now dangerous bonfire of aggression that was raging within him.

After getting dressed, loading up our rucks, and getting our weapons ready, I think I could safely say that we were all slightly refreshed from the river but were starting to show signs of fatigue. We walked for a good hour before coming to a very thick spot in the jungle that would provide proper cover and concealment for the team to stop and rest. I tended to Jesus's wound, applied a new dressing, and gave him some antibiotics. The affected skin on his wound was now open and folding back just like a chainsaw had cut it. With the help of some steri-strips (similar to butterfly bandages), I knew that I had to relieve some of the moisture or this open wound was going to seal his fate.

We took turns on watch starting out with Koz, Scout, Ron, and I taking the first shift. I don't think anyone else had even laid their heads down before they fell fast asleep. I spent my watch anticipating the pack of banditos following us to creep up on us at any time. Every sound that the jungle made caused an almost overcompensated reaction as we stood guard. After two and a half hours, the sun was starting to set and Koz got Tom, Danny, and Petie up to take their watch while the rest of us tried to get some sleep. I know I don't even remember falling asleep, but when we were awakened, the air was slightly cooler and our bodies were sore, cramped, and stiff. As I rolled over and pushed my hands in the ground to prop my tired body up, I felt a pop in my back as my hands immediately gave way, plummeting my face into the undergrowth.

I really was starting to feel the fatigue, as well as excruciating pain, and I struggled to get my hand under my t-shirt to feel what had popped on my back.

As I moved my hand around, I felt a huge bump that had to have been at least an inch and a half high, with a three-inch diameter base. It felt kind of like a huge zit; the blood, puss, or fluid was now leaking out, making the surface very slippery and wet with a small crater at the top. I took my pointer finger and thumb on each side and squeezed. An invigorating pain shot through my body like lightning, forcing my back to arch and my legs to extend out stiff and straight. It literally took my breath away, somewhat choking me, as my eyes squinted shut from the pain.

I pulled my hand up to my face to look at whatever I popped out of it. It was a combination of very thick white paste and blood that had the consistency of a thick cheese spread and had a foul ammonia-like smell to it. I asked Todd if he could come over for a second to give me a hand as I lay on the ground, thankful that no one had seen me collapse. I didn't want to give the impression to anyone that I was injured or that I would slow us down. As he came up to me, I explained how I had thought that something had bit me in the back when I was asleep. As I rolled over, he pulled my shirt up and said, "Damn, that is fucked up!" As he started to probe around the affected area, I squeezed my fists and closed my eyes as hard as I could from the pain and planted my face in the soil. "Okay, Doc, now lay still for a moment, I see what it is." He pushed and squeezed around it in a circular fashion like a zit and I felt another pop, but this time, it was a relieving pop in which I let the trapped air in my lungs now flow freely into the night air as I let out a gratifying sigh. It ended up not being a bite at all, but an inch and a half splinter of wood or bamboo that had lodged in my back at some point earlier in the mission and when I was soaking in the river, it must have softened the tissue around it, allowing it to come out.

As I looked up, Koz was standing over me and questioned, "You alright Doc?"

I gave another long sigh, shaking my head yes and said, "I am now."

He shook his head up and down and said, "Good, we need ya, Doc, don't go doing anymore crazy hero shit. We've gotta go assist some US agency that has been compromised and gotten themselves into a bit of a pickle. Get him patched up, sergeant, and get ready to move out." Todd acknowledged the command and began to apply an ointment and eventually a dressing on my back. We were all showing fatigue as we loaded our packs and began to head out. At first, the pressure from the pack hurt against the now enormous welt, but diminished with time.

Our feet were still continuing to catch on the grass and the thick underbrush as we worked to make up time to get us to our destination to come to the aid of whomever. I couldn't help but wonder why they didn't use the choppers from El Pongo or the Marine post we had visited earlier. Maybe we had to meet up with another contact or even a re-supply. We eventually slid down a steep hill onto a paved road. There were a few cars and trucks loaded with men that passed by intermittently as we staggered the team across the road between vehicles, making sure to not be seen by any onlookers. We could now hear gun fire coming from the south which was where we were heading directly for. There was a sign slightly down the road that read Jiquilisco, so I figured we were in the deep south of the country and somewhat near to a large town or city.

We stashed our rucks in the middle of a patch of neck high bushes as fast as we could, making sure no one would find the cache. Then we started to move faster and faster, almost at a double time, as we cut through the foliage in a wedge formation. Our pace was so fast, that we would be just as surprised if we ran into someone as they would be running into us. We were closing in on the gun fire, which was now directly in front of us. I could smell the ocean with every step now as we headed into more rugged terrain. I was catching my feet constantly as they slid off of rounded stones that seemed now to be everywhere in our path. As the rocks gave off the slight sound of hitting each other, I could feel my face redden with worry, knowing that we were making too much noise in our approach, even with the heavy gun fire in the background.

Koz was on point and brought us to an unexpected dead stop, directing the team down immediately for concealment. My palm rested on a rounded rock that reminded me of the river stones found on the banks of most rivers up in Wisconsin. But as I laid there, steadfast, I realized that Wisconsin seemed a million miles away from us now. I couldn't enjoy the luxury of sitting on those Wisconsin river banks, looking high in the sky for bald eagles that frequented the rivers for their flourishing fish.

There seemed to be sounds of intermittent bursts of fire coming from two different directions that brought me back to the present. Our problem was figuring out which was friend and which one was foe. We laid in waiting as Koz shot an azimuth; with an eight-digit coordinate from an azimuth, you can get yourself within ten meters of your destination. The problem was what was within those ten meters. We started to high crawl towards the fire fight traveling across large jagged and smooth rocks. All of a sudden, the firing came to a halt. We froze like statues as we looked amongst each other trying to figure out who was the victor. All I could think about was the carnage that had fully enveloped this country that I had never even thought about before coming here. Evil of every kind flourished in this country. I began to wonder… was it pulling me into its grasp? I felt so much hate, frustration, and desire to kill everything and anything in my path. I caught myself smiling at the thought of total genocide in this evil place.

Tom and Petie took out their thermal imagers, trying to assess the good from the bad or at least where all the action was coming from. After a few minutes, Petie asked what I made of it as he handed me the thermal imager. There were at least 20 men still standing around, since not only did their bodies give off a huge signature, but all of their weapons were very hot and produced a signature as bright as a street light. Rodge pulled the radio mic around to his mouth and asked whoever was on the other end to authenticate numbers and if we were in the right area to meet up with the friendlies. As we all looked to him for verification, he shook his head from side to side, basically motioning that we were too late.

As I looked into the thermal imagers again, I saw what appeared to be a cave, a Defensive Fighting Position (DFP), or a very large, covered foxhole. The hollow was producing a large amount of heat inside that was either from the previous day's retained heat within the rock walls or there were people within the holes giving off a very distinct heat signature. As I scanned the area, there were a few DFPs, all occupied by at least two to three men each. The numbers seemed to be larger than I had initially thought. All we could do now was lie in wait. There were several radios going off in the background, some were in Spanish and some were in English, as strange as it may seem, none of the men around this area acknowledged any of the radio traffic. If these were foes, they were only feet from sure death and if they were friendly, they were some of the dumbest sons-a-bitches I had ever seen. Either way, we were in a predicament ourselves; there were very few trees in the area and the vegetation or undergrowth was very limited and extremely dry; so, in a matter of words, we were sitting ducks and couldn't do a damn thing about it.

All of us laid there, motionless, waiting for something to happen. After about 15 minutes of jabbering and laughing as they looked over their victory, the men who were walking around started to remove several bodies from the DFPs I had noticed earlier. One of the groups dragged a man out, stripped him of his clothing and laid him out on what appeared to be a 20-by-20 stone or concrete slab. I then knew that the good guys had lost. There are very few factions that are associated with the United States that would lay someone out like that on display. I was getting anxious with all the movement just in front of us. I was starting to wonder if this was going to turn out like the "O.K. Corral," considering how confined the space was in which we would be confronting each other.

11

CONTACT BY THE LAKE

I INSTINCTIVELY FROZE AS I CAUGHT MOVEMENT COMING FROM IN FRONT OF our wedge formation as a man walked only ten feet to the to the right of Koz, who was on point. He walked by and stopped parallel to Danny on his right. I very slowly lowered my head those extra few inches, trying not to be noticed. I'm sure from a bird's eye view or careful observation by the guy walking towards us, that all of us must have looked like at least ten men or darkened figures laying in a V formation. My body started to tense up as the man took a couple steps more and stopped only three or four feet from Danny. I was holding my breath until he unbuttoned his fly and started taking a piss, which was hitting Danny on his right calf and right boot. If any of us tried to jump him, we would be instantly compromised and would be at an extreme disadvantage, considering the position our bodies and weapons were in at that moment. These were the mistakes that were going to be the end of us if we didn't start being more careful. I now started to really notice the humidity, as the sweat started to fill my brow and run into my eyes. The only thing that hurts more than salty sweat running in your eyes is sweat mixed with sunscreen getting in your eyes, which can almost momentarily blind a man, let alone sting like hell. But thankfully, due to a lack of sunscreen, my problem was I could feel the bead of sweat running down my forehead and as it got to the corner of my eye, it was instantly sucked in across my eyeball, blurring the little vision I already had from this position. At least the rounded stone I was now resting my chin on was cold and provided a somewhat pleasant feeling as it cooled the underside of my jaw.

Not one of us moved, not even a fraction of an inch, for the next few moments. If the circumstances were different, I would look at Danny getting pissed on as comedic gold, but in our current position, we were about an inch away from being in some seriously deep shit. As the man tapped and tried to push any remaining urine out, I was thinking to myself, "For God sakes, you shake it more than once and you are playing with it." I wished he would hurry the hell up; it felt like time was standing still as he leisurely took his time, creating suspense that I'm sure was driving all of us crazy. As he started to put it back in his pants, he stopped and froze holding his dick half in his pants and half out. I got a huge lump in my throat and knew that under no circumstances could I swallow or we were fucked. Had we been compromised? And then all of a sudden, he let out a huge fart that sounded like if he hadn't put some thought into that, he would have shit his pants. He clinched his butt cheeks together ending it, prematurely. I'm sure he did that so he didn't shit himself and then he stuffed his pecker back in his pants. As he buttoned it back up, a few of the guys behind him commented and complimented him on the fart that I, personally, would have given him a seven on a one-to-ten-point scale. Thankfully, he turned to his left to rejoin the rest of his patrol. If he would have turned a half step to the right, he would have surely stepped on Danny's legs or back and at that moment, all hell would have broken loose, all over a piss. The one thing that I did know was that, given the opportunity, Danny was going to fuck that guy up for pissing on him.

We were now waiting for verification from JSOC as to the current situation and we even heard the radio in the background trying to call the individuals we were here to assist. I heard some of the men in front of us tearing a piece of clothing or fabric and shortly after, seeing a torch light up as they lit the fabric on fire. I figured it to be the clothing of the men that now lay dead that we were sent to help. We were so close to them that I could smell the fumes and the toxins that were now burning within the fabric. With the lighting of the torch, I knew that we were desperately running out of time because once the area was lit up, we wouldn't be able to sit in the shadows for very long. I could see the team and our outline very distinctly. If we were going to make a move, it was going to have to be soon.

Three of the men started to gather wood for a fire that brought them dangerously close to us since there was very little wood in the area. They started reaching into the trees and pulling branches down, which made a great deal of noise, and as they were stripping the trees of their foliage, I saw movement out of the corner of my left eye. As I very carefully, and slowly, picked my chin up off the rock that was now sticking to the underside of my jaw, I turned my head and saw that Tom had taken what looked like a concussion grenade off his tac-vest and was straightening out the pin on it, very similar to closing a cotter pin that had been open to remove it from its purpose. I got the picture and carefully did the same, only I grabbed a TH3 incendiary grenade. Our time was running out and it was time to make a move. As soon as they lit that fire, the area would surely be bright enough that they could see us and we would be sitting ducks.

I don't know how many of us had caught on to the fact that we were about to light these fuckers up, but I did know that even if we only threw three concussion grenades, it would be truly devastating in such a small area. I moved inch by inch, removing the grenade off of my vest almost like a robot, making incredibly small and concise movements. After I got it off, I had to slowly bring my arms up in front of my face making sure not to disturb the rocks. I then slowly worked the grenade pin out with my left hand, making sure to hold the spoon confidently with my right, so I wouldn't cut anything short on time. We were looking to ensure that our team acted simultaneously with our grenades, when suddenly, I heard a bunch of splashing in front of us and slightly to the right. As I pulled my head down again, I realized we were almost right on the fucking water. If we would have gone 30 feet to our right, we would have walked right into the water. Call it luck or what you will, but as far as I was concerned, it was pure sloppiness on our part. The splashing appeared to be from a few guerillas taking a dip in the water to wash off or get some relief from the humid night air.

Meanwhile, I had pulled the pin out and was waiting to slowly lift the spoon up as we timed our grenades at approximately the same time when I heard a loud "pling" come from behind me to the left, followed by a whispered, "SHIT!" So, I said "fuck it," and let her fly. I then raised myself up to my left knee, as did several others, and started to unload my 60 in the direction I heard the splashing, making sure not to cross over too far in Danny's direction. It was awesome to see the tracers as they penetrated through the water and disappeared as they went into the silt or into the depths of the lake. Seconds after that, at least four grenades went off in front of us, exploding with an enormous bright orange light, followed by an intensely bright white explosion that looked more like a huge firework with white balls of fire mushrooming and detonating on the ground. The blast literally blinded me, at least temporarily, setting me off balance as the concussion hit my face and chest. I reestablished myself back on my left knee when 5.56 brass from Petie's 249 showered all over me, hitting my face and hands, with the hot brass burning my skin. I stood up and reengaged the water when the ammo belt pinched off and dropped to the ground. I dropped my 60 and pulled out my side arm and started to walk forward, trying to find a target but it was over in a matter of seconds. Whatever the grenades didn't get, the hail of flying lead did. Here we were again, standing in the dark with small fires burning in front of us, illuminating the hollow doors of the DFPs.

Scout picked up the torch that the bandito had lit earlier. As he slowly passed the flame from side to side overlooking the carnage, I could see the bare feet of the man that was sitting on top of the small pillbox. As I walked over to him, I noticed that he was obviously white and that he had sustained a couple of shots to his right shoulder and one through his neck as the blood pooled beneath his neck region. Of course, I stood there for a moment or two, observing the man as he laid there, but the question that kept going through my head was, who was this guy, where was he from, what agency was he working out of, and most of all, why was he here? I looked at the bottoms of his feet and noticed that there wasn't any rough skin or even a callused heel or ball. I got up on top of the pillbox where he had been laid and took out my flashlight. I removed the red lens cover that had been there and just used the white bulb. His hair was black, conditioned, and well groomed. His hands were soft, not callused, his nails were cut, and he barely had any dirt underneath them. This guy was obviously either FBI, NSA, or from the Agency. The question I had was why was a desk jockey out here in the middle of El Salvador?

Koz walked over to me and reminded me of Martin Sheen walking through the jungle in the movie "Apocalypse Now." His hair was full of all kinds of shit and his face was still covered in dried blood and dirt. He rested his arms on the top of the concrete pad of the pillbox and asked, "Any ID or tags?"

I replied, "No, and by the looks of his hands and feet, he was a desk jockey that was either sent out on his first mission, or he was supposed to have been a Listening Post/Observation Post (LPOP) and was compromised for some ungodly reason. It doesn't make a bit of sense to me, how 'bout you?"

He shook his head from side to side and wiped his brow with his left hand and said, "There isn't a whole lot of anything that makes any sense on this mission, besides there being hostiles around every curve and everything we have come in contact with since we have been here has ended up dead." He picked his head up to look at me and said, "I think that this is a war that we're not supposed to be in." Then he put his right thumb up to his right nostril and "farmer blew" out some seriously chunky snot and then did the same to the other side and walked off.

Todd, Ron, Trout, and I were volunteered to throw the dead bodies and weapons into the water, as a few of the other guys went back to get our rucks. We started a small fire using the wood that the earlier combatants were nice enough to get for us and set camp. I figured we would let the turtles and fish get rid of the rest of the bodies as we tossed them in the shallow water. I think that one of the reasons why we didn't see the water was we were moving at such a fast pace to get here that we simply hadn't noticed. But another reason we failed to notice the water was because of all of the lilies that disguised the water, giving it the appearance as a huge open field, even as you were standing right on the shoreline. Regardless of why we failed to see the water, I kept feeling that everything was about to come to a violent end. I worried that when our luck ran out, we wouldn't have any power or control over the situation and our fates would end abruptly.

Ron helped me drag one of the banditos over to the water. I had his feet and Ron had his arms. As we were walking down to the water to throw him in, his body violently jerked twice to the left causing us to drop him immediately and draw our side arms to put an end to this asshole. When we dropped him, his first two right fingers started to move up and down several times before I walked up to him and grabbed his throat to check for a pulse, as well as have a good grip on this fucker if I needed to rip his throat out. I was to the point that I needed to sleep or at least rest long enough to refer to it as a nap. We were all showing every sign of fatigue, only some hid it better than others. The guy was dead by every definition of the word; it must have been his nerves still contracting. Sometimes humans are a lot like a chicken. You can cut the head off and, of course, they're dead but the chicken will still run around in circles, just as a human's muscles and joints still flex and contract. When you are touching, or in our case carrying, someone and they move when they're supposed to be dead, it will seriously freak the shit out of you. And the worst thing about it is that you will dream about those times when they jolt around and you'll wake up covered in a cold sweat. Ron called out, "It doesn't matter which end you're on, these guys still smell like ass!" I re-holstered my side arm, leaned over and grabbed his feet again, and dragged him down in the water. I waded in slightly to submerge his entire body. I stood there, grumpy as hell, exhausted, with wet fucking feet, and it honestly took everything I had to keep my composure.

The other guys from the team came back shortly after we had disposed of the rest of the bodies. As the fire lit the area up better, I realized that this was probably at one time a really nice place to have been posted. The DFPs were well fortified and large enough that you could fit two to three platoons in here easily. A few of the guys brought out MREs to warm up or cook over the fire. As we all sat there, the violence, hate, and evil of this place finally paused. There wasn't one of us that wasn't sitting on the edge of our seat, waiting for the next barrage of bullets to come down. Oddly, I felt so at ease that I was more afraid of losing my mind than confronting another ambush.

Everything was still, without movement or sound, outside of a couple crackles from the fire. It was the actual calm in the storm; why had everything stopped? Every night in El Salvador, there was gunfire going off in the middle of the night, perhaps a fiesta or an armed confrontation, but it was present every night except tonight. Our surroundings had eerily become very calm, quiet, and contained; now I was really starting to worry and wonder if they had finally pinpointed our position. But every one of us sat there as calm as one could be, appearing or acting not to have a care in the world. I think that some of us, or at least me, looked at all of the moments leading up to this as somewhat of a game more than a battle. It was like "Robin Sage," a training scenario we used. Oh, there was a hell of a battle going on with that! But that was only a game. In "Robin Sage," you were graded and evaluated, but moments like these sometimes felt the same, because the outcome was so important, but when it was over, it was over.

I took a seat on top of one of the pill boxes and pulled out an MRE. Pork with rice in BBQ sauce... that's what I'm talking about! If you pull out an MRE that's worth heating up, it's a good one. I leaned forward and asked, "Hey, Rodge, you think you could heat this up for me?"

"You need anything else there, Captain America?" he replied, causing most of the team to let out a well overdue laugh, even if it was at my expense. I threw him the pack and he immediately responded, "Hey, Captain America has pork and rice in barbecue sauce."

I replied with a stern, "Hey, yourself, Rodge, I need that like you couldn't believe."

And with a small chuckle, a quick nod of his head, and a bad Asian-influenced accent, he said, "Don't worry there, Doc, I cook it just perfect for ya, not too pink and not too charred." I sneered and told him how much I oh so appreciated that. I sat there with my left arm supporting my weight while my right arm sat comfortably on my right knee. One thing about this country was that regardless of how sick and twisted it was in the heat of combat, when it was calm, especially at night, it was so beautiful. The irony was almost palpable.

Koz walked over to me and jumped on top of the pad to join me. He sat very similar to the way I was to my left side and asked, "You alright, Doc?"

I turned slightly, and in a very quiet and concerned tone, whispered, "I'm having a hard time with the fact that we left the LT behind. It's our code, our creed, our foundation that no one gets left behind even if it was their last request. We arrive as a team, we all fall together and stay behind in the end, or we leave as a team."

"Ya, Doc, I know, but there wasn't enough of him to bring back."

I felt the skin on my forehead tense up and I was sure I was expressing a frown, or even a look of anger, as I started to reply, "What do you mean there..."

He leaned in closer and said, "Look Doc, I don't like what happened any more than you do, but as for the LT, there wasn't enough to send home, that's the way he wanted it and that's what has been told to the rest of the team. I'm sure that wherever he is, he's raising all sorts of hell and let's just leave it at that. He was a good man and even more so, a good friend, so I'm asking you, for the both of us, to just leave him where he lay. I'm askin' ya to let this one go and lay it to rest for yourself here under God. Let him take care of the rest. I'm askin' ya, Doc?"

I hesitantly shook my head and said under my breath, "Alright, we'll let it lay, but it will be with protest between us." And so, in this part of the book, I'm saying my final goodbye and finally letting this go with a final prayer of God speed to the LT, to "Randie," and may he lay in peace. Koz tapped his hand on my left leg that was extended out, thanked me from him and on behalf of the LT. He said that he was going to go down to the water and rinse off a little bit before the corpses started to reek and the turtles and fish got so thick that they would feed on him as well.

I considered my conversation with Koz. He and the LT had a relationship similar to Tom and me. They spent a lot of time going over maneuvers, different exercises for us to do, and coordinated a lot of "special training" for us. But it wasn't all shop; hell, I heard that they were even on a bowling team together.

They were the kind of guys that would be talking amongst themselves, laughing and carrying on, and whenever you or someone else would go over to them, they would stop what they were doing, look up and say, "What can I do you for?" or "What's up?" They were both very private, professional, and proud. I can see where the LT would have had a conversation with Koz about "Where he falls is where he lays." Koz would know better than anyone and would never disgrace, slur his name, or do anything improper when it came to the LT. That's why I didn't push the matter too far and if there was a formal inquiry, you'd be surprised how fast all of our memories on any pertaining matter would just disappear.

I know that Koz carried a burden from that fateful day forward and it had to have been terrible and unimaginable. The way Koz was, he'd likely never vent about it or even talk to anyone about it. He'll keep it in forever. I feel for the emotional load that he must carry with him. He always took on everything for the team, always. But this was different. We all lost a teammate, a leader, and a friend. But with Koz, because of the way that they segregated themselves, I feel he lost more than we did that day and for that my heart goes out to him.

After Koz left, Rodge got up and started to walk over towards me, tossing the hot MRE pack from hand to hand to keep it from burning himself. He threw it up on the concrete next to me and leaned back to see where Koz was getting in the water. He then leaned in towards me and in a soft whisper asked, "What the hell was that all about?" I gave my best stupid look and asked back what he meant. He tipped his head down to the right and said, "Come on, man, what the hell you think I mean? I saw the meeting you guys were having. Was it about the LT?"

"Ya, I guess you could say that. He wanted to let me know he was going down to wash off and that he just wanted a couple of minutes alone. So, I said, sure thing."

Rodge shook his head from side to side and said, "Oh, so, it's gonna be like that?"

"No, dude, that was it." As I started to pick up the MRE pack, it was so hot that I dropped it back down on the concrete. I shook my hand up and down because of how hot it was and said, "Holy shit, what happened to not too pink and not too charred?"

He turned and said, "I didn't want to interrupt your little meeting."

"Oh, for God's sake, Rodge, give me a fuckin' break!"

He replied with his usual shrug of the shoulder and sighed, "Ya, whatever, man," as he turned and walked off. One thing about Rodge was he could see through clouds and bullshit better than anyone I ever knew and he loved to get the low down about everything. But this was something, at least at the time, I thought that I was going to take to the grave. So, I let him think whatever he wanted and sure as hell didn't give any perception that I really gave a shit, even though I really did. I needed to put this into one of those little rooms in my head that I hoped would stay locked up for eternity and I would never be able to retrieve. After I ate, I laid back on the pad, looked into the stars, thought about what happened earlier to the LT and what Koz and I had talked about. Somewhere in the middle of all that, I fell asleep.

I awoke to the hot sun beating down on my face as I was lying on my back in the middle of this concrete pad. The air was pure and clean, with the distinct smell of the ocean. As I propped my body up, squinting from the bright sunlight, I rubbed the rough whiskers on my face and saw Koz, Tom, Jesus, and Rodge enjoying a cup of hot java. Rodge was in the middle of putting his M-4 back together, and I swear, if there was anyone in the world that never needed sleep, it was Rodge. That son of a bitch was up when everyone was bedding down and he was up before anyone else. I don't know if it was because he didn't want to miss anything or if it was because he didn't need that much sleep. But he had to be like a camel, except instead of water, it was sleep he stored.

As I looked around, the DFPs looked more like Civil War bunkers in the daylight. They were amazingly simple and almost ancient. They were constructed with river rock and some kind of cement or extremely strong baked mud. The roof or top was a prefabricated slab of concrete that was lowered on top because they never pulled the cables out from underneath. As I considered the construction of the fort, I noticed that there was a piece of concrete that was sitting on top of a sandbag that had something etched into it. I kneeled down, twisting my head to see it better. It was only about 18 inches long and four inches thick, but on the left side, there was an etching of a pineapple grenade and on the right, there was a figure of a person holding a gun that was twice as big as the figure's body. It was only the upper torso with a head, two eyes, and ten lines going up from a top of the head to symbolize hair, or at least, that was my perception. Someone must have taken the tip of a bullet or some small instrument and etched it in on their down time.

It gave me a sort of morbid feeling of all the horror and combat that these walls had seen. There are certain places where I have gone in my lifetime and you can't help but travel back in time and think of the soldiers, their feelings, what they saw, and their fears. I have always tried to take myself back to another day and time to stand where others have fought and died for their beliefs, even though it may be impossible to feel the moments and reconstruct the battles. We had one thing in common and it was the one and only thing we needed to have in common: we were both soldiers. We both followed orders and would fight until the last drop of blood fell on the battlefield. But it certainly would be something to be able to see through their eyes, feel their fears, and experience their anger as it unfolded during the carnage of battle over a piece of land, religion, or just the mere fact of mutually believing in something. It was such a weird feeling, standing where history was made, let alone making it yourself. And, as so many generals and world leaders have said, "History will repeat itself."

I jumped off of the pad and brought myself back to the present, setting aside my historical imagination and asked if they had another cup of coffee. Tom commented on how it was great to get caught up on some Z's and he was right. It was great to finally sleep, let alone wake up from the sunlight and not from gunfire. As I picked up my cup of coffee, I walked around the encampment. Rodge joined me for the tour as, of course, he had already walked it several times, I'm sure. He brought me over to the far west end to show me a bunker we hadn't even seen, luckily no one else saw it either, referring to the banditos. It was masterful, truly a work of art. It had sump holes for grenades and hidden ports to every side, making an aggression on the position truly impossible. The foliage that concealed it was perfect as it butted up against the water to its rear. One thing that I found to be impressive was that it did have a brick trench line that ran in an "L." The first run was a good 35-feet and then cut back into the DFP with a 20-foot jaunt.

It was very obvious that these bunkers had been here for a very long time and were clearly used in the war that was sadly initiated from a soccer game due to the amount of bullet holes and places where the wall lost some of its integrity. As we walked the grounds, we found mass piles of brass littered all over the place, some from years past as they were coated in dirt or oxidized, and heaps from our previous conflict the night before. From a distance of 50 feet, I saw another bunker to the east that had its roof more fortified for a heavy weapon. Another thing that I found to be interesting were the different areas around the fortress in which the ground had been reinforced, almost paved, with the same kind of construction where the walls of the bunker were. I couldn't understand why they had done that, except that they would have had to reinforce the ground to prevent erosion or prevent heavy weapons from turning this area into an island. Regardless, I thought it was a nice touch and gave the area a more nostalgic feel to it.

As Rodge and I got back to the small fire, the area was starting to turn into a small congregation as more people from the team joined the circle to enjoy a hot cup of java. Koz and Tom each had several different maps out, evaluating the terrain as well as trying to find the most direct route to the radar site with the least amount of resistance. Meanwhile, Todd and I had to check out members of the team who had sustained injuries. Tom and Ron looked great and couldn't have looked better even if we had been on post. Jesus, on the other hand, was not doing well. His leg wound was now dripping with seropurulent discharge or more commonly referred to as a puss-like substance, with a foul sour smell to it. The medical term for his condition is called "clostridial cellulites," which basically means that the tissue and nerves around the wound are producing a gas which causes the foul smell. As it interacts with oxygen in the air, it turns to the puss-like substance in and around the wound. There was still good tissue around Jesus' wound; his physical and mental states were also good, which told me he wasn't suffering from toxemia.

The best thing we could do at that moment was to find a chicken or raw meat. I needed the chicken to kill it, take strips of raw flesh and muscle and put it into a baggie with the end open to attract flies. Once you have flies, maggots are soon to follow. I needed the maggots to eat the dead flesh out of the wound and help prevent further infection. I covered his wound with an antibacterial ointment and put a clean, dry trauma bandage on it. I needed to keep him on the antibiotics and Tylenol; I switched to Tylenol now instead of Motrin, because the Motrin would thin his blood and could make the matter worse. He was going to need medical attention from a hospital within a few days if I couldn't get this injury under control. I could keep him alive indefinitely, but keeping him mobile was going to be a more difficult task.

As I was finishing up with Jesus' dressing, the rest of the team started to file out of the bunkers and Danny came out of one of the trenches looking like someone just pissed in his Cheerios, no pun intended. He looked funny when he woke up anyway, but this morning, his eyes were swollen and he almost looked Chinese. Scout was quick to chime in and tell Danny how bad he looked, only to get a hateful sneer combined with a good, solid "Fuck you!" We all laughed and then Tom called us in. He showed us a topo map of the area, where we needed to be, and what time we needed to be there by this evening. We sat around for another 45 minutes, taking the time to eat and tear our weapons down while we completed a healthy function test of all our equipment. We also took inventory of our grenades, explosives, and ammo, all of which we were running dangerously low.

Rodge made contact with JSOC, and shortly after that, we started to load up our rucks and charge our weapons. Even though some of us looked like we were still asleep, you could see that everyone, with the exception of Jesus, looked and acted replenished. The air still held the slight odor of the ocean, but was dry, with low humidity. It was like waking up in Florida and stepping outside for a nice breath of fresh air. One nice thing about where we were was that there were very few insects, for some reason, but there was also a lack of any other creatures, such as birds, and more so, frogs. Something was different, I just couldn't put my finger on it.

12

THE QUARRY

AS WE STARTED OUT OF THE FORTIFIED AREA WHERE WE HAD STAYED THE night, we didn't even get 50 feet down wind when the rotting stench of the corpses overtook us. It was bad enough to make us gag and it made the air thick enough that you felt like you could feel yourself inhaling the germs and bacteria that was now flowing through their dead bodies. I found it interesting that some of the bodies had drifted considering there were no waves, undertow, or movement; the top of the water was covered in lilies, which should have prevented the bodies from moving. Several of us stopped and watched a turtle as it tried to pull an eyeball out of its socket. It slowly stretched its head out and bit the eyeball; then tugged on the eyeball, trying to get it to break free but tearing it open as the grey vitreous fluid from inside of the eye now oozed out floating on top of the water. I was momentarily mesmerized watching the turtle fight for its morning meal, when Trout nudged my elbow and said, "Dude, that's fuckin' cool, but we got a big nut to crack, Doc, so let's get outta here."

I agreed that it was cool and had started to walk in the direction of the rest of the group when Petie immediately brought us down. The weight of my pack leveled me onto the rocks populating the shoreline. As soon as I got my pack off of my head, I looked up to see Scout with his rifle raised up peering through the scope at the adjacent shore. He slowly pulled his rifle down and gave us the okay. I left my ruck on the ground as I stood up. I looked in the direction that Scout was pointing his weapon and after a couple of seconds, I noticed a small man on the adjacent shoreline, washing his clothes in the water. He had to have been at least a hundred yards away, kneeling over in the water. I tell ya, Scout could tell you if a mole had a hair out of place from a few hundred feet away, but that's what made him one of the best in the field, let alone in the world. We were lucky to have him in addition to the rest of the team. And that's why we were here, to do a job that maybe others wouldn't have been able to do, not making us any more expendable, but certainly more dependable. The guy washing his clothes had no idea, and will never have any idea, of how close his laundry duties came to ending his life. But today was his lucky day. We hadn't been seen, and he didn't pose any threat to us, so we left him alone to live another day.

We quietly and slowly packed our gear up again and moved due south. As we were walking, I caught the sweet aroma of a patch of pink and white flowers that was growing around the base of what resembled a large bonsai tree. The tree stood out all by itself, surrounded by yucca plants and dried, dead shrubbery. It gave me the perception of the Garden of Eden since it stood out all by itself, encompassed by its own little touch of paradise. The sight relaxed me and helped me put some of the past into a better perspective. Seeing the tree standing out alone reminded me of when I was in Bahrain and saw the supposed tree of life. This tree looked like a huge oak standing out all by itself in the middle of the desert, with no plants of any kind around it, just sand. The locals had told us that there had been numerous environmentalists that had checked for a water table or water supply that kept that tree alive. They determined that there was actually nothing beneath it, so locals came to believe that God had kept the tree alive for the coming of the prophets. Perhaps they had the right idea. Regardless, as I passed the tree in El Salvador, I felt the ground get drier and harder the farther we got away from the water. The plants were dry and wilted, making the walk through them loud, as they crunched under our feet.

I felt almost as good as the first day we got here, outside of the bruises, scrapes, and rub marks from our gear. As we walked, no one said a word, making the trip seem longer than it probably was. After a couple hours, we came to an area that had one small abandoned pillbox and a gravel road. The further we walked along the gravel road, we saw a roundabout only a couple hundred feet in front of us. We split in half, with two linear in-depth lines on each side of the road in 50-foot intervals. We walked up to the roundabout and three of us from each side ducked into the jungle for 360-degree coverage to cover our asses. At the far end of the roundabout, there was a little shrine with a 20-by-10-foot corrugated roof over it with a small, two-foot wall extending 30 feet to each side with several painted flowers on it and the words "Virgin Madre" (Virgin Mary).

As we neared the very small shrine, which only stood about eight feet tall and five feet wide, with an arched top, I noticed that the front of it was decorated in white, green, and grey tile. A white steel fence protected a glass paned window that stood before a three-foot statue of the Virgin Mary, with a wood and silver crucifix. There were yellow and red flowers that had been entwined in the steel mesh throughout the fence. A small, and very short, altar stood before the Blessed Mother, with a painting of a chalice (cup) and a four-way divided circle wafer to symbolize the blood and body of Christ and Communion. A small white bulb was affixed at the top of the inner ceiling of the shrine.

The statue of the Virgin Mary was very colorful and pleasant to look at. Her robe was blue and her garments were white as snow. Her hair was a soft brown and her face was well-defined, with rosy cheeks and blue eyes. Both of her arms were slightly extended out in front of her and her hands were open with her palms seemingly reaching out to us. I freely admit that I was instantly warmed by the sight and found it interesting, when Koz immediately dropped to his left knee and made the sign of the cross on his chest with his head bowed in respect for the Virgin Mother. There was a strange feeling of peace within this area. There wasn't any noise at all... I mean, nothing. It was so comforting; it almost made you feel uncomfortable and uneasy. I think that each of us took our own private moment of prayer and display of respect for the sight. Something in me wanted to stay here in the protection of her grace, which made me wonder about what lay before us. But we were soldiers and we had a job to do; that didn't mean that we couldn't take her grace and love with us, however. It meant with or without her, we needed to confront our fears and hostilities in order to finish what we had started.

While the peace and serenity of this shrine was pleasing, I think that it gave us a false sense of protection. We stayed at the shrine for almost an hour before heading due south again, having to pick up the pace a little now to make up for some of the time we had lost at the shrine. When we started to leave the sight, I felt the tension and anger start to build up in me again, for which I have no explanation. As I looked throughout the rest of the team, they appeared to almost look hypnotized. Danny's eyes were like glass and his face was without expression. Petie looked like he always did, but more concentrated. Tom walked frigid, with his arm muscles bulging as he squeezed the pistol grip of his M-4. He also had those glassy eyes. Koz was the worst; he had a grin, almost a smile, with a beet red face. His lower jaw was shaking and his eyes looked almost like they were full of tears. What in the hell happened to us within the last hour? I didn't know if it was the carnage, payback, or just a yearning to finish these banditos as we were ordered to do. Our walk for the next few hours was very quiet and without incident. It almost seemed like everything around us stopped and we were the only people in this country. We did not see even one person, child, or animal anywhere. I could feel the anxiety grow within the silence and the not knowing.

Tom had us stop for a few minutes while they checked their azimuth and topos to find our current position. As we stopped, all of us took a knee and looked almost frantically into the jungle, wondering what had happened to cause the world to stop. I don't know if it was the heat or if it was the not knowing, but I caught myself questioning our existence amongst the living once again. Were we alive and about to get into some of the worst shit we had ever been in or were we amongst the dead, walking the Earth eternally, never coming to an end? As I knelt there, I looked down to catch myself spinning a piece of grass with my finger, very much like a high school girl would spin her hair trying to calm her nerves on her first date.

The loud crowing from several roosters, from very close by, quickly brought me and the team back to reality. We scampered in all directions to take cover. Within the next couple of minutes, more roosters sounded off in the distant background. My blood was pumping at an exhilarating pace. I never thought that I would have loved to hear those fucking roosters, but at least for the moment, I knew I was still alive. As I laid there, I actually had to concentrate on controlling my breathing. The sweat was pouring down my face and my chest was soaked. Holy shit, was I having an anxiety attack? What the hell was going on? I knew that I needed to get a grip and, like, now! I looked up to see Rodge calling Koz over to his position. Within two minutes, we were up and moving again in a traveling over-watch formation, being cautious as to our surroundings. Meanwhile, I was still trying to get my composure under control.

We started to slow down and with each gaining step, I could hear running water, much like the sound of a waterfall. We stopped at the edge of a paved road and took a position in the ditch looking directly at a hydroelectric power site. Well, I guess we just found our power supply for the radar site. I knew we were close. There were five, huge, 50-foot towers, carrying approximately 12 to 15 wires across a huge quarry. The dam had to have been at least 150 feet tall. It was amazing to see something so huge out here in the middle of nowhere. Where the generators were housed was a well-fortified compound. The fences surrounding the generators had to have been at least 30 feet tall and, on the outside, there were at least 20 rows of intertwined c-wire. It was like looking at the world's largest briar patch. Regardless of how stupid of a question it might be, I kept wondering how in the hell could anyone get in there to do maintenance work? It was a spectacle to say the least!

My next question was: where the fuck was everyone? There wasn't a soul in sight. I would have thought that a power station this large would have been more fortified with guards and perhaps even assault vehicles. We walked across the road toward the power house in a bounding type movement. Then, when there were only a couple of us left to cross, we realized that there wasn't any reason to be so strategic and stealthy in our movement because there wasn't anyone there. The generator compound was about 75 feet to the southwest of the dam and roughly 40 feet lower in elevation. As we stood at the top end of the dam, we could better see the DFPs and four pillboxes that were positioned at each corner, like turrets on a castle. You could look straight down and see every foot of the compound and, more so, the impressively gigantic quarry, as the water slid down an enormous concrete slide, emptying out into the quarry. There were several large rock islands sprinkled throughout the quarry. It was an impressive sight, as we stood on hundreds and hundreds of tons of concrete. If you followed the power lines across the quarry, there was another small concrete building on the other side that I imagined helped hold the lines up and then distribute the power to wherever it was needed. The mere distance from the power station to the other side was enormous. I wondered how the lines kept their integrity without anything in the middle to hold them in place to distribute some of the weight and help hold them in the case of a high wind or a storm. The construction was genius and left me dumbfounded on how they could have pulled off something so complex in the middle of nowhere.

That powerhouse building stood out against the jungle like a sore thumb. The trees and foliage were light green and brown while the mountains hugged the other side of the dam, following the contour of the quarry. The building itself was covered in what looked like two enormous trees that were a very dark, rich forest green. All of us took a concealed position on the bank as Koz and Rodge got on the radio to advise JSOC as to the position and status of the dam and powerhouse. In our briefing back at El Pongo, we were told that as soon as we took possession of the power facility that a couple teams from Second and Third Ranger Battalions would be sent in to hold and control the area. I didn't know where they would be coming from or where their staging area was, but I knew that they couldn't be that far away. But I must say, that after all we have been through, this was the best "conflict" we had been in yet. We walked up to it and it was ours. How long that would hold true was unknown, but at least for now, we were in possession, and in control of, one of our highest priorities of the mission.

The word got passed down the line that we were going to stand fast for approximately 40 minutes while the Rangers were in transport. Even though Special Forces Soldiers and Rangers have had our conflicts on post and at many an NCO club, they were by far some of the most highly trained and disciplined soldiers in the world. I remember we used to call them skinheads and they would call us pretty boys. Shortly after we exchanged our pleasantries, we would commence in a slight to major brawl, that I determined was merely keeping up esprit de corps within the ranks. I have to say that when it comes to aggressing airstrips and taking airports, they are amongst the best and certainly vital to the US arsenal.

As we sat counting down the minutes, there was some splashing and yelling coming from the quarry. As I looked down, there was a group of men who had stripped themselves of their clothing and were enjoying a swim in the quarry to beat the summer-like heat. They splashed and dunked each other playing child-like games. They didn't have a care in the world because they didn't know we were here and the area appeared to be deserted. As we laid there watching them from afar, all of a sudden there was mass gunfire coming from the adjacent shore. It was pathetic watching the bullets dance on top of the water as they slaughtered the men, who seconds before, were having the time of their life. I was sick how fast something could go from being a fun memorable moment to your last breath amongst the living. Koz yelled out, "Shit, they're PMs! The guys in the water are the good guys. Hit the shoreline! Scout, snuff those fuckers!" Scout quickly pulled up his .257 Roberts and rested it atop the railing that vaulted the top of the dam as he worked to sight the aggressors across the quarry.

Scout shouted out, "I got you, son of a bitch!" And then four shots, in succession, rang out and echoed through the quarry. Scout shot each of the men, with one shot each, putting an end to their aggression on the swimmers. Unfortunately, we were too late and there was only one man in the water that was still alive, slapping the top of the water, trying desperately to get to the shore. I shook my head in disgust, because all I could do was watch him fight for his life when automatic weapons fire went off directly behind me. I hit the deck, rolled over, and drew my side arm pointing now at Jesus' head.

I yelled out, "What in the fuck are you doing man, I almost dusted your ass!"

Jesus yelled back, "I cannot just stand here and watch him drown, as you obviously can. He is a soldier of this country, as am I." As I slowly stood up, watching Jesus' every move, he lowered the barrel of his weapon. His head despondently followed, conveying the deep sadness witnessing the scene had caused Jesus. I looked down into the quarry to my right only to see the red circles of where the men were swimming as their blood diluted in the water. As my breathing slowed, I lowered my sidearm putting it back in the holster. I could feel my arms shaking and the adrenaline rushing through my veins, similar to when you are driving and someone pulls in front of you, almost causing an accident. The aftermath takes a while to come down from because your chest and body are so tense that it is difficult to breathe, much less move. Man was I pissed; to this day, I still think that I should have dusted his ass. It's situations like that where you can think about it years later and the hair on the back of your neck stands on end and the rush comes back almost paralyzing you, even though it happened so long ago. The memory still scares the shit out of me. As I sit here writing this, I can feel my arms, more specifically, my biceps tense up, with the feeling that I should consistently keep looking behind me. That is one moment that I desperately hope, someday, I can leave behind.

Petie walked up to Koz and said, "Hey, man, let's get the fuck outta here. Second and Third should be here within a half hour and we've been waiting for almost an hour," as his thumb wiped off the crystal of his watch and took into account how long we had been hanging around. "Besides, I think that we have drawn enough attention to this area."

Tom shook his head in agreement, suggesting to Koz, "We have a timeline that we need to follow. We can't do anything else here."

Koz turned to his right and said, "Alright, guys, I think that that's a good idea. Let's get across this dam and get to a more fortified area. The site should be on the other side of those mountains." He raised his hand and pointed to the other side of the dam and up the mountain as our eyes followed his finger. There was a walkway and a road that was approximately 20 feet wide to the other side of the dam. It looked like it could easily support the weight of almost any vehicle. After the concrete ended on the other side, it looked like it stayed flat for only 20 or so feet and then went straight up the face of the well covered mountain. That meant that as we crossed the dam, we would be sitting ducks from both sides. We had to keep a close watch on the elevation and trees on the other side and the thick jungle behind us.

Scout and Danny crossed first without any incident. Even though they were cautious, it almost seemed that we should just walk across it and not worry about it. Vigilance, I thought to myself, vigilance: we needed to keep our minds in the game. But, as I thought about it more, it wasn't a matter of "we" at all; it was a matter of me. There were so many emotions and mind games that this mission had triggered within me. I had the LT in the back of my mind, what Koz had said to me about him, and the realization that around every corner we turned in this country had seemingly ended in a blood bath.

We crossed in twos, leapfrogging, and covering both sides of the dam as the team crossed. Todd and I crossed next. As we were inching our way across, I no longer felt like we should be able to just cross it as you would cross the street in your neighborhood. I felt an overwhelming feeling of vulnerability and weakness. We were almost all the way to the other side when I noticed a huge teal colored wall with large print colored in gold. As our feet crossed over the concrete onto the gravel, Todd and I walked straight over to the monument. The words, "PRESA 5 DE NOVIEMBRE" loomed large; they had to be at least a two-foot font. There were several broken tank or bulldozer tracks lying about the front of the monument. There were leaves scattered all over the ground making it look more like a fancy US National Park sign. The words that followed were, "Estudios Preliminaries 1945. Planificacion 1948 – 1950. Consejo De Gobierno Revolucionario. Ejeccucion 1951 – 1954." It listed many more specific dates and times when events had happened in this area, as well as individual names of prominent people who were assassinated or executed because of their contributions against the government of El Salvador. The top, in large letters, translated, "Redeem or pray for the date of five November." Then, under that it said, "Preliminary studies 1948, Pontification 1949, Revolutionary Government Council's execution 1951 – 1954." The other side had some writing on it that equated to: this land is now under the control of the Military Police of El Salvador.

Todd and I stood in front of the sign while Rodge snapped a quick photo of us. To our left, there was some commotion as Petie ran around, humped over trying to catch a couple chickens that had been walking through the jungle in back of the memorial. We could always count on Petie for his intermittent acts of comedy. Every one of us broke out laughing, to include Jesus, who was dripping with sweat, fighting off sheer exhaustion and infection. The irony was the very act he was laughing at could be the very thing that was going to save his life. Petie made a comedic leap, mixed with tripping, towards one of the chickens and caught it with nothing outside of luck. As he stood up, he had a huge shit eating grin on his face as he spun its body around by the neck, snapping it within a split second.

Scout, on the other hand, walked right up to the second one and caught it within five seconds as Petie said, "Well, fuck you Scout, what in the hell was that? You practice catching chickens while we're out catching women?"

Scout laughed and said, "You're damn right." All of us shared a good laugh while we considered the art of catching chickens. We now had not only a great meal for the morning, but I had the raw meat I needed to get some maggots for Jesus. I cut one of the chicken's legs off and put it in some plastic wrap and tied it off to the top of my ruck to allow flies to get to it while we walked. That was the first, and the last time, I had ever seen that monument. Maybe someday, I will have the chance to visit it again and say some final goodbyes.

13

RON'S FALL

WE FOUND OURSELVES STANDING IN FRONT OF THE TASK OF CLIMBING this very steep and rugged mountain that would lead us to our final destination, the radar site. Rodge said that there was a small cache that was stashed on the other side of the mountain next to a small stream for re-supply and then we would be on our own. As we moved upward in elevation, I suddenly heard the sound of birds and insects intensify. I would have thought it would have been the opposite as we moved up the mountain. The incline of the mountain was so steep that Koz brought us to a halt after only moving a few feet and looked at the adjoining mountain slightly to the south. But, after several minutes of contemplating, he decided that it was the same climb and we didn't have time to search for an easier path. We needed to get over this mountain tonight, before early morning set in.

In spite of the ground being very dry, it was slippery and difficult to get any good footing. The jungle was becoming denser and the steep sides yielded some strange looking, and partially uprooted, trees. I felt like a flea climbing up the neck of a huge dog. Our slow progress was punishing, but we couldn't be scratched off. The weight of our packs made it excruciatingly difficult as we grabbed the small trunks and roots of some of the trees to help pull us up the mountainside. The undergrowth started to dissipate after the first 1500 to 2000 feet, but it slowly was changing to jagged sharp volcanic rock. The rocks were shiny black, but very sharp, and mixed with some kind of dark grey ash. As the terrain transitioned to those volcanic rocks, the team seemed to take turns sporadically falling down on the steep landscape.

As I looked up in front of me, I noticed that Scout had blood running down his hand and dripping profusely. I stopped the team to take a look at Scout's hand and arm. As I pulled up his blouse, I saw that he had a four-inch laceration on his right forearm that had cut down to the bone. That wasn't good, so I had to stitch it up and stop the bleeding or he wasn't going to make it up this mountain, let alone to the radar site. I put at least ten stitches on the inside of his arm in the muscle tissue, so he hopefully wouldn't lose mobility and would still be able to fire his weapon. I put a good 20 stitches on his outer skin and fatty platelets and as I was finishing up, Koz called over to me, "Hey, Doc, I know you have to do what you do, but we have to move out before we lose any more time." I cut the final stitch and told Scout that he was as good as new, even though in the back of my head I knew that if we didn't nip this one in the butt soon, he could lose feeling and perhaps even some mobility permanently if we didn't treat this the right way. I told him that when we got on better terrain and had a little more time, we could get him started on some antibiotics.

I put a simple bandage over his wound and we started up the side of the mountain again. The trees continued to thin out a little, but the problem now was that most of those trees had fallen, so we had less to grab onto for stability. We also had to make our way over the trees without causing them to break free and roll down the steep incline. If, by chance, one of us got caught under a rolling tree, we would be crushed and, I'm sure, the outcome would be fatal. As I tried to pull myself over a downed tree, the rotting bark and wood broke free causing me to slip and the weight of the pack threw my head into the side of the tree. Luckily the wood was soft and outside of a slight bruise on the forehead, I was okay, but I did feel the laceration, aka my "crater," on my back tear open, sending sharp, almost electrical pulses down my arms and legs. It wasn't long before the puss and blood-soaked through my shirt and ran down the crack in my ass.

As the elevation got higher, the air thinned slightly, but not enough to slow us up by any means. It wasn't that bad, but more noticeable toting the kind of weight we had on our backs. We now had to side step up the terrain because of the incline. The effort of the climb lessened as the rocks were getting larger. I stopped in my tracks, smelling death somewhere around us. I knew if there was death, then there were maggots, and there were two of us now that were in need of them. I called out to Tom and we all looked around trying to find the carcass. And, of course, Scout found it about 20 feet to the south and a good 40 to 50 feet down.

The carcass turned out to be a dog. I took my pack off and carefully stepped through the rocks to the dead dog. The smell was pungent and the flies were so thick, that I accidentally inhaled several of them. I realized it was better to just try to swallow them than cough them out. My eyes squinted tight, trying to keep the flies out, and I started to move my hands through the grayish fur, trying to find an opening or wound. As I started to try to lift some of the fur, the top layer of fur, skin, and all literally slid off of the dog. I gave a couple of dry heaves as I turned away from the smell and the sight of thousands of maggots causing the entire surface of the dog's innards to crawl. I could actually hear them moving around. I took in a couple of deep breaths, held it, and skimmed the surface taking a hand full of the larvae. I struggled up the steep slope with one hand to join the others and tried to ignore the slithering of the larvae against my palm and fingers. I focused on the importance of getting these people relief from their injuries and these maggots were the key. When I got up to them, I ordered Jesus and Scout to remove the appropriate clothing and to take their bandages off exposing their injuries.

Scout immediately said, "There's no fuckin way you're going to put those things on me!"

I went over to Jesus and sadly saw that his injury was turning gangrene. I took a handful of the maggots and scraped them off of my fingers into his wound. I took out a trauma bandage and cut it to size over the wound and sealed the maggots in with a waterproof surgical tape. I tried picking up some of the larvae (that had now fallen onto and in-between the rocks) to take over to Scout. He looked at me and said, "I'm not fucking kidding, Doc!"

And I got right into his face and yelled, "Neither am I, stop being such a fuckin' pussy and let me see your arm! You want to get gangrene and lose your arm?"

He pulled his head back, then turned it from side to side and said, "No."

"Then shut the fuck up and let me do my job so we can get off the face of this fuckin' mountain." Everybody stood there, in awe, as I lost my usual calm composure. I put a few maggots on his wound and handed him a trauma bandage and tape and said, "You tape it up." Scout had a hell of a look on his face and I was sure that if we made it out of here, that this rift would be addressed at a much later time.

The top was only a couple thousand feet up and the ground was very hard. Huge boulders stood out where rain and time had washed away the earth. Walking had become much easier and we were making good time now. I squeezed myself between two boulders when bullets suddenly ricocheted off the large rocks, causing us to hug the base of the boulders for cover. I couldn't help but yell out, "Son of a bitch!" Now this was just fucking great. We were on the side of a mountain with an extreme slope and we were taking fire from above.

The first thing that came to my mind was when I watched movies and documentary specials on the Omaha Beach invasion in World War II. For a moment or two, time stood still as I replayed some of the footage in my head and thought of the immeasurable bravery that the men on that beach displayed. They went against all odds and even defied those that said it couldn't be done. The one thing that I have always depended on in situations and unbeatable odds like this was that I believe God has a book with every name of every person who has walked and does walk this Earth. Inside that book is the day and time we are born, the day and time we get married and everything in our lives, but most of all, is the date and time in which we will die. So, I figure that if it's already been written, then it's inevitable; why fight it or fear what has already been put into stone?

I threw my pack off at the base of the boulder and took out another hundred-round belt for my baby, while I could feel several pieces of rock hit my back as the bullets hacked away at the stone. I attached the belt to the one I had already wrapped around my left arm and leaned back against the rock with my head looking to the heavens. I wasn't really thinking about coordinating with the rest of the team... just rehearsed the words from the movie "Platoon": "It ain't nuthin but a thang. It ain't nuthin but a thang. We all have to die sometime." And, sure as shit, I rounded that boulder and started to weave in and out of the rocks, showering the top with a hail of bullets. Petie and Trout stood up and engaged the small nest on top as well. Trout pitched the barrel of his 203 and lobbed some HE right in the middle of them. Thankfully, the fight was over almost as quick as it started. Smoke rose slightly off of the top of my M-60 as the light coat of oil burned on the surface of the barrel. My chest was pounding as I tried to catch my breath. This time, I do think that the elevation had something to do with it. I could hear my heartbeat pounding in my ears. I felt like I was going to puke. What had I just done? I drank some water out of my Camelbak as I felt the sweat pour down my face. Now the only thing I could think of was how fucking stupid that was and that I had endangered the lives of my team in a very selfish, insane manor. I worried about the repercussions of my actions from Tom, Koz, or basically anyone in the team. But, much to my surprise, it was never brought up, even to this day.

I went back down and grabbed my pack and flung it on my back, immediately being reminded of my "crater" that was starting to infarct with my every move. We all advanced without saying a word. My legs felt like jelly and I could feel the sores on my feet start to inflame as my boots were now rubbing the skin off my heels. When we reached the top, I think we all felt a moment of accomplishment, like Rocky at the top of the stairs as he jumped up and down. We had to have been at least 6000 feet above sea level. I swear I could see Guatemala, Honduras, and the Pacific Ocean all from this point on top of the world. Rodge pointed out where the river was and where we would look for our cache. But now we had to figure out how we were going to get down there. Looking down the steep face of the mountain made it look like the dark side of the moon. We took out our rappelling ropes and tied the packs off so we could slowly lower them down the face of a couple cliffs. Trout, Danny, and Petie then quickly repelled down, making it look as easy as saying your one, two, three's.

Scout stood on watch for any movement or hostiles in the area. As the last of us repelled down the cliff, Scout bounced his way down without incident. I felt very uneasy as we moved through the boulders, knowing well that we stood out like a sore thumb to anyone who would have been below us. But we made it to the wood line without even seeing an animal. Things were much too quiet for my blood. Once again, we fought to go over the downed trees and logs that littered the ground. Behind me to my right, I heard rocks falling and Ron yelling, "Ooohhh shit!" He was sliding down the face when his foot caught on a large rock and propelled him face first onto a jagged boulder. All of us heard the snap as we struggled to get to him. As I rounded the rocks fighting to get to him, I noticed the blood on the boulder.

Ron was lying there, with his eyes squinted shut, obviously in tremendous pain. As I got even closer, I saw that his left arm was either being held on by his torn shirt or a very small amount of flesh. The humerus bone was snapped in half and his bicep had balled up higher on his arm under his shirt. I knew this was really bad and he could die right here if we didn't act fast. I had Todd get out the sutures and a tourniquet, while Danny got some morphine. I was trying to keep Ron conscious as long as I could, but the pain and shock soon overtook him. I was already beyond using morphine. Ron's collateral ligaments were flopping around like rubber. I was going to have to amputate his arm.

The team made a 360-degree perimeter to protect us from any oncoming fire. I didn't have the option to move him to flatter ground because he was losing too much blood, too fast. Tom was O negative blood type, so I had Todd stick him and get us some blood. Petie got the surgical kit out of my bag and helped me apply pressure while I threw a C-Collar on Ron, in case he had any neck injuries. I didn't have to make too many incisions due to the arm almost being severed in half. The incised muscles had already retracted off of the bone. I had to keep as much of the superficial tissue as I could. The next thing I needed to do was clamp off the blood vessels and ligate them as I found them. I had to move to the brachial artery, because it was spraying blood everywhere in a pulsating manner. I had to dig in the appendage following the spray until I was able to find the brachial artery by touch. I had Petie leaning overhead to monitor his breathing and assure a good pulse through his carotid artery. I had to clamp off the brachial artery, which was bordering on impossible because of the amount of blood: it kept slipping out of my fingers.

As soon as I clamped it off, it was much easier to apply a transfixing suture and massively slow down his loss of blood. Todd stuck him on his other arm and started to transfuse Tom's blood. I told Todd that it wasn't going to be enough and to tap my left arm while I worked, considering I was also O negative blood type as well, a "Universal Donor." I realized that I was now in my realm and my demeanor returned to even and very calm. I felt confident and collected in my every move.

I moved entirely by instinct, as I had not only practiced this to a tee, but I could have done it blindfolded. I knew in my heart that Ron was going to be alright and I could do this; I just needed for the enemy to give me the time to finish this.

It was now much easier to find the stray blood vessels that I needed so that I could clamp them off quickly. "Okay, I have your bleeding under control; now just stay with me Ron," I said aloud. As I was clamping some of his blood vessels off, I looked up to him and said, "Thank God you got great veins, you carrot top son of a bitch." I had Petie try to bring some of the superficial tissue to a cone around the bone to stop some of the oozing and capillary bleeding. The break had already torn off the major nerves high enough that all I had to do was pump in some temporary anesthesia to dull the pain for his future postoperative recovery. I could only pray that it would hold him long enough to get him out of here.

Without needing to say anything, Koz and Rodge were in the background already on the mike to med-evac him out of here. I overheard Koz yell, "Bullshit, I don't care how you do it; you get a fuckin' chopper down here and extract him! Right, I will take full responsibility!" He threw the headpiece down and said, "Assholes, trust me, they will have their day if we ever get outta here."

I looked up to Koz and asked him, "We got wings?"

He talked as he exhaled, "Ya, Doc, we got wings. Patch him up and let's get him back to the other side."

I grabbed my pack of gauze and as I opened it, it went flying to the ground. I clinched my fists and yelled, "Fuck!"

Petie lifted his head and looked me dead in the eyes and asked, "He's gonna be alright isn't he, Doc?"

With a deep breath and a slight nod of my head I replied, "Ya, man, he's gonna be just fine; don't worry, he'll be fuckin' nurses left and right, while we're out getting our asses shot off."

Petie gave me a big smile and said, "I can live with that."

I took out another pack of gauze and applied the mesh loosely around the stump and soaked it in Betadine to help prevent infection. I applied several trauma bandages loosely around the outside of the nub. I didn't have any pantyhose or something with some elasticity to it to pull over and secure the bandages, so I had Trout give me some of his elastic football shorts to secure the dressings. They worked like a charm. All we had to do was wait around until the chopper arrived. I relieved Petie from applying pressure and assured him that Ron would be fine and Petie's eyes turned to stone right in front of me. His face suddenly filled with hate. This was a side of Petie that none of us had ever seen. I have to admit that I was somewhat intimidated from the look on his face as he picked up his 249 and started to walk back down through the boulders. Danny and Scout followed close behind. Even though Ron was looking a little pale, he was going to be alright. I let out a long, and possibly loud, exhale as I looked over my friend and comrade. As I kept pressure on Ron's arm, I looked around the team and noticed Koz with his leg propped up on a boulder looking as cold as ice. I worried as I studied the soldier, because his eyes never blinked. He had entered a place where all of us would soon join him.

In the distant background, I could hear the rotors as they cut through the air with all the aggression and hate that every one of us now possessed. Not even one member of the team flinched as the AH-60 Blackhawk dipped her tail slowing as she got in a position to hover above our wounded. They sent a basket down while Todd and I tried desperately to catch it and bring it close enough to Ron to get him in it, but it kept swinging over our heads and spinning uncontrollably. The ground around us looked and felt like we were in the middle of a tornado as the rotors threw anything and everything that wasn't weighted down all over the place.

We needed to get a hold of that basket quickly before the chopper became an easy target, which could compound our casualty ratio. Finally, Todd jumped in the air and caught it with his left hand and pulled it over to Ron. I took Ron's upper torso and Todd grabbed his legs and we moved him into the basket, strapped him down, and guided the basket out of the boulders, sending him on his way. It seemed like it took forever for us to get him secured in, but once we finally did and gave the thumbs up, they brought him up quickly, pulling the basket and cable into the guts of the chopper where they were able to provide him with immediate medical care. Several of us saluted as the chopper sped off. Now, we had a problem; our position had most certainly been compromised. But, as I looked at each member of the team, it was clear we were not the ones worried; from the looks on the faces of our team, those guerillas who were between us and our objective... it was they who, for the love of God, should cower in the face of death.

Silence had settled among us after the helicopter departed. There were no words or sounds made by anything, to include the surrounding wildlife. It was a matter of reckoning. The sheer reality was people were going to die. It was simply that black and white. Every one of us grabbed our packs, checked our weapons with a function test or whatever the individual chose and stood tall, as mighty giants that were going to crush any opposition, regardless of status. If we had to die trying, we were going to make some things right. Petie took point and, with his machete, thrashed through the undergrowth and vines as we walked through the vegetation. There wasn't a sound of any kind; it was like God had left this battle to be between us and the opposition. There wasn't any religion and there wasn't any mercy. It was personal and we were ready for anything. We were now the walking dead and we were going to take down and welcome any henchmen or any force that would dare to stand in front of us. Every one of us had a different score to settle. If it was from years past, or had happened within the last several hours, it was our time of reckoning.

14

THE CACHE

RODGE ADVISED US THAT THE STREAM SHOULD BE WITHIN A FEW MILES. As we walked further down the face of the mountain, the undergrowth on the jungle floor became almost impossible to walk through, as different species of plants intertwined with each other, using their different construction to strengthen their bonds. We had to pick our feet and legs up as high as we could, still catching our boots, more frequently than not. With what seemed to be every step, I saw snakes scurrying through the foliage, with hisses coming from my every side. I stepped on several as they tried to strike or coil under my feet. The squirming feeling under my feet was unnerving, but I had no choice but keep an even stride and keep going. I couldn't help but think of the Bushmaster that spared my life when I was taking a shower at the Marine Corp base camp. Hopefully, we would be just as lucky today.

When we got to what seemed to be the bottom, the ground leveled off very quickly and the thick lower canopy of plant life seemed to end. As I looked behind me at the intense vegetation, it looked more like an inconsistent rug woven with green and brown yarn; to call it a briar patch would be a gross understatement. For smaller animals, this had to have been the most secure place to live as I had ever seen. It was so thick that even a deer would have all kinds of trouble. Almost every member in the team had tears throughout their pants thanks to that vegetation while some of the pockets were even torn and hung by frills. The only thing that I could do was shake my head and thank God that we were through it and would, hopefully, never have to go through it again.

As we cleared the thistle, Koz shot an azimuth and I noticed a mango tree several feet to my right. I veered in its direction to grab a few mangos to munch on for the next few miles. I picked up several off of the ground, stuffed them in my blouse, and double-timed it to catch up to the team. As I fell in behind Trout, I called for him to slow down so I could hand him a mango. As he turned his head, his eyes widened almost like the sight of me scared him. When I got next to him, I asked him if he was okay and he replied, in broken words, "Ya, ya, I'm okay, I kinda zoned out there for a minute." I held the mango out and pushed it toward him several times before he took it and thanked me. His face was pale, like he had seen a ghost. He tossed the fruit up several times and took a huge bite. As he started to eat it, the color started to come back in his face.

The landscape opened up with trees standing sporadically in front of us, giving us little cover, but made for a pleasant walk. The one thing that I thought of was how the vegetation changed so quickly and dramatically from one extreme to another. The temperature and air of the day was turning out to be rather pleasant. I now got the feeling of a glamorized Boy Scout Troop again as we walked in a straight and very leisurely manor, admiring the beautiful mountains, hills, and lakes throughout the land. I pulled a mango out of my blouse and rubbed it on my pants several times and took a delightful bite. If you think about it, so many people rub an apple or fruit on their shirt or pants several times to give them a false sense of cleanliness. Did the rubbing actually clean off the surface of the fruit? Probably not, but just like combat soldiers do impulsive things that have no bearing or significance to the job or task, the act somehow or another calms the psyche. An example would be being at a casino and rubbing the side of the slot machine before pulling the handle. Did it bring a better chance of winning? No, but it may have made you feel more lucky or secure in justifying spending money that you likely won't see again.

Every soldier has a ritual they turn to in order to bring them luck or guidance. Considering that a major aspect of combat was psychological, it's interesting how we can manipulate our minds to think a certain way. By shifting the mind, we can affect the body, such as giving ourselves huge amounts of adrenaline or superhuman strength, like the proverbial old lady that lifts up the back of a Cadillac to save a child's life. The human body is one of the most complex and deadly machines on the Earth. But it all really does go back to the old saying, "You can do anything you want if you put your mind to it." Like being or becoming a Special Forces Soldier; it isn't something for just any man, in fact it's something that's for a very few men. And with our unique, but rare, physical strengths being mixed with our superior psychological ability, we can almost surpass the title of being totally human. I know that this sounds surreal, cocky, and maybe a little conceited, but you would have to live a few days in our shoes to totally understand.

We were starting to lose daylight and had not yet arrived at our cache, which we hoped was only a few minutes away. Rodge took point and walked very confidently, almost like he was the one who had placed the cache there himself. That brings us back to the ability of instinct. I don't know how Rodge would know exactly where it was considering he wasn't even using a compass. But within five minutes, he led us directly to it without even a slight turn to the right or the left. The cache was under some tall grass at the very edge of a river, with some of it even being partially sunken in the water. Danny, Trout, and Todd worked on trying to pull it up on the shoreline. As they lifted the ends a little at a time, the immense size of the cache was truly unbelievable. They worked on getting it up and secured for a good 15-20 minutes as the sun set.

As I observed the actions of the team, I realized that everyone was exhausted or, in better terms, spent. I reminded everyone to take their salt tablets, malaria tabs, and try to increase our water intake within the few minutes we had as we waited to dig into our immense re-supply. I thought it would give us the possible boost we needed to get to the site, let alone the fact that intercepting more guerillas was more likely as we neared our final destination. Our packs would be heavier now than they ever had been and we were certainly more tired than we ever had been, so I offered the team a shot of Amphetamine Sulfate, or in generic terms, Benzedrine or Ephedrine. This would give us the extra energy we needed to move forward and better prepare us in case of another confrontation. I personally wanted and needed it, so I was the first to inject myself after carefully measuring the dose, knowing well that too high of a dose was toxic and could result in death. After my injection, the team didn't need a second thought and, with the exception of Danny, Trout, and Todd, as they were pulling the cache up onto shore, every one took the injection with only one rejection and that was Rodge. He didn't feel like he needed it and or just didn't want it and I felt confident that he would be alright without it.

As the other guys drug the cache onto the bank, it turned into Christmas morning. It had everything for a platoon to live off of for a month. There were freeze-dried meat, fruits, and vegetables galore. There were more claymores than we'd even be able to carry, even if that was the only thing we took with us. There were boxes of ammunition for each type of weapons we carried, to include 203 HE and Law Rockets. If an adversary would have beaten us to it, it could have been truly devastating. We intermittently took several things out of the bags and took them back to our rucks to either pack or prepare for our final walk. We sat there for a good hour, filling up on everything we might need, and I gave the other three their injections. Mosquitoes were getting unbearable now, being so close to the river. The team was slapping their faces and necks because we were unwilling to donate the blood the bugs were striving to get. Within minutes, the team was ready for anything. We helped each other get our packs on as the weight was a tremendous burden. Hopefully, we didn't have far to travel or that the terrain would be easy enough that the walk would go fast, without too many obstacles.

We took the remaining cache and hid it back in the weeds along the shore, making sure that it wouldn't be found and that the enemy couldn't use the remnants against us. We also wanted to be able to come back and get the rest, if the opportunity presented. Cache secured and hidden, we set off for our destination. The sky was pitch dark and we would be traveling now using only hand and arm signals and whispers, of which the moment required. I reached up and scratched my neck and felt the numerous welts that the mosquitoes had left within those short minutes before we took off from the river. The mood of the team was quiet and serious, with a slight decrease in morale. Now that we were so close to our mission destination, I felt a very slight bit of anxiety or panic over what we were going to find when we got there.

Our necks and faces were itching like crazy from all of the mosquito bites. Even our faces looked somewhat swollen. One couldn't help but wonder how many of those mosquitos were carrying malaria. It was difficult for us to walk in a stealthy or strategic manner, considering the weight we were now toting. The enormous weight we carried on our backs often led one of us to stumble or periodically careen from side to side, despite the level path. As we walked, the ground seemed to open up in front of us and resemble that of a cow pasture. The smell of cow excrement was present all around us. I call that a farm smell and back in Wisconsin, we surely had plenty of that. I loved it; it actually calmed me because I felt more at home and reminded me of my grandmother's farmhouse that we would visit every Fourth of July. It didn't take long for one of us to confirm it was a cow pasture, and of course, it had to be Danny, as he whispered, "Awe, fuck," then attempted to kick and rub the manure off his boots in the dry grass. Even though we were crossing a pasture, which many would think was relatively safe, we needed to take into consideration that there was little to no cover. Not only did we have to worry about an ambush being out here, but we needed to be conscious of any pissed off bulls or cows. You might think that they couldn't hurt you, but a cow can trample you in a matter of a minute and a bull can spear a man and kill him in a split second. Sometimes, you have to be more careful with the wildlife than somebody shooting at you because they both have the ability to kill you, but humans are much more predictable.

We walked through the field without incident or even seeing any animals. As we crossed, I could tell that we were going up in altitude again and the field ended against the side of another mountain. There was a large silver cattle gate that we used to get on the other side of the pasture. It opened onto a gravel road that would skirt the side of the mountain, only gaining in height very slightly. I thought that the road would give us some relief in walking, but it didn't at all, as our boots caught on small stones that were trying to roll our ankles over. It only took us about five minutes to get to the other side and then suddenly, we were there. I let out a relieving sigh, we made it… for the love of God, we made it! The ground was very flat and from what I could tell the area would suffice for the site. We needed to take advantage of the darkness and get set into our new home for the next, God only knew, how many days.

We sat there, digging our foxholes and hasties (a basic foxhole), in the humid air, under a beautiful night sky, and what was a perfect night to catch some Z's. We worked fast and knew if the guerillas had followed us, the guerillas would be here soon and would start to probe the area. After we got our DFPs constructed, I rested my arms on the upper lip of the foxhole and waited while I took in the evening air. I hoped that they were ignorant of our position and that they were going to miss us or even better, never find us; I sat there contemplating those options while the sweat was dripping off my nose and my anxiety started flowing again.

Petie and Trout went out and strung every inch of the perimeter in early warning devices (EWDs) and were confident that not even a gnat was going to get through. They strung the perimeter with empty cans, with rocks in them, to M49A1 Trip Flares, string pops from your local fireworks stand, and claymores that would let the world know if a cricket was taking a shit. There was nothing that was getting close to us without us knowing. There was one thing that had my nerves on edge and that was an enormous crop of sugarcane that was about 50 feet in elevation below us and south of us by 70 feet. The crop was very tight and high, and could provide an oncoming force with perfect camouflage and concealment. If I was going to aggress an area like this, that's where I'd come from. It had the potential of a very high and dense corn field, which we have used in the past quite comfortably. I could hear Rodge in the background advising JSOC as to our position while several of us worked on Petie and Trout's positions. All of us knew that there wouldn't be any sleep tonight; all we could do was stand and wait for morning. Everything in the evening air and surroundings was very peaceful. But the heat tonight was unreal and the darkness of the night sky didn't bring us any relief. All of us stood in our positions and evaluated our wounds, took stock of our weaponry, ate some of our freeze-dried food, and completed a function test of our primary weapons.

Morning seemed to take forever to arrive. The evening was uneventful and quiet. I was so stiff and sore, I had to pop a few Motrin to loosen up a little. Koz, Rodge, and Tom got out of their DFPs and walked around sizing up the area. There was a house that couldn't be but a hundred yards to the south of us and paralleled the sugarcane crops. From our elevation, I could see a huge lake below us that was only a hundred feet to the south of the house. As I looked down toward the house, it looked like the walk down from any direction would be tough due to the decline and almost a sheer rock ledge. This position took a lot of looking to find and had to have been sought out by Green Berets or a Ranger team. It was as flat as a school playground and the ground was dense enough that it could hold a mass amount of weight. Tom and Scout took off to do a small recon of the surrounding area and find any weak points in the camp so they could be better watched or reinforced with EWDs. With the exception of Petie, Jesus, and I, the rest worked on cleaning up the DFPs to ready us for the evening hours, because from this position, they wouldn't be able to make any sort of aggression in the daylight, without full compromise.

A couple hours passed before Tom and Scout came back. The camp was pretty close to being completed and we could look to our wounds, shave, and prepare to catch a few Z's. With the exception of Tom, Scout, Trout, and I, the rest of the team was able to drop into sleep almost immediately. I know that it wouldn't have taken long, because we were all at the brink of sheer exhaustion and dehydration. I took to the middle of the camp with Tom as he started to plot our DFPs and range of fire. I started to dig out a small bunker (large hasty) while the others walked the perimeter and Tom set up our defensive grid. My hands were blistered from digging out our DFP the night before and I found it difficult to manipulate my hands to a position where I wasn't rubbing the existing blisters or creating new ones. Either the ground was much harder in the middle than it was over where we had dug our DFPs, or I was quickly running low on energy due to exhaustion. I drank a tremendous amount of water, taking breaks more frequently, and after I got the area to a good hasty position for cover, I used a poncho to cover the hole for shade and try to cool down.

Going on four hours, I caught myself getting rubber neck and fighting to keep my eyes open. I had to move out from under the poncho and walk around a little and try to wake up. As I threw the sling to my sixty around my neck, I could surely identify every rub mark that I had resulting from our huge packs. I had several deep scratches on my legs and abdomen from the undergrowth that we had to fight through to get down the mountain. They itched and stung as the salt in my sweat ran over them. My face, hands, and neck were terribly welted with mosquito and insect bites and scratches. I took out some ointment and applied it to the affected parts, and boy, did it burn as I applied it. It quickly woke me up, but gave very little relief. A strange memory suddenly resurfaced as I found myself wishing for some horse urine. I had once used it to soothe mosquito bites as a boy on our farm, based on the advice of my great uncle, and it had taken 100% of the itching and swelling out. I certainly would have bathed in a vat of horse urine at that moment, if given the chance.

Rodge stood and stretched his sore arms as he awoke from his nap. Tom went through and got the rest of the team up. You could tell that every one of us was sore as hell from the hard-driven march, our bites and lacerations, and our intermittent moments of confrontation and hand-to-hand combat. The team appeared a lot better now than they did when they laid down. I seriously felt like I was going to fall over. I was to the point where my feet felt like they weighed a hundred pounds each and with every step I took, I was fighting with everything I had to stand erect. As Todd climbed out of our DFP, he gave me a slight pat on the back and said, "Don't do anything I wouldn't do." I gave him a simple nod of the head and slid into the foxhole. To this day, I don't remember falling asleep or passing out, all I know is that as soon as I hit the floor of the fighting position, I was down for the count.

I awoke to the sound of laughing in the distance. As I tried to lift my body from the side of the foxhole, it felt like I was hung over and had been beaten to a bloody pulp the night before. I rolled over and pushed myself up with my hands and as I did, I think that half of the bones in my body cracked simultaneously, feeling actually quite good. I grabbed my two-quart canteen of water and finished it off. The corners of my eyes were seriously crusted with eye boogers. They were hard enough that I probably could have used a knife to cut them out. I gave a huge yawn and flexed my pecs several times before climbing out of the hole. My right butt cheek hurt like hell, since part of it was half in and half out of a grenade sump. When we constructed the DFP, we covered the ends for flank cover and to block out some of the sun's heat. As I climbed out, the sun was unbelievably strong and the air was humid and stank like something rotting or decaying. It smelled a lot like the morning breath of some of the girls with whom I had enjoyed a great night of drinking and hard-core sex.

I walked toward the center of the camp and noticed that the hasty I had begun was now turned into a very fortified fighting position, communications DFP, and HQ for the duration of our stay. Tom and Scout were still asleep. I squinted down at my watch and it read almost 1600 hours local. All of the DFPs had aiming and limit-of-fire stakes put in and the camouflage had been dressed up immensely. From the looks of things, everybody had been really busy as I dreamt of large women, in grass skirts, with very tiny coconuts covering their breasts. Koz was reading range cards to plot positions on our camp map. A range card tells specific details about a certain DFP. It has to include information like dead spaces in front of that position where the enemy could approach, undetected, or where the weapons in that hole were unable to engage. It has to show certain targets in front of a DFP to assist the shooter in low or limited visibility. It also includes a Final Protection Line (FPL), in which the occupant of that position would lay down a constant line of fire to assist in evacuation or to tie down an aggressing force that has overrun the camp. Then you plot your primary and secondary sectors of fire with the occupant's types of weapons and give all of the information to the unit leader so he can better his defense plan or strategy.

I stood over the group for a couple minutes and decided to go and check on the status of Jesus. I went to the far north end of the camp and saw Jesus sitting on the edge of his foxhole, cleaning his weapon, with his pants off. As I approached, his head quickly turned in my direction and after verifying who it was, he slowly turned back around to continue what he was doing. At a safe distance, as I neared, I asked him how he was doing and how his leg was. He turned and looked up at me and said, "Look at it!" in a heightened voice. I was almost reluctant to look but I readied myself for the worst. I knelt down by his left side, minding to stay clear of his weapon hand, because some people get touchy when they are out on a mission and you crowd their means of defense of life. So, I kept to his left and looked at the wound.

My eyes just about popped out of my head as I said, "Holy shit, you've got to be fuckin' kidding me!" The wound now appeared to be just a deep scrape. The maggots had eaten all of the dead skin out and left what I would define as a minor wound. Nature has wondrous ways of healing the heart, soul, and body, and this time I think it did so for the both of us. I told him that the air was good for the wound and that I would be over again later with another dressing and antibacterial ointment. All I could do was look in awe; I had never seen a wound heal like that ever in my life. But thank God, it was for the better, because we needed him for many different reasons.

As I walked back to my fighting position, I quickly pulled my side arm out and pointed it at a small boy that was hiding behind a tree about 70 feet to the south of our camp. At this range, my pistol was basically ineffective, but hopefully, he didn't know that. As I held my pistol up with my right hand, I motioned with my left to have him come out from hiding. I caught Danny out of the corner of my eye, standing on point, and looking to each side for any others. Jesus limped over in his fucking underwear, I'm sure really confusing this kid, and if not, making him think of many things that this wasn't. Jesus told him that we weren't going to hurt him and that it was safe to come out. I lowered my side arm and holstered it as a sign of good will, even though for safety's sake, Danny wasn't moving and that was fine with me. We didn't know why the child was here and we certainly did not want this to turn into something really bad. Jesus told him that we were there to help them build a school and that we weren't there to hurt anybody.

The boy stood up and slowly came out from behind the tree. I rolled my eyes and sighed. This kid couldn't be any older than five or six. He was wearing a blue, white, and red striped polo with red cotton shorts that appeared to be slightly too big for him. He was bare-footed and approached very slowly. Obviously, outside of Jesus' appearance, I'm sure that we looked very different to him. Jesus asked if there was anyone else with him, for our safety as well as his safety. He said, "No," in a very soft and scared voice. I told him that we were from the United States and we were here for them. His posture eased and he walked a little more calmly toward us, so he must have had a good experience in the past with Americans. We asked him where he came from and where his parents were. He pointed at the house that was just south of our position down by the lake. He told us that he lived with his father, younger brother, two sisters, and that they were doing their chores. He was going down to the small stream to get some water. The child had a very strange look on his face as he looked at Jesus. You could see the confusion on the child's face in response to Jesus' present condition. Jesus looked down at the boy and said that he would be right back with his pants and that he had them off because of the wound he sustained on his leg. As he pointed to the wound, the boy looked up at him and immediately became frightened. As the boy neared, he looked at Jesus with wide eyes, scared to death, and while pointing at his face, asked him if that was from the banditos. Jesus looked up at me and with a slight nod, he told the boy that that was none of his business and stormed off. I don't know if it was the embarrassment over his appearance or the reminder of what had happened to him, but nonetheless, he was infuriated by the boy's question.

The boy stood there with me for about 15 minutes, asking me about my weapon and the gear on my tac-vest. He was mesmerized by all of the "cool Army stuff," like most boys his age. And like any other boy, he wanted to touch everything and that is where I had to draw the line. I told him in a fair, but stern voice, that I was a professional soldier and that no one could touch any of our things without repercussion and with that, he stepped a couple of feet back and the expression on his face went hesitant to our presence again. Tom and Jesus walked up from behind us and as soon as the boy saw Jesus, he once again became scared. I told Jesus that it was nice of him to put his pants back on for us and Tom and I laughed. Jesus' expression was numb to anything and he just stared at the little boy. Tom said, "I'll go first since you have such a way with children." Tom put his hand on the boy's shoulder and led him towards his house, with the boy constantly looking behind at Jesus in fear. As they walked away, Danny lowered the muzzle of his weapon and walked to the north side of the camp.

I turned and went to the now established bunker in the middle of our camp. I could hear Rodge on the radio and intermittent talking from within. I stepped down into the hole and Koz asked how I was doing, just like we were at some biv-wac in the States or just outside of base. His actions were without emotion; like nothing had happened up to this point and that we were just having a jolly of a time. I responded to him questionably, "Yeah, I'm doin' alright, how about you?"

He smiled and said, "Great, we're here, we got the bull by the balls, and the El Salvadorian Special Forces will be here in a couple days."

I nodded, raised my eyebrows and said, "Great, that's good to know." I turned back around, somewhat confused, and climbed back out. Now squinting from being under the poncho, the bright sunlight partially blinded me.

I noticed Scout in his hole on the northwest side of the camp, playing with something at the back of his foxhole, as he kept touching something then quickly jerking his hands back. I had to investigate; it was either something really funny or something really stupid. I looked down to see Scout pushing two black scorpions toward one another. Kneeling down to him, I couldn't help but ask, "What in the hell are you doing?"

He smiled and looked up with a, "Hey Doc, check this out. This little fucker here almost has this big one dead, but I can't get them to finish it off."

I closed my eyes and nodded my head quickly from side to side and asked, "Why don't you push them together with your knife instead of your finger?" "Hey, good idea," he replied, pulling out his knife from his side. The handle and blade were covered with dried blood, skin, and bone matter. All the experiences from our previous conflicts rushed back to me in one huge painful memory. It literally sucked the life out of me within a second. For some reason, I now felt tired and didn't feel much like socializing with anyone. I clenched my teeth together, swallowed, nodded a couple times, stood up, and returned to my foxhole.

When I got back, Todd was content with himself, cleaning his side arm and humming a tune. I climbed back in the foxhole with him, opened the feed tray to my sixty, relayed the ammo belt in, closed the cover, pulled the charging handle back, and secured it to the front. I laid my left hand on the fore stock and let my chin rest on my hand. I looked out into the void and couldn't stop thinking of the sacrifices we made to get us here. Ron was a damn good friend and I hated what had happened to him, but I did know he was going to be fine. He was a tough son of a bitch and I looked forward to seeing him when we got back to post. (As you the reader read through this book, I don't know if you realize it or not, as I am for the first time, but every time I think or talk about Ron, I refer to him as a "son of a bitch." If his mother sees this, it's only a saying among comrades and nothing to do with anyone's mother.) I hoped that he was tagging several nurses and would have some good, juicy stories for us when we got back. All of us thought about him and the LT; we just did it in different ways and didn't express it out loud.

I turned my sixty in the direction of some movement coming up the hill. It was Tom and Jesus. Tom came to the back of our position and told us that the family down in the house below was on our side and that they lost the mother when they refused to dump dead bodies in the lake at the bottom of their property. He told us that the locals call this place "The Lake of Ten Thousand Souls." The expression on Tom's face changed to a more serious, cautious one. He then said, "The property owner down there said that they dumped load after load of dump trucks full of bodies in that lake." He stood and pointed just beyond the house.

Jesus stepped forward rubbing his wounded leg that was now bleeding through his pants and said, "This land has been damned by the devil, as we soon may join him." His head hung down as he walked back to his DFP.

Todd sat up saying, "What the fuck was that supposed to mean, damned by the devil?"

Tom explained that the farmer below said that anything outside of his family that has come here has died a terrible death and that we were now going to meet the devil face to face. I looked at him and said, "Say what? The devil, huh? Well, I've never been properly introduced."

Todd laughed and said, "The devil, I told you that this was not going to be good."

"Oh, for God's sake Todd, relax!" bellowed Tom. One thing that did cross my mind was the fact that I said we hadn't been properly introduced. It took me back to when I was a teenager working as a bouncer a few nights during the week and weekends during football season. One night after closing, the manager brought out a Ouija board and we played with something we shouldn't have. That's all I'm going to say about the actual incident. Let's just say that I have never had the shit scared out of me more than that night. Have I been introduced to the Devil? Maybe, if not him, someone real close to him. After that, I found it very hard to be frightened by man or animal. I honestly don't ever want to go through anything like that ever again.

Tom leaned over and said, "Doc, Doc! Earth to Doc." I shook my head wildly and acknowledged him. "Hey man, are you alright?"

I shook my head again and said, "Yeah, yeah, I just was thinking of something from a long time ago."

"That must have been some thought. You turned as pale as a ghost and I was going to bet money that you were going to pass out." I lifted my head and said I was all right.

Tom pulled his head back and said, "Doc, please tell me you don't believe in this devil shit. Do you?" I again told him I was alright and asked what else the farmer had to say. Tom pulled out his "Blood-rag" and wiped his face of sweat, then knelt down again and in a whisper said, "The locals call it 'The Lake of Ten Thousand Souls' because there were over 78,000 people that were dumped in that lake. And, unfortunately, his wife was one of them. He protested them using their property to back the trucks in and dump the bodies, so one of the guards walked straight up to his wife and shot her in the head right in front of the kids and all. Then, they threatened to kill his children if he didn't comply with their demands. So, basically no one goes anywhere near this place. All of the locals say the ground has been damned by Satan himself and if they touch the unholy soil, they will die 10,000 deaths and a bunch of other mumbo-jumbo bullshit." The hair on the back of my neck stood straight on end. And by the look of Todd, he wasn't too pleased with the briefing either. Tom shrugged his shoulders and said he was going to talk to Koz. The first thing I thought about was that I was sure Koz was gonna love the shit out of that, considering he was also a Catholic; I certainly wasn't jumping for joy, to say the least. I think that Tom's outer shell is so thick that it seems like everything and anything bounces off of him, but I personally have caught moments when I could tell something bothered him. This definitely bothered him.

Todd looked over to me and asked, "You believe in that shit, Doc?" I leaned into him and replied, "I believe in a lot of things, Todd. But right now, I believe we're gonna finish this thing, go back home, get fuckin' wasted, and bury our faces in a million curls."

I had to go get some air bad, so I made something up so I could escape for a few minutes. Todd asked if I was alright and I shook my head and smiled with a, "Hell yeah, man, I'm just kinda fidgety. I mean we haven't really done a lot since we've got to the site. Give me a few minutes and I'll be right back." I picked my feet up and down several times and stopped for a minute and listened. I could hear him take the slide off of his side arm and start humming again so I leaned over and yelled, "Oh shit!"

Todd dropped everything and wasn't but a half an inch of literally blowing my head off as he yelled back, "Fuck you, Dave! You asshole, I almost shit myself. Fuck!"

I apologized and said, "Sorry, man, bad timing." He flipped me off, said fuck you, and told me to get out of here. So, I did.

As I walked, Petie, Danny, and Trout slid down the rock face as they left camp to go gather bamboo shoots to use as booby traps. I personally found bamboo to be an attractive native plant in this area, but I also have seen the true devastation that it can do to a human body. It slices through skin with the ease of surgical equipment and if the shoots have been tainted with anything, as they usually are, they can cause an almost guaranteed death. Most of the countries that use them use very simple toxins such as human excrement, poisonous tree frog skin, and viper venom, all things that are found right in the general area of where the very shoots themselves are found. After heating, drying, and hardening the shoots, then applying the toxins, if the initial puncture wounds don't kill you, and if they are not treated with the right anecdote, the victim will certainly die a very painful death.

I walked the perimeter carefully to study where everything was and if there were any natural positions that could be used for cover in the event that we were somehow overtaken. The ground yielded sharp rocks throughout the area, making any crawling devastating and sure to tear not only the clothing but also the flesh of the individual. There was so much about this country that was left unexplained or questionable. As I circled the very outer edge of the camp, everything was so peaceful. There wasn't anything anywhere that would suggest the mass amount of destruction and death that we had encountered since we'd been here. It seems to turn on and off within a second; there wasn't anything in-between. It was always one extreme to another. I stopped when I got to the farmhouse below and watched as the children played, throwing sticks to a white dog that resembled a very malnourished greyhound. I looked past the house and saw the lake in the background. I thought it not only looked beautiful, but was very inviting for a swim, if time would allow. And if it wasn't a burial ground.

I looked into the sky, where there were very few clouds, but the colors were awesome. The night was soon approaching, and in my mind, I was hoping for another uneventful night. The air seemed to be almost extra fresh tonight and had a very low humidity but it also had an unnerving calmness to it. A yellow outdoor light that hung by the front door turned on and was followed by the father telling the kids that it was time for them to get ready for bed. My eyes were mesmerized, but not focused, as I stared at the farmhouse, almost in a trance. As I looked at the house, I hoped and prayed that we would not be the ones to bring any harm to this tight knit family. Tom spoke like we were the ones who may be in danger; if it meant a physical confrontation with the banditos or supernatural utter chaos, that's one thing. But I didn't look at it like that. We were being hunted by a faction that wanted us dead with our heads on a stick and truly, I didn't blame them. We killed a lot of them and as far as they were concerned, unless they had found the LT, their body count still stood at zero. The silence that surrounded me snapped me out of my trance and, as the sky was quickly darkening, I walked back to the center of the camp.

15

HERE COME THE NATIVES

As I neared the bunker, I saw a small fire burning that had at least three or four people around it. I could hear Rodge in the background talking on the radio. There now stood a 40-foot antenna protruding from the Command bunker, and knowing Rodge, he was probably talking to some chick in Argentina. Scout sat with his legs bent and spread, while he pushed a pebble back and forth with the tip of his knife. I asked him if there was ever a fatal victor in his scorpion match. He never lifted his head but said, "I claimed no glory and cut both of them in half," as he continued to push the pebble from side to side. Morale was dropping quickly and I think that all of us felt just as trapped in this compound as we did in El Pongo while staying in the small jail. Our lying-in wait provided very little stimulus and we were more accustomed to our own command and control versus sitting under the thumb of a foreign diplomat.

I knelt down at a fair distance from the fire and rested my weight on the carrying handle of my sixty. As I sat there, I began to think that everything felt so far away. I mean, I felt like we had been so detached from the modern world for so long that a million things could have happened stateside and we would never know it. But then, I already thought of this place as home. I felt comfortable here and maybe Bill knew something that we didn't. But for now, this was home and I was going to do everything I could to preserve that. I rehearsed a part of our Creed in my head: "I know I will be called upon to perform tasks in isolation far from familiar faces and voices; with the help and guidance of my God, I will conquer my fears and succeed." And that most definitely brought my shoulders back, my chest out, and my head back into the game. Koz walked out of the bunker and called off the nightly guard duty. We were only going to keep two up at a time so we could concentrate on bringing our health and demeanor back, and by the sound of it, I was going to have the entire night off. I was going to take full advantage of every minute of it. I stood up and said, "See you guys on the flip side." They all mumbled something, nodded, or just said, "Later." The walk back to my fighting position was relaxing and all I had on my mind was getting this sixty off my shoulders. I slipped back into the foxhole, kissed "Mother" goodnight, pulled my poncho liner out of my rucksack, and fell fast asleep.

I was quickly awakened to the sound of chopper blades as they whipped through the early morning air. It was dark as hell and the choppers were coming in on stealth mode with all lights off and full power to their destination. Petie and Scout walked up to the back of our position and stated that the El Salvadorian Special Forces had sent a huge amount of men to help us protect the site. I could only imagine the cluster fuck that we would now have with these guys running all over the place. Petie and Scout ran out to the field to guide them in and, within minutes, an AH-60 Blackhawk touched down directly in front of our position out in the field behind the camp. To my surprise, they only dropped off three or four people but were shortly accompanied by a MH-47 Chinook and, holy shit, if that thing didn't throw every piece of anything that wasn't tied off all over the place! If you haven't had the pleasure of actually being up close to a Chinook when it was landing or taking off, I will tell you, it is quite an awesome sight. And when she came down, people poured out of the back of it like angry fire ants pouring out of their hole.

Petie, Scout, and three other people, very casually walked through the booby traps with the guidance of Petie and struggled up the rock face as they approached our position. I wasn't sure who was coming but, with the exception of Petie and Scout, I was definitely ready to light some of these guys up if the occasion demanded. Scout brought up and introduced us to a Major Woods, Colonel Lira, and a Navy Seal that went only by the title of Chief. After they left our position and walked to the center of camp, I couldn't help but laugh and shake my head, saying, "Great, now we got the fuckin' Seals here." Don't get me wrong, Navy Seals are by far one of the best and elite forces in the entire world, but sometimes we had a tendency to hold differing opinions. Petie walked through the labyrinth of booby traps, but all of the others stayed on the outer perimeter. I asked him in passing why they weren't coming in and he said that they are going to set up on the outer perimeter. We would now be the final line of defense.

As I looked out towards the field, I honestly couldn't tell you how many new troops had arrived, but I did know that there was one hell of a lot of them. Many of them snapped glow sticks to help illuminate the area and as they moved out, one soldier knelt at their landing sight holding a glow stick in each hand. They didn't seem to need any sort of noise control after the helicopters and they sure didn't display it by any means. The bulk of their forces all moved to the west. Things in front of our position had just started to calm down slightly when I heard another group of choppers coming from the north. I said out loud, "No way?" Just after saying that, the short man in the field stood up and raised his glow sticks straight up in the air. Dust, grass, and tree limbs flew in every direction as I tried to cover my eyes. Another Chinook landed, dropping off at least 20 to 30 more men. If I didn't have any anxiety towards a hostile attack or attempted infiltration, I sure as hell did now. If the numbers were strictly a precaution, that was one thing; but, if they anticipated a force large enough to actually need these kinds of numbers, blood would surely stain the ground here for an eternity.

The yellow light down at the farmhouse lit up again, and if I had to guess, I would say that several members of the first wave went down to talk to the occupants. It wasn't long before their voices got louder and the farmer was once again forced to yield to their wishes. I couldn't get back to sleep for many reasons, but the most obvious reason being that the guys that were now skirting our outer perimeter were loud as hell and walked around like they were setting camp to buy tickets to a rock concert. By the looks of things, I figured that we would be out of here within the next few days considering that the area was now being secured by their native government. Todd told me that he was going to go and heat up a cup of java and asked if I wanted one. I accepted the offer with gratitude. For the next couple of hours, I sat and watched the soldiers set their camps around us like the Sioux did right before they destroyed Custer.

As I watched the sun come up, it was difficult for me to conceive how many soldiers actually came in last night. They were everywhere! Tom called out to me in the distance, yelling for me to diggy up to the command bunker. At first, I was worried that we already had a medical emergency, but when I got up there, all of our guys were cutting up with each other, each giving their own opinions as to the happenings during the night. Tom called us to attention as the major and his cohorts came out from underneath the poncho covering the bunker. The major called at ease and said, "I know I don't have to piss around or glamorize anything with you guys, but I do need to express our concern as to the importance of this mission. It is vital that we proceed with this in a very quick manner. I would like to start out with my condolences for the loss of your lieutenant. Randie was a damn good officer and he will most certainly be missed. I would like to introduce to you Colonel Lira, who will be head CO of the El Salvadorian Special Forces." He took a step forward and bowed his head, then stepped back.

"And I would also like to introduce Chief, who is one of JSOC's leading advisors in this theater of operations. His men brought you your cache, which I have a good reason to believe you found to be okay?" Koz nodded to verify. "We will need you to conduct recon patrols with the native SF as to any movement in the area. I'm not going to sugar coat anything; you guys did exactly what we needed you to do and that was find the local guerilla factions and to destroy them and eventually provoke them to bind forces to take you guys out. And from the latest intel, you did just that and they're lookin for ya. Now we have to destroy the bulk of their organization and take full control of the country for the benefit of the United States as well as the El Salvadorian people. This could get really messy, but we all hope that we can defuse a lot of it through other means. You will have the support of our AH-60 Blackhawks; we just brought some more into theater within the last week. There will be construction machinery and supplies beginning to be brought in, as early as today. Almost every bit of it will be dropped by chopper, but we do have several convoys that are already on their way, so I ask every one of you to do what you do and help assist the equipment and supplies to get in here safely. Are there any questions? I have had the opportunity to further brief Sergeant Koz on some more specific matters and Chief will be here for the next few days to help get things started. Okay," he concluded, as he quickly looked around, raised his eyebrows, and went back down into the bunker followed by the chief and the colonel.

Koz took in a deep breath and said, "I will get with all of you individually. Anything else for right now?" as he stretched his open palms forward. He scratched his five o'clock shadow and said, "Dismissed." I could tell already that we were in for a hell of a time. Scout brought up the fact that the native forces would have to be briefed about the rules of engagement for our safety, the safety of the family in the farmhouse, and even to protect the lives within their ranks. We couldn't risk some cherry lighting up the whole fucking area over an animal setting off a trip wire. Koz stated that he was going to address that very point right now; he ducked his head and went back down into the bunker.

Jesus waited for Koz to disappear into the bunker then told us that Colonel Lira was a very hardened man. He also shared that Lira was the one who mostly governed all of the mass executions and that it was his order to dump all of those bodies here. So, he basically had returned to the scene of the crime. I couldn't believe all of these things that kept coming up. Something was going to happen here and Uncle Sam didn't want his boys at the front of the line when the shit hit the fan. I greatly appreciated that, but I didn't know enough about the native SF to feel comfortable with the current situation. They could be just as much of a threat as the banditos if they weren't trained to confirm their target or the many disciplines that were necessary to fight in this kind of situation. But, like they say, it's just another day in the Army.

The air was getting more humid as the day progressed. As I looked out at the DFPs the soldiers were creating on the outer perimeter, I got the feeling that they weren't going to be using them too much or that they needed to be able to get up and out in a hurry considering their construction or lack thereof. Petie was given the job of briefing the native NCOs of the EWDs on the perimeter, making sure we didn't have any friendly accidents. I gave "Mother" a once over and went out again to walk the perimeter. As I got out in front of our DFP, I noticed that the little boy and, I assumed, his brother and his older sister, were down at the water hole filling huge jars and what looked like a five-gallon gas can with water. The little boy was wearing the same thing that he had on earlier and his little brother had on long denim shorts without a shirt. None of them were wearing any shoes and the sister had her back to me since she was hanging some laundry on a couple of branches just to the rear of the water hole. I guessed that this was not only their only source of fresh water but it also served as a safe place for them to do their laundry and brilliantly use the trees and shrubbery as a drying rack. The older sister was wearing a red shirt with black print flowers on it and denim shorts as well. She was much older than I had guessed earlier when I was talking with the little boy. She had beautiful long black hair that she had pulled up in a ponytail.

The little boy looked up and saw me standing there and gave me a big smile and a wave. He tapped his sister on the back almost to introduce us at a distance. She bent over to ask him what he wanted then turned around and looked up at me. I swear my heart and throat dropped straight to my stomach. She was absolutely beautiful. Her smile almost killed me; her dark skin and black hair created the most beautiful aura. I was heartbroken the minute I saw her. She waved and I had difficulty raising my arm, which now weighed a thousand pounds, so I picked up my hand and moved it back and forth several times as the only reply I had the strength to do. I then immediately felt like I was thirteen years old again as my face blushed, and inside I was thinking, "God, she's going to think I'm stupid," like with every move I made I had to try to impress her. It was so juvenile; I wish I could have slapped my face to avoid any other embarrassment and to stop acting and feeling like I was in middle school again. I gave them a quick nod of the head and moved out as fast as I could to walk the perimeter.

As I walked away, my heart pounded like a deep bass drum and I could feel how red my face was from the embarrassment that caused me to sweat profusely. As I looked up into the sky, an enormous blast rang from the other side of the camp. As I immediately fell to the ground, my face hit the barrel of my sixty and split my mouth open. I was pissed as hell from the start to even let my emotions cloud the mission. This is exactly what happens when we don't separate our heart from the job, people get hurt, hesitate, or get themselves or others killed. "Doc!" rang out from the west side of camp; I jumped to my feet and ran toward the voices. At that moment, I also noticed that I must have cut my left forearm open on a rock as the blood ran down the outside of my arm.

I could see the smoke rising on the far west side of the camp but clearly was on the outer perimeter and down closer to the sugarcane field. I slid down the rock face like a skateboarder riding a railing. As I approached, I saw that one of the native SF was down and it looked like his guts had been totally removed from his body. I couldn't help but say, "Ssshitt," as I moved over his now open thorax. I cut the rest of his blouse and shirt off of the front of him and the first thing I saw was his gall bladder flopping around at the top of his diaphragm. His gastroepiploic artery vein was severed so bad it would take me an hour to try to stop it off. I told one of their SF guys to go up to the camp and get my surgical kit while I tried to make heads or tails of this. I started to dig, trying to find the end of the artery, and part of his now cut in half colon fell to the ground. My blood from my left arm was now mixing in with the horrendous pool of blood from the patient. There wasn't much I could really do for him in this sort of environment and I didn't have my kit with me to start clamping off veins and arteries. My head started to pound, and as I clenched my fists together in anger, I said as calmly as I could, "God, what a mess. I don't even know where to begin."

I pulled out three tubes of Morphine from my right cargo pocket and gave him two right away to dull his senses and to calm him so I could get inside of his abdominal cavity, without him rolling from side to side and convulsing. I stuck the needle at the end of the two tubes through his right chest pocket on his blouse and bent them over to keep them visible on his chest. I, as well as other medics, do this so they can keep track of the injections and how much and of what was administered. Sadly, it was over within two minutes. He either died from Hypovolemic or Neurotic shock. In layman's terms, he lost too much blood too fast and the shock caused his heart to seize.

I regretfully took a lot of my frustration out on the NCO that was with him, yelling that they had been told that the perimeter was booby trapped and that this was his fault. He had an expression of horror and hung his head. I stood up and yelled, "Fuck! How are we going to be able to get through to these people? Cock sucker!" I turned and walked up toward the camp, as the soldier I sent to get my surgical kit ran to me with it outstretched in front of him. I grabbed it from him and said loudly, "You're too fuckin' late!" I walked right past him and he couldn't do anything but stand there. Jesus stood motionless as a statue as I walked up the rock face and asked, "Is he dead?" I looked up at him and said, "Fuck yeah, he's dead! You can't get any more dead than that!"

From what I heard, Jesus was able to talk to the colonel and had him explain to his troops that they had to stay on the outer boundary without moving in, only out. It was impossible to teach them each spot that held a trap and even if we did, we could still be endangered if anyone was to get a map or grid of the traps to the outside. Koz caught up to me and told me that Tom and I were going out on recon tonight and to rest up. I walked back towards the stream to see if the girl was still down there. And, of course, she wasn't; I'm sure they hightailed it outta there when the booby trap detonated.

I looked down at my feet as I peripherally noticed movement. It was a good size black scorpion in front of my right boot. I pulled out my knife and laid it width wise across the top of it. Its tail went tick, tick, tick, tick as it struck the top of the knife with its tail and then I looked at my hands as they were covered in blood. I crushed the scorpion under my boot and walked down to the stream where I saw the children earlier and washed my hands and shirt cuffs. The laceration on my arm was about four inches long but luckily wasn't too deep; it was more superficial, but caused a lot of bleeding. I would have to get Todd to stitch me up because of the angle; it would be almost impossible for me to set the sutures. I sat there bent over for about 20 minutes while I tried to regain some composure.

I could hear another chopper in the background coming from the north. They were moving much slower than they did last night. I was at too low of a vantage point to get a good look so I started back towards the middle of our camp. As I stood just outside of the HQ, I could see a chopper that looked a lot like it was missing all of its innards with the exception of the rotor and turbine and had a huge either backhoe or front-end loader attached below it and at least two or three AH-60 Blackhawks escorting her in. The hollowed-out helicopter looked a lot like a Sikorsky CH-54 Tarhe. It took quite a while to get here, but when it did; it proved to be an art to get the machinery down in one piece.

The Blackhawks hovered in the background as if to stand watch and to protect the shipment. When the front-end loader touched the ground safely, the huge cable that was carrying it broke free from the under belly of the chopper. As it fell, it sparked and cracked as it fell across the roof of the end loader and the hook crashed to the ground with an enormous thud, followed by a huge plume of dust. It did a one eighty and then flew back in the direction it came from. But the Blackhawks stayed and hovered in place, making us all curious about what was going to happen next, as almost every one of us looked to the sky. And without hesitation, another helicopter of the same construction as the first brought in an earth mover or plow, however you define it. All I knew was that it had the ability to grade enormous amounts of land within a short period of time. They dropped it in a similar manner to the first. If there was anyone in this country who wondered where we were now located, their curiosity was answered that afternoon with the transporting in of these huge pieces of machinery and the detonation of one of our booby traps.

I got a handful of freeze-dried fruits (my favorite is still the pears) and walked to the west end of camp and overlooked the sugarcane field for about an hour. I considered how easily a large force could maneuver through the cover and be on top of us within minutes. I personally didn't realize how tall sugarcane grew... the stalks were huge! As I bit off a chunk of the fruit, it dissolved in my mouth as it mixed with the saliva. My thoughts once again returned to the girl who lived below us in the farmhouse. The fact that she was so close, yet so far away, was spinning in my mind at a horrendous pace; what was her name, how old she was, and more than anything, how could someone like her end up here, out in the middle of nowhere. I must tell you; it was a serious mind fuck. I stared into the field like it was supposed to give me an answer when I noticed several people walking together in what appeared to be dress clothes for this area. I went up to the HQ tent and told Koz I was going out on a very small, and close to home, recon with Trout. He looked up to me and said, "Later, man, and don't do any crazy Captain America shit." I knew I was never going to live that down and, of course, Rodge thought it was funny as hell.

I walked down to where Petie and Trout were and told Trout to get his LBE on and that we were going out for a scavenger hunt. He looked at me and said, "Yeah, whatever."

"Seriously, man, grab that M-4 and let's get going."

He said under his breath, "This is not good." I smiled and walked out several steps toward the sugarcane field, which reminded me of "Children of the Corn." You never knew what was going to jump out at you. He finally emerged out of his DFP and asked where we were going and I said simply that we were out to exchange foreign relations. He just laughed and followed me down the rock face, towards the cane fields. We walked to the very north side of the field, where I had noticed the movement of several locals. We skirted the north end of the field and at a safe distance, followed what looked like the farmer, just below the radar site.

As we followed them, we came to a makeshift stone wall that had to have been just as ancient as the country itself; it stood only a couple of feet high and had no consistency in its construction. It looked more like a very long pile of rocks that had been placed there by a farmer that turned them when he plowed a field. We made sure to step carefully so as to not to disturb anything and alert anyone that we were following them. When we rounded a few low-lying trees, we noticed a building, if you could call it that. It was about 50 feet long and looked like one of the most unsecured buildings or structures I had ever seen. I couldn't tell the width from where we were, but I could tell that the roof was a mixture of thatched branches and corrugated metal. There were a few spots on the side walls where it looked like they tried to thatch it, or at one time, it was thatched and time had taken its toll. I couldn't believe how healthy the sugarcane looked but then the outer boundaries of the crop were all dead, surrounded by burned plants and grass.

After the family went into the shack or whatever you want to call it, what looked like a black man in a long white robe came out the side and waved to us to join them. I didn't know if I should have felt some hesitancy, but I felt none; I actually felt very comforted. And sure as shit, Trout and I walked over towards where the man was standing. He made the sign of the cross to each of us as we stood before him. The black man was older, his grey hair announced his age but also gave him the appearance of a scholar or a very wise man. His demeanor was like no one I had ever met before. His heart was pure and his soul strong as iron. After making the sign of the cross to both of us, he said in fluent English, with a very comforting voice, "May the Lord be with you." And, we both replied, "And, also with you."

He smiled and welcomed us into his church. It didn't have any plumbing, any electricity, no floor except the ground, no actual church or building representing one, or even any pews or seats, just tree logs tipped on end. And still to this day, I feel it was one of the most inviting and humbling churches I have ever been to. I truly felt not only at home, but I felt the strength and love of God so strongly in that holy place. I have never felt its equal, even to this day.

I had to lower my head because the ceiling couldn't have been any taller than an even six feet. There were about 20 people in the church, each sitting on a log, positioned in four straight lines. Trout and I preferred to stand in the back, which didn't seem to bother anyone. We got a few concerned looks throughout the parish as we walked to the back, but the people seemed to be too intimidated to dare turn. I thought of the Geneva Convention and how the presence of weapons in a hospital or a church was forbidden, but under the circumstances, it was going to have to do.

The people in the surrounding area were very religious and content in their faith. Their faith helped soothe some of the horror that they had been forced to be a part of and witness. This was definitely a good thing and helped Trout and I to ease some of our anxieties and troubles that we had gone through in the last week or so. One thing about being Catholic is that it doesn't matter where you are or what language is being spoken, the Mass is the same and can be easily followed by memory. The priest was very passionate in his preaching ability and pronounced the word of God with such strength that you felt like you were in the Vatican listening to the Pope. It was one of the most humbling experiences I have ever had in my life.

As Mass ended and the parish filed out, the Priest came to the back where we were standing and crossed his hands in front of him and said, "You have brought the Demon with you when you came to this country. You must protect those who look onto you and search your very soul within both of you to make it out of here. The Lord is with you, but you have brought many of the happenings onto yourselves. This will not be a battle between weapons, it will be a battle within the Book and may God have mercy on your souls."

Trout tilted his head to the side slightly and asked, "Father, what's going to happen here?"

He smiled and slowly put his hand on Trout's left bicep. "Look to the Book and strengthen your relationship with the Father inside of each of you. As soldiers of

God, you have to protect those who walk in our path. Now, please go and may the mercy of God fall upon all of you. Peace be with you."

Trout and I both knelt and made the sign of the cross on our own chests as the Priest did the same to each of us in reply, "And, also with you."

The priest turned and walked toward the front altar and started to put some of the things away and lit several candles as the sky was turning dark. Trout tipped his head and said for us to get going back as it was getting dark and reminded me that I was going out on patrol with Tom and some of our new native team members. On our walk back, the air seemed to be very peaceful and I felt the peace that I always felt after attending church. It was crazy how dark it got so fast after the sun passed over the mountains. At least it wasn't like the Middle East, where you had to hurry and change your clothes from the sweaty ones to nice dry ones, otherwise you would freeze your ever lovin' ass off. Nights here cooled slightly, but remained the same temperature but without the beating sun. I tried to look into the sugarcane field as we passed it and was unable to see anything beyond three feet. As we walked back to camp and struggled to get up the rock face, I'm sure we were both thinking about what the priest had said and wondering what the other thought about it, but neither one of us ever spoke of it again. We went to the HQ and debriefed Koz about the sermon and found out when we were going out tonight. Koz told us that the recon would be heading out in a couple of hours. I told them to tell Tom, if anyone saw him, that I would be down at my DFP.

I got something to eat and checked my gear and water rations for the night's adventure. I had no idea what to expect nor had any intel or pass-ons about what our local banditos had been up to. I took the belt of 7.62 ammo off and brought it down to 200 rounds, locked and loaded, and prepared my tac-vest with concussion and fragmentation grenades. I took out a roll of electrical tape and taped off anything that made a sound or shifted as I jumped up and down. I tied my blood rag around the top of my head, pulled tight on the knot, and asked Todd if he could check on Jesus' and his wounds tonight and to apply some antibacterial ointment, with a good dressing, to help in the healing process. He said, "Sure thing, Doc. Be careful out there." I told him, "Later" and climbed out of the foxhole. Tom and I met in the middle between his DFP to the east and mine on the south side of camp. We walked down to the far south side of the base, manipulated our gear and weapons through the booby traps, and went to the west to meet up with three El Salvadorian Special Forces Soldiers.

We stopped and waited only about 50 feet from the farmhouse when I noticed that girl again; she was sitting under a small ransacked carport reading a book and twirling her hair. She was sitting in one of those old aluminum framed chairs that have those hideous seventies colors printed across the plastic like fabric. The light in the carport reflected off of her hair and even though it was too dark to see any of her features, I could still very easily remember everything about her as if she was standing in front of me at this very second. I'll tell you, she was a hell of a heartbreaker, but I needed to divorce myself from my hypothalamus and get back to protecting these people instead of admiring them.

Before long, Tom and I were joined by three native SF soldiers. I explained to them several times before we went out that they needed to verify their target and not to shoot unless absolutely necessary. I told them that they needed to follow our lead and that we needed to use sound discipline, which I knew that they were not very accustomed to because one of their primary strategies with the banditos was to make it appear that there were twice as many of the SF troops then there actually were. I could respect that. One of the only ways a small force such as an American Special Forces team can engage a large group, possibly three to four times the size, is to terrify them, keep a constant momentum without relief, because as soon as you do let up, even if they start to fall back, you will create a false sense of victory. At the opposite end of the spectrum, if you let up even slightly, it could give you enough time to even doubt the odds within yourself. Momentum is the key to victory and just like with almost any sport; you need to follow through to the end.

16

BRINGING IN SUPPLIES

A FTER OUR LITTLE PARENTAL BRIEFING WITH THE LOCAL SF GUYS, WE headed towards the north so we could get back on the gravel road and back track towards the cache. Tom and I had each brought several bags within an empty rucksack to bring the remnants of the cache back to the base. Tom and I found that our pace was too fast for the others, because they kept sliding on the rocks and couldn't get a solid footing on the gravel. We stopped and I asked one of the guys to come over to me and let me see the base of his boot. As he put his weight on my shoulder, he picked up his right boot to reveal just what I thought: no tread whatsoever. Their boots were so worn that it was like trying to keep your balance on a two-by-six laid over a hundred marbles. Tom and I slowed our pace and reinforced to the others how we needed to keep absolute sound discipline so "we wouldn't end up in a fire fight on this road where we had no cover and would be sitting ducks." I then had to spend a few minutes trying to describe and translate what "sitting ducks" meant. I finally told them to forget it and that it really didn't mean anything.

When we started up again down the road, I noticed that things were just too quiet and that I was getting a feeling in my gut that told me to hold up. I motioned to Tom and the others to stop and drop; we laid there for about ten minutes until some of the others were getting fidgety and we rose up. Tom brought us right back down and took out his thermal imager, and sure as shit, there were two guys walking down by the edge of the river. Tom and I told the rest of the party to stay there and not to make any sound at all or Tom would cut their throat. And that went without question; they understood that just fine.

We slipped our packs off very slowly and took our time standing up. I took my sixty sling off from around my neck and set it down on the road. Tom did the same with his M-4 and unsheathed his knife, that was comparable to "The Widow Maker." Meanwhile, I reached into my cargo pocket and pulled out my garrote. I made the toggles out of ash wood and had three 16-inch strands of piano wire. Some people say that they keep theirs at 12 inches, but not me; I made that mistake once because the guy's neck was too big and the wire didn't cut in right away. So, to say the very least, it was like riding a bull. I couldn't let go of the toggles and it took forever to strangle him out. So, I went with longer wires so I can cross over and fully absorb the weight.

We took our time walking down the road until the ground planed out and we could get into the grass. The men looked to be armed with AK-47s and were walking with hesitation, but never looked behind them. As we got within a few feet, I held a toggle in each hand and minded where my feet were when I whipped the wires over his head, turned around crossing the wires, and held them to each side of my neck as I took the victim's full weight on my back. I yanked the tension of the wire several times as I walked with him on my back. I could feel him wiggle and fight trying to grab the wires that had now penetrated at least an inch or two into his throat. He gurgled for a couple seconds then grew silent as his now dead weight slumped over my back. I could feel where the blood had soaked through my blouse just below my neck and was quickly running down the middle of my back. I let the toggles go and the man dropped to the ground with a big thump. As I turned and looked to Tom, he was wiping the blade of his knife in the grass. I walked over to Tom's kill and noticed that Tom almost cut the guy's head clean off. He was so strong that when he cut a person's throat, he literally almost takes their head off. There have been times in which he had cut himself because the knife penetrated straight through either to his arm, chest, or hands. I walked over to my kill to retrieve my garrote and noticed that the guy's eyes were bleeding. As I was yanking on the garrote, the blood vessels in his eyes must have burst. It was kinda cool looking, like a Halloween mask, and the wire cut through like warm butter. I grabbed one of the toggles, placed my foot on his face, and pulled it out from within his windpipe with a wet sucking sound as the little air left in his lungs bubbled out.

I was always glad to get the little fuckers because they were much easier to pick up off the ground. We walked back to the local SF we had left in the middle of the road to comically see that they hadn't moved an inch. Tom told them that it was okay for them to get up now and with much hesitation, they did so slowly. All of us got comfortable with our gear and putting on our packs, as Tom and I divvied out the bags for the rest of the cache. Tom and I both had the feeling that there would be more sentries to come in the very near future so we needed to get the cache and get the hell outta here. When we got down to the river, the rest of the men saw the remains of what we had done to the roaming patrol. They whispered amongst themselves until I told them to zip it up. Tom and the three others pulled out the still huge cache out of the river while I took an AK off of one of the dead and stripped them both of all their ammo and pulled them into the water along the shoreline. I knew that time wasn't on our side and that there would be more down here soon or certainly, someone was going to be looking for these two within a couple hours. We had to fill our packs and take everything we could back with us and sink the rest into the river. We got everything, with the exception of a few claymores, and with our packs and all pockets full, we started back to the camp up the gravel road.

The extra weight on the others made walking even that much more difficult. I knew we didn't have time to help them with the load or help them sidestep up the gravel, so I told them that they needed to get the fuck up this road or we were sure to be compromised. I also explained that there wouldn't be any help and we would have to take all of them on alone with these explosives strapped to our backs. And wouldn't you know it, they moved right up the road. Sure, they were still slipping around like crazy, but they moved. One of them even used his hands as he humped over and clawed at the gravel to help him move at a faster pace. Tom and I watched the others as they kept looking to the rear like we were being chased by wild dogs. Their paranoia seemed to worsen with every step. After watching them for a few minutes, I caught myself looking back as well, wondering if there was something there that Tom and I had missed. There is nothing worse than letting the mind play tricks on you; you could be looking into an empty swimming pool and after staring at it long enough, you would swear that there were snakes or fish swimming in the shadows.

As soon as we got to flatter ground off of the gravel, Tom and I had to hoof it to keep up with the others. Tom used our FM 21-75 on the run to rush a call into HQ so that they wouldn't open fire on us as the three other soldiers ran like hell. They were scared shitless and wanted to get back to camp in one hell of a hurry. As we got back, the others dropped the bags off and went to their fighting positions to tell everyone what had happened. We sort of did the same thing except we just needed to let Koz know that the banditos were sending out feelers looking for us and that we had to take a couple of them out prior to retrieving the remnants of the cache. They weren't far behind now and we knew that we would be seeing more of them moving closer each day and inspecting our perimeters. Koz mapped out the area where we saw them and told us to get some rest. Tom and I emptied out our rucks at the HQ and went down again to the cane field to bring the rest of the cache up where the others dropped it and high tailed it out of there. When Tom and I were walking back through the booby traps, Tom mentioned how much he really liked it here. I had to agree, but also reminded him of all the things that had happened to us up to this point. Tom stopped and said, "Now, why did you have to go and ruin a good thing? I was enjoying the night air and the peace of being home again and you have to go and bring up the crazy shit from the past! I'm goin' to bed. See you in the morning."

I felt like I just got kicked in the balls. One weakness that I have had all of my life was that I looked at everything from a more realistic position instead of an optimistic one. It was always too late before I watched what I said. I shook my head, let out a big sigh, and just said, "Fuck it!" and walked back to my DFP. As I stood over the hole, I noticed that Todd was fully engulfed in bliss as he slept with a big smile on his face. I tried to be as quiet as I could as I slid in from the back of the foxhole. I sat with my back to the left of the hole and rested the top of my head against the wall as I looked out into the dark sky. I pulled my poncho liner out and fell into a deep sleep as well.

I awoke to the birds chirping in the background as my eyes squinted to get into focus. I wiped the sleep from my eyes and looked straight in front of me to see Todd still smiling in his sleep. I thought to myself that had to be some dream to keep a smile like that. The evening left a slight dew on all of our gear, weapons, and clothing. I jammed my blanket into my ruck, grabbed "Mother," and walked to the center of camp. Scout was sitting on a rock drinking a cup of coffee as I extended a "Good morning." He looked up at me and asked how I slept. I continued to tell him, "I slept pretty good, but not as good as Todd." He asked what I meant by that and I told him how he had a shit eatin' grin on his face from the time Tom and I got back well into this morning. Scout laughed and asked me if my ass was sore this morning. It took me a couple of seconds to catch on and I replied with a sarcastic smile and a "Fuck you." He laughed harder and I walked up to the HQ to get a cup of coffee. Koz was standing in the rear of the bunker looking out into the sky. He said good morning and commented on how beautiful this country was. I agreed and grabbed the empty coffee pot. I could just tell that it was going to be one of those days. As I started a new pot of coffee, Koz told me how busy the day was going to be and how we were supposed to get a convoy and additional troops into the site. I sat at the back edge of the bunker waiting for the coffee to boil when I heard choppers in the distance. It wasn't even daylight yet and I guess we were getting this day started in a hurry.

Thankfully, I was able to get a cup of coffee before the chopper got to the base. It was loaded with enormous amounts of wood. As I turned to my left, I noticed two native soldiers walking towards the east side of camp. The helicopter set the wood down and they released the cables, sending the chopper back in the direction it came. They had two different patches on each shoulder that I hadn't seen before. One patch had a red background with black stitching around the border and writing from within that said, "BTN. DEINGS. DE CONST." across the top, with a black and white stitched bulldozer in the middle, and the numbers, "06 FEB. 1993" across the bottom. The other patch, on the opposite shoulder, had a yellow background, black border with the engineering castle in the middle, stitched in red and black. It also had a green wreath cupping the bottom and sides of the castle with red berries on the leaves and a blue bow placed at the middle base of the wreath. Under that were the words "CONSTRUYENDO, Y, DESTRUYENDO VENCEREMOS" (Building and Destroying We Will Overcome) following the rounded bottom contour of the patch. It was obvious that these guys were with some sort of civil engineering battalion to start the construction of the radar site, which surprised me. I thought that they may have had a "Seabee" unit come in instead, considering the supposed importance and urgency of the project. But, hopefully, Uncle Sam knew what he was doing.

As the wood fell to the ground, the noise was intense and left your ears ringing for hours. It was within a couple of hours after that when the first convoy pulled up. There were approximately seven US five-tons loaded with wood, supplies, and more native engineers in addition to a sixty mounted Hummer at the lead and one bringing up the rear. The Hummers and trucks were being driven by US engineers, attached to the 160th at Fort Campbell, Kentucky. If I had to make a guess, I would have to say that they were transporting the wood from the Marine post we were at in the beginning of the mission, and if they were, there were going to be convoys running around the clock for a good length of time. The methods they were using to get the materials into the radar site also seemed to be kind of primitive. There had to be a faster, more effective way of bringing all the supplies out here, but hey, who in the hell am I to criticize? I'm here to safeguard the site, not maintain tabs on how the engineers do things.

Later in the day, it was made known to us that intelligence from El Pongo and via satellite confirmed that a mass of guerilla movements had occurred across the country and they seemed to be heading in our direction. Koz didn't pass on any specifics on numbers, but he did say that Major Woods and Colonel Lira were concerned that they had grossly underestimated the actual size of the foreign factions. Which, of course, is the thing that everybody wants to hear when you're stuck in the middle of a third world country. The colonel felt that it was becoming too dangerous for them to be there and they hopped into one of the supply choppers to return to El Pongo.

The "Chief" told us that he had a few more things to do in the camp and he also would be returning to his base camp. We never really knew what he was doing in the camp anyway. He used his fancy-dancy Seal magnaphone to convey information to whomever and carried a green plastic binder around with him everywhere he went. What were the contents of the binder? I will never know and really don't give a shit, but would like to thank him for taking off right as things started to heat up.

The helicopters ran consistently for a couple days bringing in wood, steel I beams, gravel, and even GP large tents. The native CE guys took a lot of the wood and made base floors for the GP large tents, which housed all of the Civil Engineers and even several cooks that were brought in from El Pongo. On the third day, we got a shipment of PMs; there had to have been at least 20 of them, half brought in by chopper and the other half went back and forth, guarding the convoys. We didn't have a lot to do except try to stay out of everyone's way and monitor the outer boundaries with the native SF. We helped them with several exercises to further assist them in safeguarding the area after we left. Petie and Danny gave several classes on setting up EWDs to buy them time, in case of an emergency, and tactfully take out large numbers of the enemy before they got the opportunity to get inside the area. They were also able to better fortify the sugarcane fields as that was the obvious weakness in an attack or attempted infiltration.

Meanwhile, Todd and I worked with several of their medics to teach them emergency medical techniques in the field. I was surprised that they were fairly proficient in the field medical techniques which made it easier for us to further teach them how to sustain life in a combat arena. The one thing that I definitely appreciated from the native soldiers was their professionalism and their desire to learn what we had to offer them. The only question that we seemed to get several times a day that we didn't have an answer for was what they were in store for and why weren't there more US soldiers coming to help. I hoped that they had enough confidence in their own abilities that they could feel like they didn't really need us anymore and that they could now handle anything that was thrown their way. But they seemed reluctant, like they knew something that we didn't.

We made several attempts to get local intelligence to find out what the word on the block was, but the locals kept in a stage of seclusion, not willing to talk to us anymore. If we were losing the support of the locals, we could be getting set up for something huge. I know that the farmer down below us had harsh feelings toward Colonel Lira because of the hell that Lira put them through, and quite frankly, I didn't blame him one iota. They took so much away from their family that nothing could ever replace. If it had been me, I would see to it that I pissed on his grave before I bought the farm, no pun intended.

After a few days of walking around watching the progress on the concrete base for the radar unit, I decided to ask a couple of the PMs in casual conversation if they knew anything about the girl who lived in the farmhouse below us. One of them explained that her name was Anna and that she was the hottest girl in the entire country. Personally, I had to agree, but I didn't tell them that. In my ranking, she was one of the hottest girls I'd ever seen, even in the States. It was nice to know that I wasn't the only one who was infatuated with her. The guys continued to tell me that there was one of their troops that had a date with her tomorrow. I would be lying if I told you I wasn't jealous, because I was, so bad that it kind of hurt. It was for the better anyways. That was the last thing that I needed to be thinking about, but I changed the topic of conversation anyways.

Danny's team was going out tonight with the native SF to conduct a recon patrol of the area. The CE guys strung barbed and concertina wire around almost the entire camp, making infiltration even that much harder for the banditos. I walked the fence line, checking for openings and where the weak areas were, in case of an urgent situation. The sun was going down against the mountains that turned the sky yellow and orange with the perfect touch of white clouds mixed within. This was the kind of sky that you sat down with a couple of buddies and a few beers and enjoyed the peace of it while watching the tapestry change before you. I stopped on the west side of the camp and stared into the cane field once again, wishing that they could talk to me or tell me their future.

I was proceeding down to the south side of the camp when I heard some groaning coming from one of the immense piles of wood and building supplies. I slowed my pace and approached with caution. I hugged a pile of two-by-twelves with my left side as I silently inched my way around the stack. I couldn't believe my eyes! It was Anna lying totally naked on her back on a stack of wood with one of the native soldiers slowly screwing the hell out of her. Her breasts were perfect; they didn't roll onto her sides or in her armpits like some women's do. They had to be at least a triple C, if not a D, and they rested perfectly on her chest, with very little movement. If I was in the US, I would have said that they were a dead ringer for a boob job, but not out here, they were real and they were perfect by every definition of the word. They were so round, with her small darkened nipples centered perfectly on top, delicately mounted on such a small frame.

When I saw her earlier wearing that red shirt, I would have never imagined her to look like that. Her skin looked so soft, reminding me of cocoa butter and she didn't have an ounce of fat on her; on a one to ten scale, she was an eleven. Instead of being a native of El Salvador, she was more like the perfect "Penthouse" model. Her lover was standing at a perfect height and held her legs across his forearms as her calves moved slightly against his outer elbow and bicep. He glided in and out of her, slowly arching her head slightly as he grinded in the heavens of a million curls. Her arms were at her sides, gripping the wood beams, as both of them enjoyed, I'm sure, the fuck of a lifetime. As stupid as it sounds, my heart broke like a beer bottle being thrown off the side of a building. I would have never attempted anything with her, but the image of her innocence always left everything to the imagination. Now, that was shattered.

I rolled out of their line of view and backtracked into the heart of camp. As I walked, I started to get pissed off, not because he was tapping the best piece of meat I had ever seen, but because he had brought her into the camp, violated our safety zone, and could have possibly compromised the integrity of the inner camp. Now I had to decide if it was worth mentioning to the higher ups or just let it go and talk to him personally, making sure that it never happened again, at least not in the direct vicinity of their positions or ours.

I sat in the HQ bunker listening to Trout tell a story about a girl he fucked that only had one leg and that if she would have tried to run away, she would have run in circles, only gaining inches. I have to admit that it was funny as hell and especially how Trout's eyes would go crazy every which way when he told crazy bullshit stories. For a little while, I sat feeling sorry for myself with the thought of Anna. I don't know how someone I had never even talked to could have a grasp on me like she did. But, after listening to Trout for a while, it faded into one of those little rooms in the back of my head, that holds insecurities at bay. We sat there for a couple of hours, telling stories that were either half bullshit or all bullshit, like every group of soldiers does. There is never absolute truth to any story when a group of American Soldiers sit and tell tall tales. They may be close, but never all the way true.

Todd started to tell us a story about a girl he knew named Camille in Idaho, when automatic weapons fire burst throughout the night sky. I think that the first word out of all of our mouths was "Shit!" I rolled over into the pit in the bunker and Petie ran down to his DFP. Several of the outer positions beyond the camp engaged God knows what. We had no choice but to hunker down and wait for things to slow up a little. The area was an instant cluster fuck and we couldn't tell who was firing at whom or the direction of where the initial shots came from.

I laid my chin on my left hand on the fore stock of my sixty. The firing slowed slightly when, suddenly, a flare shot up on the other side of the sugarcane fields and everybody outside of us was firing in the direction of the flare. We waited a couple of minutes before moving out to our DFPs and made our way down to the outer positions to tell them to cease fire. After we stopped all of the gunfire from our end, we explained to their top NCO that our guys are out there, too, and if they start shooting again, we would cut them down.

Tom, Petie, and I moved out of the camp in the general direction of where Danny's team went. All of the gunfire created a cloud of smoke too thick for us to see through into the cane fields, so we were blind and approaching a possible unknown force or perhaps we were heading toward Danny. Either way, anything out there was going to be just as blind as we were. As we skirted the northwest side of the field, we ran into one of the native SF soldiers that had tripped the flare and was probably cut in half by friendly fire coming from his own troops. He was alone, which made us believe that the rest of them had either been gunned down or the guy took flight in a panic and got himself killed. All I knew and cared about was finding Danny and the rest of our team.

As we walked along the gravel road, I could hear talking from down below by the river and it sure as hell wasn't American or more specifically, Danny. "Fuck!" I knew that this could really be bad. Petie led us down the far-left side of the road, stepping slowly through the limited vegetation. All of us were bent over and very cautious of every move we made considering that we didn't know the size of the force below and we needed to find the others without provoking another shootout. When we got to the bottom of the road, we spread out, took cover, and hugged the ground. From my vantage point, I could only see five of them and only had a clear shot at one. We had to wait. The sweat trickled down my face as I turned my head from side to side, only moving an inch at a time to view the surroundings, in case they moved up behind us or flanked us from the right.

After about ten minutes, which felt more like ten hours, I heard a strange bird-like noise coming from in front of the group of banditos and every one of them snapped around, whipping their weapons off of their shoulders or from hanging at their sides and started yelling in the direction of the noise. They ordered whomever, or whatever, to come out and surrender. They promised that they would spare their lives if they did so now or that they would gun them and every one of their family members down. I laid there as a smile crossed over my face and motioned for Tom and Petie to hit the dirt. I smiled because the only thing in the world that could make a sound as fucked up as that was Danny. The sound rang out again as the banditos took point with their weapons; at the same moment, Scout popped up from their right and took two of their heads clean off with his Ithaca. Then Danny's SAW ripped into the rest of them, to include the two headless, cutting them basically in half. Scout and Danny now stood straight up and called for the native soldiers in back of them to get up there with them. The three of us knew that we would have to wait a little bit and let Danny and Scout cool off a little before we dared to try to make contact or we risked being lit up in the same manner.

After about a minute and a half, out of nowhere Petie yells out, "Penis!" I jerked my head in his direction then jerked back looking for a response from Danny and Scout. I felt a huge lump in my throat like we were about to perish over the word penis.

Scout cocked his head and responded, "Penis? Who in the hell is out there? I know that if you're not a friendly, you could have come up with a better word than penis."

"It's Petie, Tom, and Doc," Tom yelled out.

I leaned over to my right side propping my head in my right palm and asked Petie, "Where in the hell did that come from? Penis? Really? What the fuck are you thinking about?"

He brought himself up to his knees, as Scout and Danny approached and said, "I have no idea. I was trying to think of a word that would let you know it was us and out of nowhere the word penis popped in my head and directly out my mouth."

Scout started laughing, as we all did, and said, "Man, I'm starting to really worry about you. Does Trout know that you are having these thoughts?"

Tom snapped, "Alright guys, let's get back to camp. They have to be sending more as we sit here with our thumbs up our ass."

As we all stood up and walked toward each other, the El Salvadorian guys looked like someone just pissed in their Cheerios. They had no idea what just transpired and not one of us was about to try and explain it. I think that all of our hearts were still pounding from what happened in the last hour. But we couldn't help but laugh and Scout kept saying, "Penis? I still want to know how in the hell you came up with penis? Something's just not right about that."

After we returned to the camp, we invited the native soldiers into the camp to help them calm down a little. They looked seriously freaked out. They followed us in, either because they were terrified or because they were still in a daze. Either way, they needed a debrief and a cup of something. Probably something that was at least 150 proof. But for now, a cup of coffee was going to have to do. When Scout walked by the HQ, Koz looked out at us as we filed in and said, "Penis?"

Koz looked out at us and yelled, "What the fuck is that supposed to mean?"

Tom walked up and said, "I'll have to tell you about it later."

As Koz put his hands on his hips replied, "Thank you, I would appreciate that. Fuckin' penis, where the hell did that come from?"

"Trust me, I'll tell ya later," Tom replied as he took a seat at the back of the bunker and wiped his face off with his blood rag. I walked down to our DFP and soaked a washcloth in water and laid it on my face. Todd wasn't in the hole, which was good, because I really needed a couple of minutes to myself. I let out a sigh, caught my breath, and poured the rest of the canteen over my head and God, did it feel good. I rubbed the washcloth all over my head and face, then rolled up the towel and placed it across the back of my neck. The night air felt even cooler as the air hit my moistened head and face. I looked out into the jungle in front of our position and scanned from left to right several times, not exactly expecting to see anything, but to just take a minute to myself. All of the native SF positions were either asleep or taking a quiet moment for themselves as well. There wasn't a noise to be heard across the country.

The sky was pitch-black and there was not a star to be found. I reached into the right front pocket of my ruck and took out my cleaning kit for the sixty. Being a professional soldier meant that everything you owned or are issued has its exact spot and can be found without effort. Organization is an essential prerequisite that you have to live by or the one time that you slack, you will either die or get someone else killed and there wasn't any room for error. I broke down my sixty and cleaned it slowly periodically looking into the distance just like an old man sitting out on his front porch on a cool summer night cleaning his 40-year-old

12-gauge that was handed down to him from his father. It wasn't just a material object of convenience, it was a sentimental part of who you are, and that's how I felt about my weapon. We had been through so much together and I felt that I owed it respect for not only saving my life, but also because it was one of the only things in my life that had never let me down or pretended to be something it wasn't, leaving me insecure of its potential. I checked every part with precision, not needing a speck of light to guide me through its numerous and small parts. The smell of the brake free filled the foxhole as I rubbed it down, put her back together and wiped all excess oil off. I performed a good function test and she was ready to rock and roll once again. I grabbed the 200-round belt, fed it back in the feed tray, and added one more hundred round belt, just in case all hell was to break loose.

I sat on the upper left side of the foxhole and pulled out my notepad from inside of my left breast pocket. It had taken a beating from all of my sweat, blood, and the elements as the edges were frayed and the thick cover was only being held on by three of the minuscule metal rings. I started to write a letter to one of my best friends who lived in Chicago, even though each page was only about five inches long and three inches wide. I wanted to tell him some of the things that we have had to endure since being in El Salvador. As I wrote about several of the conflicts we had been in and even a little note about Anna, it couldn't have been four pages from front to back when the sound of the roosters cackling to our north started and ended my writing. I immediately dropped the note pad in the hole and slipped down the side and pulled the stock of my sixty in tight to my shoulder. I knew that it may have been ridiculous to rely on the roosters, but your environment can sometimes warn you of an upcoming situation or problem before the EWDs would. The sounds of nature were more reliable because they stretched out much further than the camp and had readied us more accurately than modern intelligence and warning systems recently. Now, it was a matter of a waiting game.

I noticed Todd swiftly walking to our DFP as he was hunched over and came from the left rear and quietly slipped into the foxhole. He went into his pack and cargo pockets and took out several clips for his grease gun and laid them on the front edge of the DFP.

"See anything yet?" Todd whispered as his hands cupped the edge of our position.

"Not yet," I answered, shaking my head from side to side. The call of the roosters now spread throughout the countryside. I could hear some moving around from within the farmhouse below. Either they were preparing for the worst or the farmer was conducting a check to account for all of his children. The roosters kept it up for almost an hour before quieting down and then everything fell into silence. I know that Todd and I were as jacked up as you could get. Not only were we ready, but at this stage of the game, we welcomed it. We were ready for the final showdown with these factions and as far as I was concerned every last one of them deserved to die for all of the terror that they had spread through this country and all of the suffering hundreds of families had to surely endure every day of their lives. My gut told me that the end was near. But what the final outcome would be, I didn't care. I wasn't afraid to die; I would never allow myself to ever be captured and I was ready for whatever the future would hold. My insides were so pumped up that I was ready to get it on.

17

THE LAST STAND

THE EVENING PROVED TO BE UNEVENTFUL AND BY MORNING, I WAS worn out. Whenever you have that much adrenaline pumping through your veins, it will suck every last bit of energy out of you. I think that you would use less energy if you actually contributed in a confrontation than waiting for one to happen. The air was pleasant and had a sweet smell to it. There was a bird off to our far left that sang an addicting and calming tune. Tom came down to our DFP and told us that he needed us to go down to the lake, take some water samples, and evaluate how safe the water line was down there. We responded with a nod of the head and prepared our weapons, then retrieved our water test kits from within our packs. We did test a lot of the water sources on many deployments to measure the water safety for the locals in the immediate area. We often would test the wells and even the water table if we had the tools and machinery to get access to it. Tom stood over us as we prepared to move out. My body felt beat up and I was sore from several of my wounds sustained in the last couple weeks. I had an intense headache that was going to have to wait until we got back.

As I pulled myself out of the hole, Tom rested his hand on my right shoulder. I looked at his hand, then looked at him in the face. Speaking almost under his breath he whispered, "Look Doc, we had a hell of a lot of movement last night. Be careful down there and try to get a good assessment of the water line. I'm sure we don't have to worry about a full-scale navy, but we have to look at every avenue of approach seriously because as of right now, we're outnumbered by at least twenty-to-one." I felt my brows lift, and not that he didn't have my attention from the moment he got down here, but he sure as hell had it right now. He tapped my shoulder a couple of times and said, "Be careful down there." I assured him that we would, but told him that if we weren't back in a couple of hours to send in the cavalry. We both laughed as I squinted and rubbed my forehead a couple times trying to ease my headache.

As Todd and I walked to the far south side of the camp to exit where the incoming troops came in, Jesus called down to us and asked if he could go with us. I asked him how his leg felt and he responded in a very cheery voice that it was fine and then asked if I wanted to see it as he started to unbutton his pants. I held my hand out in front of me, squinted my eyes from my headache and told him, "No, no, I'll take your word for it. Yeah, come on, I'll show you how to test different water supplies." He buttoned his pants back up and waited for us to take the lead. This was the happiest, or whatever you want to call it, I had ever seen Jesus. I didn't think he could smile, not only physically, but literally; he was always so cold and withdrawn in his own world. I had thought his heart was dead because of all the things that had happened to him and because his physical being was a reminder every day of his own personal horror. I couldn't help but study his face again for a brief moment and then started walking towards the lower gate. As I passed through the cattle gate, my thoughts once again returned to what the priest had told Trout and me. Obviously, he knew much more about what was going to happen, more than we did at least, and even certainly more than JSOC, because he had talked to us before we were briefed about the latest intel about guerilla movements. I didn't dare say anything in the presence of Todd or Jesus about what a priest told me; he didn't really have any proof that anything was going to happen. But I did think that he knew something was coming and it wasn't going to be good.

As we walked through the numerous hasties that the native SF had scattered all over the place, they looked at us like we were ghosts. They never made or kept direct eye contact with any of us until we were well past their position. Some of the soldiers were said to have been terrified of Jesus and thought that wherever he was, hell was soon to follow. The words they used to describe him sounded more like they looked at him as a bad omen or something related to that.

After we walked through the maze of hasties, we walked across a small field that had very little vegetation thanks to all of the helicopters landing and taking off. I looked at the ground and noticed that the dirt was brown and looked to be very rich soil, outside of being bone dry. You could cultivate some really good crops here and even use the water from the lake to ensure that they would prosper, although I had yet to see any use of irrigation on any of the fields we had passed. Obviously, sugarcane needed very little water to grow, because the cane field looked as healthy as it could be.

We soon arrived at the southeast side of the farmhouse and walked on the outside of the carport. As I looked to my right, I noticed that the farmer was standing in the doorway peering through the screen and gave us a look of hate I will never forget. As Jesus brought up the rear, the farmer closed the door as Jesus glared back. I turned and asked Jesus what was up his ass. Jesus explained that the farmer thought we had brought the Devil back to his front steps and there was nothing he could do about it. He didn't have anywhere to go and he was stuck with the fact that he may lose more of his family before this was over. I asked if there was anything we could do to assist with their safety and Jesus simply stated that they would never turn to us for protection because everything of theirs would be gone if they sided with us. Basically, the farmer and his family were stuck in the middle of what may turn into a gruesome war; all that they could do was ride it out and keep their heads down. They had probably done the same during the war years ago, but now everything was so close to their home that it was literally in their backyard, they could be regarded as the enemy simply by guilt of association. Just our being here could cost that farmer the rest of his family. But I know we would do anything we could to prevent that from happening. The reality of it was not good, but I knew that we would or die trying.

When we reached the lake and the water line, I couldn't believe what I saw. There were bones, skulls, and mangled spines, if not directly on the shore, within a couple of feet in the water. It was a graveyard all the way up and down the coast as far as I could see. I felt my chest tighten as I looked onto all of the faceless and nameless remnants that stood in front of me. When they called this the "Lake of Ten Thousand Souls," they weren't kidding. It was hard to think of someone telling you that in literal terms. But now I had seen it with my own eyes.

Jesus tapped my right arm and startled me. As he pointed out towards the water, I noticed a snake swimming with its head slightly above the water. He pointed and said, "You have to watch out for the snakes along these shores and especially in the water. If you get bit, you won't make it back up the hill to the rest of your team and there is nothing anyone will be able to do for you." I shook my head several times up and down and side to side and thanked him for that short and brief, but well-taken, bit of warning. He continued to tell us that even though the snakes were very small, they were as poisonous as a coral snake and would kill you once the poison entered your circulatory system, causing either respiratory arrest or cardiac arrest. If the poison got into your central nervous system, you would break your own back as your nerves contracted the muscles in your body to such an extreme that the convulsing would break your bones and tear the muscles off of the bones as you redefined doing the floppy chicken. He was right though. The snake was very small and skinny, much like a garter snake, but as we have learned on many deployments, if it's in the water or ocean, it's likely to kill you within a minute. It's better to be safe than sorry.

As I looked over all of the bones, it kind of reminded me of a bar and restaurant in South Carolina that served oysters on the half shell like they were going out of style. If you walked the deck that bordered the outer edges of the bar and looked out into the marshlands, you could see tens of thousands of oyster shells that the restaurant discarded out there. It was kind of like that because the shells that were in the water were a dark gray, just like the skull that was covered in peat and algae that sat only a couple feet in front of me at that moment. The bones on the shore were stark white, much like the oyster shells that the sun had bleached. I took a stick to turn the bones over and studied some of them. A great number of the skulls had either a bullet hole in them or many had mass head trauma from someone bashing their skull in with a blunt object. On the shore, many of the bones had been chewed on by animals, more than likely after the marrow, which was very high in protein as well as many other well-needed minerals and calcium. Deer did that up north near my home, especially when they would lose their horns. Animals would eat the calcium rich horns so fast that it was very rare to find a rack that hadn't been destroyed.

I pulled several pairs of surgical gloves out of my cargo pocket and handed them out to Todd and Jesus. I got out several small bottles that resembled the ones you piss in at the doctor's office and put about an inch of water into each of them closing the lid after each sample. We have PH strips that test for different diseases as well as the actual PH levels in the water. We dip a different strip in each container and wait the prescribed amount of time before we compare the colors to the side of the bottle holding the strips. It's just like testing the different levels of chemicals in a swimming pool. The first thing to change the second I let the strip hit the water was cholera, which was a given considering the amounts of raw flesh that had been dumped into the lake. The other given was malaria, which was almost an epidemic down here as the numerous signs outside of each exposed village spread rampant.

I turned to show Jesus how we got the results and teach him how to compare the colors to the side of the bottle but he stood motionless, staring out into the middle of the lake. Because of his gross disfigurement, it was difficult to read any expression on his face. I shrugged my shoulders and threw the remaining water from the plastic containers back into the lake and told Todd that we needed to evaluate every and any way that the guerillas could try to infiltrate us from the water. He asked me what was with Jesus; I shook my head, shrugged my shoulders again, and told him that we needed to get this information back to Koz ASAP. Todd and I walked along the shoreline towards the far southwest side and found that there was a small patch of the sugarcane field that came this far down to the water. Bordering the field was a long-worn drive that dump trucks must have used at one time to back down to the water's edge to dump the bodies in the lake. I would guess that animals and water fowl spread the body parts out along the shore as they ate the meat off the bones that, I'm sure, they had fought over. After seeing the aftermath of the physical carnage that had occurred everywhere down here, I was dumbfounded. I didn't know what to say, but knew we needed to get back to the camp and let the others know that we have a weak spot down by the lake that could prove to be vital in any attempt to defend the area.

Walking back to the east, we told Jesus that we were done and we would be returning to the camp. He didn't budge and I wasn't about to tap him anywhere to snap him out of it. Todd and I walked back up the path that we used to get down to the water and once again passed the farmer as he stood in his doorway, glaring at our presence. I felt like walking up to the door and tell him to get fucked, but I thought the more composure we kept at this time could prove to be vital later. I heard a bunch of commotion just to the north of where we were walking and decided to veer over in that direction to see what was going on. I noticed that the further we walked away from the lake, the trees and plant life thinned dramatically.

Just in front of us, there were about 30 native SF circled around a tree throwing what looked to be rocks at the branches. As we got closer, we saw something fairly large fall to the ground with a thud and they all cheered. Todd and I got within 15 feet of the group to witness almost all of them throwing rocks at iguanas that were climbing through the branches up into the tree. They had obviously found a delicacy for lunch this afternoon. Every one of them appeared to be having a great deal of fun as they made a sport out of knocking iguanas out of the trees. It's interesting how soldiers can turn almost anything into a great time; all it takes is a little imagination, which is something almost every soldier has plenty to go around.

We stopped by the little water hole where we saw Anna and the children washing their clothes and collecting water to take back to their house. I ran the same tests that I did down at the lake to find that this spring was pure, healthy, and was probably better water than half of what we drink in the US. It was amazing that the farmer knew or had some kind of access to test materials and could test the water supply here. Or, maybe after a hundred years of people getting sick, they finally figured it out for themselves.

Todd and I checked several of the booby traps that had been laid on the perimeter between us and the other SF soldiers. Everything appeared to be in standing order, so we proceeded up towards the HQ bunker. Scout and Danny had another scorpion fight going on outside of the HQ bunker. Remember how I said that all it took was a little imagination? Well, there's a perfect example of it. The two of them were happier than two pigs in shit, but I needed to yield to my headache and tell Koz what things looked like down at the lake. I should go pop a couple of Ranger candies (Motrin) to ease this thing out of my head. But, before I could do that, I needed to advise Koz about how the cane field reached all the way down to the water line and what our water test results were. He mapped out the field line to reach down to the lake and sent Tom to go and get Petie and some others to secure the field by the lake. Todd joined in on the scorpion fight as I worked my way back to our DFP. After taking a few pills, I used my poncho liner to cover the top of the hole to block out the sunlight and sat back and took a quick power nap.

I woke up to a raunchy ass smell and noticed my hole had been partially covered in smoke. I was relieved that my headache was gone as I took a few drinks of water while I tried to figure out what caused the smoke. It smelled like burning flesh mixed in with some shit as my mind immediately retrieved the thought of the guys earlier catching the iguanas for lunch or dinner or whatever time it was now. I pulled the poncho liner off the top of the hole to let a huge plume of smoke overtake the position. If I had still had the headache I had earlier, I would have puked for sure. It was a heinous smell, which left me curious as to how they actually cooked them. As far as I knew, they jammed a stick up its ass and cooked it like it was on a spit. I climbed out of the hole and stretched. It was cooling down and the sun would be down in the next few hours. I lifted the sling to my sixty over my head and walked toward the east side of the camp to where Tom was. I knelt down over their hole and asked Tom what was up. He asked how my head felt and I replied that I was feeling much better now, right as a trip flare popped into the sky directly behind us.

I slid into Tom's DFP and hunkered down. Tom knelt down at the bottom of the hole and while cupping his hand over his mouth over the receiver, got in touch with HQ and asked their status. As I looked to every which side, I was grateful that those little buggers down by the lake didn't start shooting in every direction causing an absolute cluster fuck. Tom nodded and replied to whatever was being said on the radio as I watched for something else to happen. Tom said, "Copy that, out." He grabbed his M-4 and rose slowly to the lip of the hole. There was utter silence, not a sound from any direction. Tom looked in the direction of the cane field, pulled his left hand towards his face and using his pointer and middle finger, brought them to his eyes and then pointed to the field. In our language, if you hadn't figured it out, he said, "I see or something has seen movement" in the direction where his finger pointed, which happened to be the cane fields.

Half an hour passed in utter silence; there wasn't an animal, human, or insect that made a sound of any kind. The silence was eerie and created a level of anxiety throughout the camp as I looked out into the void hoping to see something or anything move to verify that there was still life here. Tom crawled out of the hole and slowly high crawled to the Command Bunker. I sat in the silence as I watched the sun fall behind the mountains. The sky turned a dark grey and the pitch-black was soon to follow. I had never experienced the pitch-black of nights liked

I had in my time here. I caught the glowing of some embers down at the other encampments out of the corner of my eye. It was so quiet that every pop from the burning wood amplified throughout the entire area. There was no light of any kind: in the HQ bunker, down at the house, or from any of the fighting positions. It felt like I was on the planet Mars, on the dark side, all by myself. It was like "The Twilight Zone" when the music starts and something freaky happens to one of the actors. I tried on several occasions to close my eyes for a moment or two to better my night vision without success. It was like sitting at the bottom of an enormous vat that had the lid on tight.

I could feel the hairs on the back of my neck stand on end. I heard the slight sound of scraping gravel coming from between Tom's position and the HQ bunker. It was Tom. He took his time in moving, trying not to make any noise, which everyone knows is almost impossible on gravel or rocks especially doing a low or high crawl. When he was about five feet from the hole, he whispered that I return down to my DFP with Todd. He stated that there were about ten guerrillas that were probing the northwest end of the cane fields. I gave him thumbs up and crawled out as he was crawling in. If there is one very specific thing in life, it is that it is absolutely almost impossible to low or high crawl with a sixty, let alone with between two to three hundred rounds on an open free belt wrapped around your left arm. I hadn't made it 30 feet from Tom's position when I felt the wound on my forearm open wide. When it splits open initially, it doesn't hurt at all. But if it splits open after a few days of stitches, it really stings like a bitch. My face was sweating to the point that it was a steady drip off of my nose and chin. It felt like it took hours for me to get back to our hole and I was only several feet away when a claymore detonated in the cane field and shook the ground like it was within a few feet of me. I raised myself up to my hands and knees and dove in the DFP.

I struggled to get the sixty and all of the ammo in the right place as I hurried to the top lip of the hole. Todd lowered himself slightly in the hole and told me that they were everywhere and he felt that this was going to be the final showdown. I smiled at him and said, "Well it's about fuckin' time."

Todd laughed and said, "You are one crazy son of a bitch, you know that?"

I felt my face grin and answered, "You damn right, I am."

Two M-127A1 slap flares shot into the sky and a M49A1 trip flare detonated at almost the same time down by the lake. The bright white flares illuminated the ground over the cane fields and small arms fire lit up the entire south end of our position between us and the lake. Everyone in our immediate encampment waited to verify what was going on before engaging. I grabbed the thermal imagers for a look to see to the south of us. "Holy Fuck!" just came out of my mouth when I saw what looked like hundreds of people already engaging in hand-to-hand combat.

Todd turned and asked, "What did you see? What's down there, Doc?"

I yelled to him, shouting over all of the gunfire, "Wait till they get inside the camp before engaging!" Todd laid his Ithaca twelve gauge to his right side and placed numerous clips for his grease gun just to the upper left of where his firing port was. I knelt down and opened my ruck to grab more ammo belts. I tore into the boxes, pulling out the belts, and hurried to clip them together as my hands were shaking. I knew we didn't have that much time before they would be in our camp. Even without the thermal imagers, you could tell that now everything was a free-for-all. Danny, Scout, Petie, and Trout were now engaging since you could hear their SAWs spit lead and brass into the darkness of hell that this night had become. There were claymores going off, mortars being fired from only God knows where, and automatic weapons fire coming from everywhere.

Todd and I ducked into our foxhole to avoid getting hit by stray bullets that were flying over our heads from every direction. There were grenades exploding in the distance and we now had no idea who was who or where anything was coming from or going. I turned my head slightly to the right up towards the top of our hole to see tracers flying overhead like fireflies in July and sounding like a million bees zipping and buzzing over our position. The ground was shaking even more than my legs were as the ground kept absorbing the concussion of numerous blasts.

There was smoke from gunfire everywhere; the air was humid that night to begin with, so the smoke lingered more than usual. There was no way to get any bearing of what direction things were coming from. You try to depend on your hearing so much that when you're caught in a situation such as this, *utter chaos,* things get even more confusing. Your ears are ringing, your adrenaline is rushing, and your eyes are burning from the gun smoke. The sweat from your forehead runs in your eyes, blinding you in a mass fury of hell. Everyone seemed to be yelling something, cursing the darkness, or shouting commands to people that didn't exist.

Despite the cacophony of noises, I could still hear the thump of bullets pounding against human flesh. There was groaning, yelling, cursing, and screaming filling every available space in the air as one sound tried to overpower another. I pulled myself up to the lip of the hole to glance down below us. There were now numerous guerrillas trying to pull the cattle gate off of its hinges and I saw a person attempt to dive over the concertina wire. I yelled to Todd, "Hit 'em!" Todd rose to the top in a split second, glanced from left to right, and engaged portions of the wired fence as people tried to either jump over or fight their way through the mass of barbs and razors. When you get caught in c-wire, the last thing you want to do is start to fight your way out. It will cut you into smithereens.

It was like every swinging dick in this country was here to be a part of the last stand. I clipped another 300 rounds to the end of the existing belt, propped them up with my left hand, and pulled the trigger. All of a sudden there was one pop. "Holy shit, my baby has turned into a one-shot wonder." My mind instinctively ran through a checklist of how to resume firing without pause. Many soldiers don't understand that when higher NCOs or Command make you do things over and over again in repetition, they do it to make it instinctive so you don't have to think; all you have to do is react. That is not only what I did, but I even seemed to calm slightly as I pulled the charging handle back, locked it in, pushed forward, and squeezed the trigger again. "Mother" now rang with precision. Bum, bum, bum, bum, bum. I had to have been smiling as I blew the shit out of everything in front of us. I could even hear the rounds bounce off of the cattle gate when I sprayed the men as they tried to pull it off. Pling, pling, plink, plink, plong!

Behind us you could see people running all over the inside of the camp. They penetrated through the line. I engaged again to our left, as they were now everywhere swarming up to the wire. I saw the cattle gate lift off of its hinges and was thrown over a patch of c-wire. Now, I knew that there wasn't any resistance, so I turned and fired everything I had straight down the middle where the gate was and where they ran through like a stampede. It looked just like D-day when the US soldiers tried to jump off of their landing crafts as the Germans pumped everything they had down the middle of the landing ramp. I cut them to pieces! I expended the rest of my ammo and noticed Todd was already blowing bodies in half with his twelve gauge. They were right in front of our position, running right at us. I pulled out my side arm and took out two with a head shot. One of the men I shot almost fell in our foxhole. I knew that I was going to have to get the fuck out of the hole or I was going to be buried in it. I used the back of the guy's shirt that fell in front of me to help pull myself out. Just as I had got out, I felt my leg get pulled out from underneath me as I fell face first into the dirt. Then the pain surged through my body like lightning. I must have taken a round in the leg. I stood back up and, obviously, my adrenaline was pumping to the point that I couldn't feel anything anymore.

At this point, all of us were fighting on pure instinct. Every one of us was instantly turned into a savage as we fought tooth and nail. I looked to my left and saw a guy running right at me, coming out of the brush, holding a knife a good 12 inches long in his hand. The first thing that came to my mind was to use my Aikido training and grab the knife hand, twist the wrist, and use his own momentum and his arm joints to flip him over then giving me the upper hand to strike down on him while his arm was separated. But instead of doing the first thing that came to mind, which seemed to take far too long to think of in the first place, I put my hands up in the air to give him a focal point and I gave a forward lunge kick, also termed as a "boot toe" (term used in SF hand-to-hand combat training) pulling my toes back in my boot as far as would go utilizing the front ball of my foot for striking. I arched my upper torso back and pushed my hips forward as hard as I could all in one very quick movement. I caught him in the solar-plexus and threw him back a couple of feet knocking the wind out of him and crushing his sternum.

It seemed that almost that all of the noise and the commotion going on around us had either meshed together or stopped, I honestly couldn't tell the difference at that moment. As I remember now, I seemed to have lost my peripheral vision and the only thing I could hear was the pounding of my heart. I could, however, see my opponent trying to rise. I ran to him and used my knee to drive hard into his kidney as I jumped onto him. I grabbed his knife hand and placed it on his chest trying to drive the knife in. The dust was stirring on the rocky surface that we were on, sticking to our clothes, and to the sweat on our bodies and faces. I started to bounce up and down in our struggle on the ground to drive the knife into his chest. The sweat from my face was dripping on his. I knew when things got this up close and personal that one of you were going to die; at this point, it was my decision who was going to be the victor. He kept trying to push me off to his left, never letting his eyes leave mine yelling, "Fucking pig!"

I pounced and pounced to try to drive the knife in feeling the tip grind on the bone. My boonie cap fell off to the back of my neck and the string was choking me. I know that I had cut his chest with the knife because you could smell the iron from his blood. I just couldn't get the fucking thing to go into his chest. I knew that the longer this went on that there was a greater possibility that one of us was apt to make a futile mistake. The knife was starting to get slippery from the blood and sweat from each other's hands. If I was going to turn the tides of this predicament, it was going to have to be now because I was tiring fast and I was worried that I was losing the upper hand. As I struggled and wrestled with him, adrenaline pounding in my ears, I pounced two more times to try to get the knife to puncture his chest wall and end this thing screaming, "Die you mother fucker, die!"

I kept thinking, "I just can't get this fucking thing to go in!" I then reached down with my left hand and grabbed his balls and squeezed with everything I had. His butt sank and his back arched and I put my weight on the top of the knife and pushed and twisted the knife with everything I had. I could feel the bone grinding in the vibrations in the handle of the knife when finally, the tip fell between his ribs and quickly sank into his chest. It felt like cutting chicken bones with a knife as it pierced through his left lung. His eyes opened wide and you could now see the evil turn to fear. That was the first time I think that our eyes left one another as he looked down at his chest. I pulled my legs and lower torso off his and in one smooth motion kneed him in the balls. I could see his stomach tighten and crunch up. No matter how hard I tried to twist the knife, it wouldn't budge. It was lodged tight in between his ribs and I knew from experience that it would be harder to get it out than it was to get it in. I arched my right shoulder back and started punching his throat. His chest was crackling with every breath and his throat gurgled. I pulled my hand back and with an open palm, I jammed his nose cartilage deep into his brain. During the entire bout, I felt nothing physically, only the emotions of hate and rage. I rolled off of him exhausted, my body feeling like jelly. Then the gunfire, the smoke, the heat, and the screaming suddenly rushed back, making my hair stand on end and bringing me back to reality. During my battle with my attacker, it felt like time stood still waiting for the victor to emerge. Time had started back up now and I had goosebumps from noticing how loud everything was around me.

I don't know if it was from all the explosions around me or if it was from the knowing that this thing wasn't over that I jumped back up on my feet and immediately ducked as something rushed me from my right side. I took the weight of whomever had charged me and propelled their body into the air, sending them literally flying. I picked up my side arm, turned, pointed, and aimed the direction in which I sent the person flying. It was one of the guerillas and he raised his hands like he was giving up. He was lying on his back and tried to push his body back inch by inch like we were on a playground and he realized that he had been tagged and he had had enough. "Fuck him!" We weren't done by any means. He quickly shook his head from side to side, trying to tell me not to do it. As I recall, I smiled and shot the hollow point right out the back of his head.

When I turned around again, I didn't know who was where, who was friend, or who was foe. Everything was spinning. I don't know how things got so far out of control so fast. I was desperately trying to catch my breath as another guerilla rushed towards me from the south. I raised my side arm and shot directly towards his head. He stopped dead in his tracks. His eyes opened wide and his face went pale. The slide on my side arm was now locked open as I just fired my last bullet. I turned it slightly to the right looking at the side of it as the man in front of me felt around his face and chest in disbelief. I discarded it by merely letting it drop. His face wrinkled in hate and he ran straight at me knocking me over back into the foxhole. We were hitting each other frantically when I noticed Todd's e-tool sitting at the back of the hole. He punched the shit out of my stomach as I grabbed the e-tool. My abs tightened as my face reflected the pain; I swung the end of the e-tool right on the top of his head. I felt his skull crack through the end of the shovel. The e-tool literally split his head open; the crazy thing was that he didn't die right away. As he went into shock, his hands whipped around futilely, randomly not hitting anything, as his mouth lay open and drool spewed from his mouth running down his chin.

I was breathing so hard that the sound of my heart was almost deafening as it pounded in my ears. I once again pulled myself out of the hole and crawled towards an AK-47 that was lying not ten feet from the hole. I picked it up and fired several shots towards the fence line again as the guerrillas were still coming in. I turned around and jumped back in the foxhole. Todd's Ithaca was lying to the right of our hole, almost where he had set it right before the shit hit the fan, but Todd was nowhere in sight, so I reached out, grabbed it, and pumped round after round into the numerous targets of my choice. There was a shotgun belt laying on the far-right side of the hole with only several rounds missing from it. After I fired the last shell, I turned the 12-gauge over and pushed the rounds up the underside belly of the weapon as fast as I could, dropping several. I filled the lower port with as many rounds as it could hold, to include placing one in the chamber. I looked out into the distance as people were running around everywhere.

It took everything I had to pull myself out of the back of the foxhole and try to make my way towards the HQ. My leg was bleeding badly and gave out again and again as I tried to regain my footing. I tried to prop myself up with the 12-gauge, when I then pulled it tight into my right cheek and sent a man flying through the air as the round picked him up off the ground. I felt like someone hit me in the chest with a sledgehammer, like I held a couple of two-by-tens up directly in front of my chest and they gave a full swing. I flew backwards, hitting my head on a rock. I rolled over and started firing the shotgun from a prone position. I heard someone yell, "Doc! Doc! Dave, Dave over here!" Now gasping for breath, I used the last of my energy to turn my head to the left to see Petie yelling, "You're going to be alright, Doc, just hang in there!" He turned and started to fire into the night again.

I was confused for a second until I could feel a sticky sensation between my shirt and stomach. I pulled my left hand down to my stomach and wiped it up and down several times and pulled it up in front of my face. My hand was soaked in blood and I knew it wasn't good. I had no idea where I had actually been hit because my entire body just felt like rubber and all I wanted to do was catch my breath. I was pissed as hell that I had been hit. I swung the Ithaca in front of me and fired the shotgun three more times, the third shot slashing open my right cheek and brow from the recoil. All I could do was look in front of me and think that if this was the end, it wasn't so bad. Every noise around me sounded muffled like it was coming from inside of a cave and every movement I saw seemed to be going in slow motion. Sometime after that, I lost consciousness and don't remember anything.

I guess a few days had passed by the time I woke up in the back of a C-130 with an IV bag dangling over my head. As I looked up at the ceiling of the plane, I realized that I couldn't, under any circumstances, move any part of my body except my head. Well, I soon found out that I was strapped in on a metal bed with a plastic spongy brown leather pad on it that looked a lot like a hospital gurney. I yelled, "Get me out of this fuckin' thing! You mother fuckers, get me out of this thing and let's get it on!" An Air Force officer ran down the middle of the aircraft in his cute little Air Force jumpsuit and put his hands over my arms, trying to hold me down. I pulled my head up towards him and yelled, "Ya, you want some, mother fucker?" trying to head butt him.

Within a second, another officer came to our side as well. This was a redheaded female. She was ugly as the hair on a mule's ass, but her voice helped me regain some composure and she was wearing perfume. I don't know what kind it was but it smelled a lot better than I'm sure I did. She slowed her speech down a little and talked in a very calm voice and told me that I was going to be alright. The first thing that came to my mind was where the hell was Todd? I asked her where he was several times before she leaned over me slightly and told me that everyone was fine. I let my head fall back on the pillow and found it difficult to catch my breath again. She put her right hand on my right arm and rubbed it up and down several times and said, "Look, you have sustained several wounds and if you keep trying to fight us, we will have to sedate you. I will unbuckle your arms and let them out from under the sheets if you promise to lay still and not attempt to get up." I shook my head and agreed.

As she started to loosen the straps, I looked down and noticed that they had put on bright blue scrubs and I uncontrollably said, "What kind of fag color is that?"

She smiled and said, "I'm sorry about that, next time I will ask you what color you would prefer instead." I could hear the sarcasm in her voice and realized that I was being an asshole and needed to get a grip. I didn't know where the hell I was or where the rest of our team was, but I was in American hands and realized that I should feel grateful instead of acting like a prick. After she started to unbuckle the straps, I noticed that the straps were made of the same material as seatbelts in cars, in other words, if she didn't want to let me out of them, there wasn't a damn thing I could do about it. There was no way that I could have fought my way out from underneath them.

The guy to my left was an Air Force major, as I now made out the bronze-colored oak leaf on his shoulders covered by a plastic see-through film. He looked at the lady to my right, talking over me, and said, "Judy, it is in my professional opinion that you don't release his restraints."

I looked over to him and said, "Fuck you, Jack."

He put his hands up in front of his chest and said, "For that very reason."

She looked over to him and squinted and nodded her head towards the front of the aircraft, like I wasn't going to notice that. He stood up and did. He walked towards the front of the aircraft. The first thing that came to my mind was, "This lady's pretty cool." But I hated how she talked to me like I was ten.

As she tapped my right shoulder, she said, "You have to control yourself or you will tear your stitches."

I pulled my head back deeper in the pillow looking dead in her eyes and questioned, "Stitches?"

"Yeah, you guys went through one hell of a lot down there. But you really need your rest. Okay, I'm taking off the belts. Are you going to be a good boy and conduct yourself like a gentleman or are we going to have to send you back asleep with princess valium?"

"All right, Captain, I realize I was acting like a prick, but hopefully I am now in enough of a sound mind that you could at least let me scratch my own face." I loved playing mind games with officers, especially medical officers. But she was right; I needed to compose myself. She let the strap fall to the floor of the plane and slowly backed away from my gurney, never letting her eyes leave mine. She actually, and genuinely, looked scared.

I looked over towards her and said, "Don't worry, I'm not going to freak out."

She let her breath out that she was holding and replied, "Okay, that's good." I started to pull my right hand up from under the sheets and felt pain shoot through my body. As soon as I took it out, I shook it a few times to get the circulation going again. When I looked at it, it was swollen and had been 100 percent drenched in iodine with numerous stitches. I put my hand back under the sheet and helped pull my left hand up and out. It was also brown from iodine, but I had very little mobility in my left hand and arm. The female, Judy or whatever her name was, looked at me like she not only didn't trust me but she was literally afraid. My hands were so swollen that it felt like the hottest day in hell. They were so tight that it was difficult to make a fist. I flexed them in and out of a fist as much as I could to get some better mobility out of them without tearing the stitches.

I looked at her and very calmly asked her where the rest of my team was. She took a very cautious step forward and said that she didn't know and I believed her. I tried to sit up and I immediately found out that that wasn't going to happen, at least sure as hell not right now. As I laid there, I pulled my right hand in front of my face and watched as it shook uncontrollably. She took another hesitant step closer to me and said, "We picked you up in El Pongo. There were several planes there and I don't know where the rest of your team is or where they were going. I really don't know anything honestly."

"I can't feel a lot of my body, am I paralyzed?"

"No, you're not paralyzed; we have you on enough medicine to sedate a horse. You really do need to rest." I shook my head as if to agree.

I turned and looked at her again and in a very softened and labored voice asked her, "Where are we and where are we going?"

Now appearing more comfortable, she knelt down next to me and said, "We are probably somewhere over the Gulf of Mexico and are headed to Lackland Air Force base to Wilford Hall, one of the best military hospitals in the world. We will land right on the base just outside San Antonio, Texas, so I hope you like Mexican food.

I closed my eyes and asked her in a worried tone, "Am I so bad that I need to go to one of the best hospitals in the world?"

She smiled and said, "No, but we do want to give you the best medical treatment that we can."

I closed my eyes and woke up in, I guess, Wilford Hall. I had to lie quite still for the first few days. I guess that the captain on the plane ride in here wasn't kidding; I was a wreck. I was shot in my left thigh, which I remember, and shot in the chest, which I vaguely remember some of. My condition was bad enough to warrant covering my body from head to toe in iodine because I was totally covered in blood and they couldn't tell right away where my actual wounds were, or what was superficial and what needed immediate attention. I had a combined total of 87 stitches.

After a few days passed looking out the inch-thick hospital window, Petie and Danny came to visit. I have never been so happy to see anyone in my life. Petie had an arm sling on his left arm, but looked as good as the day we first landed in Colorado Springs. With a quick lift of his head Danny said, "How ya feelin, ya big puss?"

I smiled and replied, "A lot better now, ya fuckin' dickhead." He smiled back and Petie said that it was good to hear me talking because they had come up several times to see me but I was out.

"Where is everyone else?"

Petie placed his hand on my right leg and said, "Everyone's fine. You get some rest and I'll give you a hundred bucks if you tag one of these nurses and it doesn't even matter what she looks like."

I put my hand over his and in a serious tone asked, "Where is everyone?" He sat in the black silver framed chair next to my bed and explained that Todd and Scout didn't make it, but outside of a couple dents and scratches everyone else was doing just fine. I felt my heart fall through the bottom of my ass. I didn't know what to say. I got that huge lump in your throat that you get when you're about to cry or are trying to hold back from crying. I don't know about anyone else, but when that happens to me like it did that day, it really hurts your throat, I don't mean emotionally, I mean physically. I wanted to cry and won't ever tell anyone that I didn't, but sometimes it just takes a little while for it to come out. Sometime later, I finally had my first really good cry while in the shower at the hospital. It needed to happen and I did feel a little better afterwards.

I asked Petie about the family down by the lake and if they made it. He nodded and said, "Every one of them made it. I don't know where the farmer took all of them, but they were soaked from head to toe when I saw them. He either hid them under something or actually took them into the lake where no one would look for them. Whatever he did, he saved his family and would now be able to live their lives in peace, outside of some little radio waves when they get that radar site up and running. But they are fine. Jesus looked like a caveman as he walked around through the aftermath, but he made it, too. Oh, I have something for you," he said reaching in his right pocket. "After you got hit in the chest, I don't know if you remember me talking to you or not, but Todd came out of nowhere and got the guy that hit you." Petie pulled a bullet out of his pocket and said, "This was the second bullet that I'm sure would have finished you off. But someone upstairs made this one stove pipe and saved your life. So here, man, you take it and don't forget that someone has bigger and better plans for you. Now, get some rest, man. We'll be back to see ya in a couple days."

I thanked them for coming to see me and they were good to their word, because they did visit often. I still have that bullet hanging on my wall in a shadow box with some of my other small trophies. And every time I walk down the hall and see it, I thank Todd for being there for me to the end.

After several months of physical therapy and a couple of awards and decorations, I actually did live to fight another day. With this being the end of this story, I ask you and everyone you know to take just a second of your life to think about the people (Soldiers) who gave their lives or shed their blood for this awesome country we all call home. Because my blood, as well as my brothers', was shed in the name of our country: The United States. Don't ever let their sacrifices go in vain.

DE OPPRESSO LIBER.

AFTERWORD

I found out when the medical unit flew me out of the country and back to the states that they first took me to Wilford Hall, Lackland Air Force Base, in San Antonio, Texas. I was then later taken to Walter Reed National Military Medical Center in Washington, DC, where I started my physical therapy. I just missed Ron, as he had checked out just days before. I was really bummed that I missed him, but I wasn't in any shape to have had a room party.

It wasn't until several visits later from Petie and Danny when they finally told me about what happened to Todd and Scout. I waited until they left, following a million "Are you okay?" questions, then I got into the shower and wept for God only knows how long. It was well overdue. I do that, even to this day: I go into the shower to cry. I do it I think because you can't feel the tears run down your face and there isn't any audience to catch you or become "concerned" because of your emotional state.

Hearing what happened to Todd and Scout was just the right amount of news to make all of the pent-up emotions flow out. It brought every feeling, fear, and memory I had of that experience and allowed me to break down those walls of denial. It was a blessing, alleviating all that pent-up pain, anger, and torment. I miss Todd, Scout, and the LT very much and I have realized through the process of writing this that I had encapsulated all of the emotions I've had tied to them.

It has been a tremendous gift to be able to admit and recognize the feelings of loss I have for them.

Tom, Koz, Petie, Danny, Rodge and myself stayed with the same team for quite a while together and received replacements from "The Unit," and 1st SFG to fill the very big shoes of our fallen brothers.

Rodge and I actually became roommates for a while after my rehabilitation at Walter Reed, which was great because we were able to help one another through periodic and incremental moments of torment and horror brought on by our time in El Salvador. We spent many of our days together out on the back deck sharing a beer, talking about nothing in general or about specifics of that mission, and we even got to go out to our favorite Japanese restaurant a few times before he transferred to 1st SFG, where he was recruited (and needed) for some specific operations. Our beauty of a server at the restaurant wasn't there and wasn't even employed there anymore once we got back Stateside, but we sure talked about her a lot before he left for his next assignment. After he transferred, we lost touch and never talked again. I think about him often.

I took some leave and went and saw Ron, that carrot top, red headed stepchild, son of a bitch. Man, it was great to see him doing so well. After we flew him out, he went to El Pongo and straight to Walter Reed, then eventually received an honorable, medical discharge. And yes, he did get to smoke that enormous Cheech and Chong doobie that he wanted so bad and I think that they even integrated marijuana into his therapy for PTSD and his PT. So, I'm sure he's loving everyday smoking his weed.

I couldn't help but feel a tremendous amount of guilt and sadness about what happened to him and I felt a great deal of responsibility for his arm. Most of all because I was the one who took it in the end and I felt terrible for that. Did it save his life? 100%, but I still feel a kind of guilt that I don't totally understand.

Tom and I were always really close, even before El Salvador, and we stayed that way and did a lot together outside of missions. Then, he was transferred out to "The Unit" and we eventually lost contact with each other. I heard that he died honorably behind some line somewhere, doing what he loved. This world lost a great human being when we lost Tom.

A little unbeknownst fact was that before we went on this mission, we were visited by a US Army Catholic Priest to read us our final rights before we departed. We had been read them three times previously, but were read them again and given a pendant of the blessed Virgin Mary after the prayer and dedication. Every one of us wore that pendent accompanied by a cross except for the LT, who literally threw it away after we got it from the colonel. Ron dropped his and Scout sighted in his weapon with his. Rodge didn't wear his, but he brought it with him (with us) to El Salvador. My thought to this very day, this very second, is a simple question: did not having that pendent make some kind of difference to what happened to us? Did the universe change or alter that day when we did or didn't take that pendent? I wear mine every day and I will till the day I die.

We got many stares and whispers while we were at Bragg. No one really approached us and asked us anything, but didn't stop talking about what happened to us until much later.

In El Salvador, we helped open up the election for Arena Candidate, Armondo Calderon, who was the previous mayor of San Salvador, to become president, because of the newborn freedoms that the United States helped provide. Some of his key projects that he was building on, included integrating former guerrillas into civilian society and continuing to work for peace. Regardless of his reputation for violence, he served the country well. He died in the US, at the age 69, in Houston, Texas, on October 10, 2017.

WRITER'S NOTE

I wrote this book purely as a therapeutic outlet. I was approached by Reverend Fowler and told that writing this could help me in letting go of the demon's that were haunting me. He stated that it would also be a chance to serve as a voice for those who no longer had one and to talk about what actually happened in El Salvador.

I wanted this story to be told, not only for my children someday, but also for others to know what happened in those fateful months. These experiences will never be found in any history book and will never be taught in any class sessions. But it will be told by word of mouth for many, many years to come, after we are all dead and gone. Because the people of El Salvador cannot, and will never, forget what happened.

As for the people of America; the US government, I'm sure, has tucked everything about this away in some filing cabinet, in some deep, dark, and never-ending bunker that no one will see for the next 60 years, where all the things go that "never happened." It is one of those stories, that even when I tried to talk to my father-in-law, who is a Vietnam Veteran, about it said, "I never heard anything about any of this and I never saw anything on the 5 o'clock news about this," so, it obviously didn't happen and was perceived to be made up. How sad.

But even though my father-in-law felt it was made up, and could have given me the support I needed at the time, Reverend Fowler ensured me of my obligation to those we lost in the field and to tell the story regardless of how it was perceived. I should have known better than to have tried to share. Most of us don't. And, I think that is because most people just don't, or can't, understand.

Our job and responsibilities to the US Army and for our country are indescribable at times. The lengths to which we have to go and what we do are immeasurable to some and unknown to many.

My sharing was to relieve the pain of loss. There is nothing good about men dying, especially for the gains, or losses of any country, for any land, and or piece of property. It's amazing what a country will do to gain a perceived piece of power, or such a small piece of land, regardless of what they want to use it for; or even if they aren't going to use it at all.

But I felt that it's important that people need to hear about the fears, hardships, laughs, atrocities, mishaps, and terrors that happen to the few for the many. I'm not trying to change history, or make a new book on history, or most definitely, change any one's opinion about the US government's actions, disrupt political ties, or cause tension between countries. Because this is history! It's done! But it does need to be told.

The evil we experienced in El Salvador was real. We were surrounded by it almost every day and it eventually started to dwell inside each of us. The things this evil drove all of us to do, including, I think the enemy, is incomprehensible to anyone and everyone who wasn't there. Our actions, and probably theirs, were prompted by fear, vengeance, adrenaline, and or for the pure fact of hate. We did crazy, unbelievable things because we didn't care about death. Every one of us believed that God held a book and within that book and pages was the date and time we were born, and the date and time of our death, and everything in-between. Everything was inevitable, it was already in stone, so why fear what was already, permanently written and published.

Our crazy acts, plus survival and self-preservation, equated into unforgivable carnage and indiscrete prejudice. Our job was to kill before we were killed and to do it by any means necessary to achieve our mission.

Will we be forgiven for our unspeakable sins? Who's to say? We will find out when we each stand before our maker at the pearly gates for judgment. All we had to do was ride the wave, take out as many of our enemies as we could before we got ours and try like hell to stay alive in the meantime. And, hope for the forgiveness and unconditional love of our Lord and God that is promised in the scriptures. Even though sadly, no-one thought about any kind of forgiveness, until after we had survived and actually made it out.

I cannot and will not say that one thing in this book is factual, and at the same time, I will not say that any of it didn't happen. The people that were there know the truth and I know the truth. The poor people of El Salvador surely know the truth. I was going to put pictures in the book, but then that would kinda sway your decision on if it is real or not, wouldn't it? I leave what happened down there up to you the reader. Do some homework; find out more about this history. This was purely therapeutic for me and I thank you for reading and letting me share it with you. All of the names in the book have been changed to include my own, for obvious reasons, so no retribution could come to me or my family. I did this also to protect my fallen brothers and their families. These factions down in El Salvador are no joke and should be treated with the utmost respect and very carefully.

May God have mercy on all of us.
Lo Que Sea, Cuando Sea, Donde Sea.

ABOUT THE PUBLISHER

TACTICAL 16

Tactical 16 Publishing is an unconventional publisher that understands the therapeutic value inherent in writing. We help veterans, first responders, and their families and friends to tell their stories using their words.

We are on a mission to capture the history of America's heroes: stories about sacrifices during chaos, humor amid tragedy, and victories learned from experiences not readily recreated — real stories from real people.

Tactical 16 has published books in leadership, business, fiction, and children's genres. We produce all types of works, from self-help to memoirs that preserve unique stories not yet told.

You don't have to be a polished author to join our ranks. If you can write with passion and be unapologetic, we want to talk. Go to Tactical16.com to contact us and to learn more.

CPSIA information can be obtained
at www.ICGtesting.com
Printed in the USA
BVHW090433030721
611064BV00018B/1052

9 781943 226597